Walter van Laack

Our Key To Eternity

Novel

Author
Prof. Dr. med. Walter van Laack
Specialist for Orthopaedics and Orthopaedic Surgery,
Physiotherapy, Sports Medicine, Chiropractic and Acupuncture.
Author of numerous non-fiction books for existential and natural philosophy

Cover
Designed by my son Martin van Laack
Master of Science in Architecture (RWTH-Aachen)

Translation
Translated by Anneliese Wolstenholme, Roetgen near Aachen/Germany
from the original German version "Unser Schlüssel zur Ewigkeit", published 2015.
Once more I thank her very much for her very kind and patient cooperation.

This book is a work of fiction and all the characters in this book are fictitious.
Any resemblance to actual persons, living or dead, is purely coincidental.
The places and locations chosen as a tribute to autobiographical aspects are,
however, real and are described authentically to the best of my knowledge and
belief. The scientific contents of this novel are also authentic. They are based on
earlier non-fiction books by the author. The same applies to selected contents
derived from numerous descriptions of extraordinary experiences with
consciousness of other people and some of my own experiences of that kind.

To all my beloved ones

**© 2016 by Prof. Dr. Walter van Laack,
van Laack Buchverlag**

www.vanLaack-Book.eu   -   www.van-Laack.de   -   www.vanLaack-Buch.de

All rights reserved. This publication may not be reproduced in whole or in part by
printing, phono or photomechanical reproduction, photo copying, microfilming,
computer processing, transfer to the Internet and translation or any other means
of recording and reproducing by existing and future media.
Exceptions only with the prior written permission by the author.

Printed and distribution: Books-on-Demand (BoD)
In de Tarpen 42, D- 22848 Norderstedt
Fax +49-40-53433584 - info@bod.de - www.bod.de

Printed in Germany
Printed on paper bleached without chlorine, Softcover

ISBN 978-3-936624-18-2

1

Sudden flashes . . . a multitude of flashes.
I can't see anything, just flashes.
I'm complettely blinded . . . it is unbelievably bright,
vivid colours surround me . . .

An ear-splitting bang shakes us both to the core.
What was that? . . . We are wobbling . . .
'Max, what's the matter?'
'I don't know, just let go of everything . . .'
' . . . I can't keep the damn thing in balance . . .'

Dizziness . . . our hearts are racing, everything seems to move so fast.
Thoughts are coming and going, circling in rapid succession.
What the devil is going on and why?

It feels like being in a tumble dryer spiralling down . . .
at lightening speed . . . going down and down . . .

Friends appear, siblings, the family,
situations from the past ...
It is growing dark,
infernal noise, just dreadful . . .

'Max? What is it? Say something!'

Then a hard blow and a muffled thump, then sliding, another blow, even harder, further sliding, broken parts everywhere,
a hard blow to the head,

and night settles . . .

2

Christmas Eve. It is already past nine in the evening.
The Schneider Family meets in Aachen to celebrate Christmas together. The Schneiders are a typical family you can meet anywhere in the country – or are they?

As far as I can remember ever since childhood we have celebrated Christmas Eve together. When we were children, my sister and I were always getting very excited when this day drew closer. I can still remember very well how, on the day before, we were allowed to do the shopping for our mother and run errands for her, only to make time pass more quickly.

My parents and we two children lived in Cologne, yes, smack in the middle of the city. And in our quarter you did not have to go far to get everything you wanted from the shops.

For a long time now, I have been living in Aachen with my family. It is not too far away from Cologne and yet completely different. From our quite spacious terraced house on the outskirts of Aachen it would have been much too far for our kids to go to the shops.

So now, I, the physicist Christian Schneider – called Chris by everyone – sit in my inherited and already slightly old-fashioned armchair in our beautiful lounge and I let my mind wander as I often do back to the distant past. I am now in my mid-fifties and my three children are already grown up ... well, very nearly anyway.

My two sons, Robert the elder, called Bob and Thomas, almost always called Tom, have already passed their finals at university.

Bob is now 30 years old. Ever since he was a kid he wanted to follow in my footsteps and be a physicist like I am. From a very young age onwards he has always been fascinated by the almost endless vastness of the universe and so he developed the ambition to further research the history of the universe beginning with the Big Bang and following it through to the distant future. When he was still at elementary school he already used to pepper me with questions concerning this subject. Later, on our joint walks on Sunday mornings, we often discussed it and fantasized together about it.

He was especially fascinated by aliens when he was young. And I can't recall how many times as a child he watched the American science fiction film 'E.T.', the movie about this funny extraterrestrial being. But it must have been quite often.

My second son Tom is now 28 years old. In contrast to Bob he was very doubtful about some of the things I told him and his brother about the universe from a scientific point of view when he was young. He always tried to look behind the matters and he thought he could detect many things which were not entirely conclusive.

Tom was more interested in philosophy. Therefore, his typical questions included issues like: Where did mankind come from? What does it mean to be human and where will mankind end up? Later on I liked to joke about it and I used to say: where we all go to is quite clear, our last walk goes to the grave. Bob was able to laugh about it but Tom never found it quite so funny.

Furthermore, Tom has always been very musical and he always wanted to be a band leader.

I must admit, music and philosophy always strike me as being rather unsuitable for earning a living, but Tom immerses himself completely therein. Not that I fundamentally detest music and philosophy, on the contrary, I especially love classical music and I also like to discuss philosophical problems. But on the one hand I think that with both disciplines – at least for most people – it is quite difficult to earn enough money to make a living. And on the other hand I believe that it is absolutely essential to take the objective results of scientific research into consideration when attempting to answer existential questions.

After completing his studies at the RWTH[1] in Aachen Bob earned a PhD in Physics before he went to Munich some years ago where he started to work as a scientific assistant in the Max-Planck-Institute for Astrophysics. His childhood dream has thus come true. Bob has been dealing ever since with all issues regarding our universe.

Despite his young age Tom is already a lecturer at the Conservatory in Cologne where he studied music. He plays electric guitar and piano among other instruments. But above all he loves to play his saxophone in a 4-man band. Thus he remained true to his chosen path which had already dominated his childhood.

Well, and then there is our 'baby': Lara is our family pet and she turned 18 this year. She is still attending school and will sit her finals next spring. Whereas Lara still lives at home, Bob and Tom have long since moved out.

When Tom started to study at the Conservatory in Cologne he took a room in a shared accommodation there right away. But Bob also thought it was a good idea to go his own way and, although he studied in

Aachen, he moved to a small apartment in the Pont Quarter, the 'Quartier Latin' of Aachen so to speak. There the students meet in the evenings and go to one of the numerous restaurants and bars which line up here in abundance.

But our house always stayed open for our sons.

My wife Helen, nee Smith, is the same age as I am and she is American.

After finishing High school and Junior College she passed the exam as a qualified nurse in Boston. She still works as a nurse here, full-time again now, but for many years she did not work at all or only part-time because of the children. Her parents and her older brother live in the USA.

Helen and I are delighted that we five are going to celebrate Christmas Eve together today. Bob's girlfriend Jenny is not with us because she wants to spend some time with her parents in Munich over Christmas. She will join us in Cologne, however, where we plan to celebrate New Year's Eve together this year.

I am not sure about Tom, whether he is in a relationship, and Lara does not seem to have a steady boyfriend.

For dinner this evening Helen has prepared an especially delicious meal: a crisp goose with dumplings and red cabbage. Well, typical bourgeois some may say. In fact, to have a goose at Christmas is a Schneider family tradition, which already existed when I was a kid. However, in those days the goose was something special for Christmas Day. For Christmas Eve my mother traditionally prepared something simple, usually sausages with potato salad or something similar. But a crispy goose is one of my favourite dishes and is also loved by all family members.

In former times our whole family used to visit my parents in Cologne on Christmas Day. But sadly, my parents are both dead now. My father died nearly ten years ago and my mother three years ago. The first Christmas after her death we spent Christmas Day with my sister in Bonn and the year after that they all came to visit us. This year and the year before, however, she and her husband decided to take a few days off over Christmas to go on holiday, since both their children have also left home and seem to have different plans for the festive season.

Therefore, this year everything is different and we are staying at home. Bob and Tom will stay with us over Christmas. They plan to visit old friends in Aachen on Christmas Day and Boxing Day or to meet them in town and, as I happened to overhear, maybe go to the movies. If the weather allows they may even take strolls through the magnificent, rambling Aachen Forest.

I don't really know what Lara's plans are for the holidays, whether she wants to join her brothers or whether she would prefer to stay with us. However, I expect her to hook up with Bob and Tom.

I am not sure but I heard through the grapevine that she has a steady boyfriend now and that she might meet him tomorrow. With her I am never quite sure – just as little as I am with Tom. They don't tell me much about their private affairs – maybe they just don't tell it to me....

After having finished a delicious dinner the five of us sit together with a glass of champagne, and it just calls for the Christmas presents to be handed out.

When I was a child we could not have waited for so long into the evening. My sister and I would have been 'exploding' with excitement and my parents would not have been able to endure us. When our three children were small the presents were also handed over in the late afternoon of Christmas Eve.

All the presents are arranged around the Christmas tree – also a tradition in our family – wrapped up in colourful wrapping paper. Sometimes one or the other present might even be hidden in the tree. Then one after the other is sent to the tree to collect one of his or her presents. This is great fun and we like to draw out the process, we tell stories and we often take the mickey out of someone, we try on presents or try them out and in general, we just enjoy the evening together.

In addition to presents which were carefully chosen and which the recipient hopefully might really enjoy, every so often there are also 'nonsense-presents', simply something one likes to give to someone as a tease.

In this way I have great fun in getting rid of things which have crossed my path as a freebie in the course of the year. Of course, I am also fair game for accepting similar nonsense. However, as I already mentioned, most presents are not only beautiful but also useful.

Usually, as with a good symphony, the suspense grows as the evening draws on.

It is the same this time, we are in a festive mood, we enjoy one another's company and have a lot of fun together and with unwrapping our presents. Only Lara seems a bit more withdrawn than usual.

At long last every present seems to have found its recipient, has been unwrapped, heartily laughed about or admired, when my children ask me to go back to the tree. Of course I follow their instruction, look around but I can't see anything at first sight. So they navigate me into the right direction – like we used to do as kids with our friends at birthday party games – with loud whoops of 'hot' and 'cold'.

Since I still can't find anything they are having tremendous fun and I go round the tree again and again, sometimes it is 'cold' then again it is 'hot'.

Then I see it. Hidden deep between the branches of the tree something is dangling. It looks like a small key, with a silver gleam and it is not wrapped up. Among the abundance of Christmas tree decorations and baubles – also tradition in our family – I did not notice it.

I reach for it and really – at first sight it looks indeed like a key. But a closer look reveals that it is a small USB stick in the form of a key. I need not look for my laptop as Lara already passes me hers over with a broad smile on her face.

On the stick I only find *one* file. I open it and a beautifully designed gift certificate appears.

I am absolutely over the moon: my children give me a one-hour flight over Aachen and the border triangle – Germany, Belgium, The Netherlands – in a small helicopter. And the most exciting thing is: I am even to fly it myself, with me on the controls.

Wonderful! At the beginning I will receive extensive theoretical instructions and then the controls will be handed over to me. I have never been in a helicopter before and of course I don't possess a pilot's licence neither for the helicopter nor for any other aircraft.

As a teenager I had the opportunity to fly a few times in a glider. A classmate of mine was a very good friend and he acquired a pilot's licence for gliders already at the age of 16. So he was proud to take his friends up with him and I was very keen to go.

A fixed date, 5th June next year, a Sunday, was already arranged.

They succeeded in preparing a terrific surprise for me. I am absolutely delighted. In fact, I always wanted to do that. With a sense of overwhelming anticipation I hug my kids and Helen with a big thankyou.

Then we clink our glasses and drink a toast to a Merry Christmas in the circle of our family.

Of course, now I know why Tom asked me a few weeks ago quite casually whether I had planned to be away in June. A vague memory stuck in his mind that next summer I was booked for giving the ceremonial address at the congress of the New International Association of Physics on the occasion of its 100th anniversary next year. And he had the inkling that I might be busy preparing for that for months beforehand and would not have time for anything else.

I was asked to speak and give an account of the current status of cosmology – my favourite subject and passion – on the occasion of this world-wide important event. For me this invitation is a gigantic challenge and also an outstanding honour. And I assume I have told my family about it more often than once.

My discourse is expected to last for about one hour. In the course of which I plan to give the audience a general overview of the most recent findings concerning the 'Big Bang', 'cosmic inflation', 'dark matter' and 'dark energy', 'black holes', 'strings' and much more, in short a 'view of the world in the 21st century'.

Of course, the presentation is expected to be as vivid as possible; after all, the spouses of the conference members would attend as well, and I would like to give everyone a good time.

Many renowned scientists are expected to follow the invitation. But the anniversary is not before September next year – so there is still plenty of time.

3

When I mention the conference only briefly in our family circle now, Bob thinks this is too good an opportunity to miss and he encourages me to enter into a further discussion about 'God and the universe and everything' – even though it is Christmas Eve.

I must admit that I like to grab the chance. Usually Tom also likes to join in but today he is rather reluctant.

Helen on the other hand dislikes such discussions on days like this, but when we start she sees herself powerless and more often than not she just disappears.

She retires to the kitchen with a strained expression on her face.

Lara rummages through her presents and listens only with half an ear. Neither does she seem to have great interest in participating in our discussion.

Over the last few days or even weeks I have had the impression that Lara often seemed distracted or even a bit gloomy. Whenever I ask her what the matter is with her she acts somehow abrasively. Sometimes I can hardly talk to her at all and she reacts like a shrinking violet.

Admittedly, I just said in a casual way 'to talk about God, the universe and everything'. I am not really a religious person. For a long time now God has been a sort of gap-filler for me, standing in for everything we don't know yet or for everything we can't explain in a neat and tidy scientific way. And in my opinion the gaps for a God will become even smaller and smaller in the course of time.

To all intents and purposes I prefer not to elaborate on religious matters – quite in contrast to our daughter Lara, and so very much to her regret.

Not only is Lara very actively engaged in the youth work of our parish and supervises groups of children preparing for their first Holy Communion but for my 'atheistic-agnostic' view of the world she sometimes seems a bit too dogmatic for my liking.

It's true, all our children were baptised by the Roman Catholic Church, since I underwent the same ceremony as a child. In a similar way my father liked to see Helen and me being married in the Roman Catholic Church and we did not object.

On the contrary to me Helen is a believer but she is not especially strict. Her parents are members of an American Baptist Church, some kind of protestant free church. And, of course, Helen grew up in that environment. However, the Baptist community is very tolerant and supports freedom of belief and conscience, so Helen was not restrained from going through a Roman Catholic wedding ceremony.

I myself, however, being an orthodox natural scientist and – to make matters worse – a meanwhile renowned physicist, a member of the most unforgiving no-nonsense faction of science so to speak – I went along with everything in spite of my profound religious unbelief – if only for the sake of peace and quiet.

However, until today I have not changed much in my attitude towards 'God and the Universe'.

Why should I? Up to now, we physicists have always been able to come up with some kind of physical explanation in the end.

Therefore, I see no reason why that should change in the future.

Particularly problematic for me is the entire sphere of 'esoteric rubbish' as I like to refer to the so-called 'supernatural'.

Sometimes you can follow a television programme dealing with it or you read about it in the yellow press.

But, apart from the fact that I myself have never experienced anything like it: whenever it seemed that there was a breath of truth in it – hey presto – a very natural explanation turned up in no time.

And – last but not least – critics of the supernatural even offer a prize of one million dollars to anyone who succeeds in proving that a supernatural, psychic or paranormal event took place. As far as I know, nobody has claimed the money yet.

Some time ago I read for the first time about experiences which some people claim to have had when they seemed to be very close to death: 'near-death experiences'.

Yes, there are even people who claim that they have had '*after*-death experiences'.

As if a dead person could ever come back to life. To me, that sounds like a whole lot of nonsense.

Of course, even I, as a lay person in terms of medical knowledge, know that, at the end of life, during the transition from life to death, the brain cells are insufficiently supplied with blood and thus much less oxygen reaches them. A friend of mine, a medical doctor, told me that during this phase the brain cells stop functioning very quickly and hallucinations may sometimes occur. At this point, many people seem to have strange dreams. Some even experience intense feelings of happiness. Fighter pilots who are exposed to high circular accelerations in hyper-fast centrifuges also know this phenomenon. In addition they often perceive very bright light and so-called tunnel phenomena.

Perhaps nature thus chose its own way to give us some kind of 'Christmas present' – a last one before we die. We then dream of a motherhood-and-apple-pie world with endless happiness and wonderful things, and thereafter everything draws to a standstill ... and that means indeed a complete, definite and final standstill.

Stephen Hawking, the famous British physicist, who, due to a terrible nervous disease, is paralysed from his head down, once said during an interview in answer to the question whether he believes in "life after death": *'I regard the brain as being some kind of computer which somewhere along the way stops working. There is no heaven, no life after death for broken-down computers.'*[2]

I think I am of the same opinion.

Bob and I quickly but intensely exchange our views on the current situation regarding astrophysics. In the first place, out of an extremely hot and dense initial condition, only the Big Bang has facilitated time and space to evolve, according to the most recent calculations almost exactly 13.7 billion years ago. Ever since, the universe has expanded continuously.

Initially, within an almost unimaginably short period of time, maybe in the magnitude of a thousandth of a millionth of a millionth of a second the universe inflated from a 'breath of nothing' to approximately the size of a football. This phase of faster-than-light space expansion is called 'inflation'.

Subsequently it grew over a few hundred thousand years to an astronomical size. Many physicists consider this initial period as being part of the Big Bang. The universe at that time was still so incandescent that it consisted of electrically charged plasma of atomic nuclei and electrons in which the radiation, caused by mutual extinction of initially existing matter and anti-matter, was constantly scattered back and forth. After nearly 400,000 years, however, the density and temperature of the young universe had decreased to the extent that nuclear particles started to form atoms. At the same time, the radiation started to spread uniformly in all directions.

Today this radiation is detectable as 'cosmic background radiation' in the frequency spectrum of microwaves.

Throughout the entire universe this shows an overall fairly uniform temperature of some 2.73 degrees above the 'absolute zero' or 2.73 Kelvin. This temperature shows only an unimaginably minimal fluctuation which is caused by gravitation – that is the gravitational pull which inevitably exists between any two masses. Gravitation was also generated by the Big Bang.

It seems that today the universe is still expanding. Strictly speaking, not the galaxies drift apart but whole galaxy clusters are flying away from one another at an increasing speed. The universe is often compared to some dough with raisins. The galaxy clusters are the single raisins. When the dough expands during baking, the raisins drift further and further apart. There seems to be no end to the universal expansion as was discussed in the past. On the contrary: the speed of the expansion is increasing as we now know. In principle however, this phenomenon remains an enigma, since the gravity of all masses should really cause the opposite and everything should at some time be drawn together again, just like on earth a ball which is tossed into the air falls back to the ground. Therefore, there seems to be a power which we cannot measure or see as yet. We call it 'dark energy'. This causes the ever faster expansion of the cosmos.[3]

On the other hand, however, even the entire visible mass in the universe is too small to explain why, for example, galaxies do not fly apart although they rotate as fast as they do. Each rotation generates a power which acts against gravitation, known as centrifugal power. We know this force for example from a chocolate centrifuge: chocolate is poured into moulds which are then spun round at high speed to produce those hollow chocolate figures which are so loved by children at Easter and Christmas. Scientists assume, therefore, that in addition to visible matter far more mass exists which obviously exerts gravitational force.

Since we are unable to measure or see it, we talk about 'dark matter'. Only in this way we can explain the actually observed movement patterns and structures.

When we now consider the entire universe, then we realise that only 5% is visible matter. Another 20% is 'dark matter' and 75% must be 'dark energy'.

Thus nearly everything is today already explainable in a plausible way. Therefore, we don't need God. Pierre Simon Laplace, the French mathematician said something similar more than 200 years ago, when Napoleon asked him where God has his place in such a scientific view of the world: *'Monsieur, I do not need this hypothesis.'*[4]

Tom had listened to all this for a long time in a detached manner. Now, however, he interrupts our dialogue rather morosely: 'Are you really sure about this? A lot of it seems to me rather far-fetched und pure speculation. Some of these theses are repeatedly supported by ever new theses, however, without any real proof. You said yourself, no one is able to see or measure this "dark matter" or "dark energy" as yet. Have you heard of a physicist called Laughlin?'

'Do you mean Robert Laughlin, the quantum physicist and Nobel Prize winner?' I am surprised that Tom, who feels at home in completely different areas than quantum physics, has obviously heard something about this colleague.

'Yes, exactly, that's who I mean. I read somewhere that he was awarded the Nobel Prize for physics in 1998. But what I mean is that in 2008, in an interview with the magazine "Spiegel", this physicist said something very remarkable about the current state of cosmology.'

Tom fumbles in his trouser pocket and retrieves his mobile phone.

'Just a second, I have it here.' He seems to look for the interview in one of the files.

'Here...., yes here it is. I took a few notes from it, so, Robert Laughlin said: *"The Big Bang scenario is nothing but marketing"*. And in reference to other alleged discoveries, such as, among others, dark matter and dark energy or the string theory he adds: *"Not one claim of these guys..."* – he means his renowned physicist colleagues – *"..... is supported by any experiment. Not one of them told the truth."*[5]

In fact such imaginations are often based on appropriate observations but nearly all of them may be interpreted in a different way. In the end we would reach completely different hypotheses which would have nothing in common with the current ones. And thus some particles or some forces, which have only been "invented" in order to support a different thesis, would then disappear in a void......

Furthermore, I believe that in many cases people try to explain something which, with closer consideration, cannot be explained...'

Tom's mobile phone rings and he leaves the room without a further word.

Lara, who only caught the last remarks about Napoleon's question and Laplace's answer, also shakes her head and points out: 'I hope one day your eyes will be opened and you all will reconsider your views. You should rather pray to God more often than to turn away from God like you do. May I remind you of the Dominican friar Giordano Bruno[6]? He thought that the universe must be *infinite* and *unlimited*, and would last *eternally*. Only a few years ago you believed the universe to be limited and finite and that it will collapse again. Now, you believe something completely different and you *invent* reasons for that. Giordano Bruno didn't need such inventions.

For him it was clear for *logical* reasons that only an infinite universe corresponds with an almighty and eternal God. Maybe that would be a better approach for reflection. To believe in God although you can neither see nor measure him never enters your mind.

But to believe in a highly questionable almightiness of natural scientific explanations – or maybe even better only "speculative theses" – which can neither be measured nor seen seems to be no problem at all for you.'

Rather in a huff she also disappears.

Bob and I smile at each other. Lara is still too young to understand the really big issues of this world.

It is an ironic twist of fate that Giordano Bruno of all people was burned at the stake by "his" Catholic Church, no less, although he was so pious – but he was also a scientist.

If he were alive today and possessed our current knowledge, he would certainly think differently...

Merry Christmas!

4

Next morning, it is Christmas Day, we are all gathered around the breakfast table. We are happy to talk about this and that and our conversation is interrupted by laughter now and again.

However, now is not the time for further discussions and least of all for scientific appeals, regardless of whether for this or for that.

Everyone seems to enjoy this family get-together, an occasion which occurs less and less often, without wanting to settle disputes.

Later in the day we all go our own ways. Bob and Tom go to visit old friends in Aachen and its neighbourhood.

Lara actually has a 'date' today.

In answer to my cautious question, whom she is going to meet and whether I know the person, she gives a short almost pert reply: 'Dirk'. I am not to find out more and I don't know any 'Dirk'.

Well, well, I think, a friend after all? Certainly, she is 18 years old, but with regard to male friends she seemed rather reluctant up to now. I mainly blame her religious beliefs for that. Especially sex before marriage is a problem for austere Christians, if not even an absolute taboo as it is in some other religions, in Judaism and Islam for example. And since Lara gives me the impression of being strongly influenced by the Catholic Church – which I as her father cannot at all understand – a close male friend side-by-side with Lara would be a tremendous surprise.

For Helen and myself it is a rather unusual experience to be alone at home on Christmas Day. Just when I want to sit down in front of my computer, Helen comes in and asks with a somewhat worried tone of voice: 'Have you noticed that Lara is often so abrasive in the last few days?'

'Yes, indeed, what's wrong with her?' I ask.

'I don't know either. Of course, I tried to start a conversation with her again and again but she just brushed me off or simply changed the subject,' she replied.

'Well, maybe there is nothing in particular. She has to sit her finals shortly and maybe she is already worried about that. And she is not really doing as well in school as Bob and Tom in their time.' I try to dispel our unease.

5

'Now then, thank God we've survived that again', my mother used to say when the festivity was over. We usually laughed about that sigh of relief.

Bob will stay with us for another few days since this year we want to celebrate New Year's Eve together in Cologne. Tom frequently commutes anyway between Cologne, where he lives, and Aachen and he usually drops in on us then. For Jenny, who plans to come to Cologne from Munich on New Year's Eve, and Bob, and for Helen and me we booked two rooms with a rooftop terrace at the City Hotel Europa in Cologne. From there we will have a fantastic view of the cathedral. Lara insisted on not sharing a three-bed room with us, she preferred to stay with Tom. Perhaps, Helen remarked, she is not coming alone...

Tom lives within walking distance of the cathedral, so he doesn't need a hotel room.

Incidentally, he moved into a new flat some months ago. It is large and spacious he says, but I haven't seen it yet.

The view from the hotel of the Cologne Cathedral, this church with its two majestic twin spires – for me one of the most amazing buildings on earth – is phenomenal. When I was a child, I often went there full of enthusiasm on Sundays with my father.

The ancient Gothic cathedral of the biggest archdiocese in the whole of the German-speaking world is one of the highest with towers 157 metres high and also one of the largest in the world in square metres.

In 1248 construction started on the burned out ruins of the previous great Romanesque building of 873. The ambition was to create a celestial building worthy enough for the hosting of the bones of the Three Kings, which Rainald von Dassel[7] brought from Milan to Cologne in 1164. Yet it took very nearly 650 years before the cathedral was finished in 1880. Between 1530 and the early 19th century Cologne Cathedral remained unfinished, there being on the one hand no money, on the other hand the spirit of the time had changed and with it came different ideas about how to build churches. For 300 years a crane loomed on the half-finished south tower of the cathedral and became Cologne's landmark of the time. It was only after Georg Moeller in Darmstadt and Sulpiz Boisserée in Paris rediscovered the old original construction plans for the facade in 1814 that the construction of the cathedral slowly regained momentum, mainly due to the initiative of influential private citizens of Cologne such as the already mentioned Sulpiz Boisserée and Joseph Görres.

Even Johann Wolfgang von Goethe[8], who was already famous in those days and played an influential role in aristocratic circles, supported the idea. Enough money was flowing in again with the help of the Prussian King Friedrich Wilhelm IV[9] and a 'Cathedral Construction Lottery' which was initiated in Cologne and in which all ordinary citizens could invest their money with the chance of rewarding winnings. Thus large parts of the cathedral were finished in only 40 years, among others the north tower and a large remaining part of the south tower. The most important religious item of the Cologne Cathedral became, of course, the shrine with the relics of the Three Kings.

According to latest research the shrine contains indeed bones of three human male skeletons: one young man, one middle-aged one and one already old adult. However, it remains a mystery as to who these persons really were.

Actually it was Lara's idea to celebrate New Year's Eve and the start of the New Year together. On the Internet she had read an advert for a big New Year's Eve party in the *'Gürzenich'*, the legendary festival hall in Cologne, Cologne's 'front parlour' so to speak.

Lara especially likes two well-known Cologne music groups who sing their songs in the local dialect: the *'Bläck Fööss'* and the *'Höhner'*. Both groups are expected to give a performance to welcome the New Year with their music which is popular also nationwide.

The Gürzenich is a large old Patrician villa located in the historic centre of Cologne. It was built in the 15th century by the town master mason Johann von Bueren. Its history is rather chequered and multi-faceted: originally the Gürzenich was a municipal festival hall and was visited by several emperors, such as Friedrich III, Maximilian I and Karl V. Later it was used as an emporium and from 1822 onwards also as a ballroom during the carnival season. In 1849 Karl Marx announced his Communist Manifesto in the Large Hall and in 1928 a forerunner of the Christian Workforce was established there. In the course of the last 150 years the Cologne stock exchange resided here as well as the philharmonic orchestra, and in 1999 the Gürzenich was the venue of the G8 World Economic Summit.

Many television viewers know the Large Ballroom of the Gürzenich from television broadcasts of carnival sessions.

In fact, it has several ballrooms and the New Year's Eve party will take place in all of them.

The offer also includes a fantastic multi-course dinner with a large selection of beverages and a number of attractive stage shows.

All of that whets our appetite. I must add that both our sons and I myself were born in Cologne and that they, not least thanks to their father's love for that city, still feel they belong there although they didn't live very long in Cologne and went to school in Aachen.

Our daughter Lara was born in Aachen but she nonetheless loves the music and the songs of those music groups from Cologne. And Helen's maiden name being 'Smith', even she might have Cologne blood in her veins, possibly inherited from her forefathers, as the name 'Schmitz' has been known in Cologne since ancient times.

Helen managed to book some tickets for us in time. 'Enough,' she said, and left me guessing as to what she meant by that and as to who would join us in the end. Perhaps she means it to be a surprise.

6

In the afternoon Tom turns up again. In answer to my question as to how he spent his day, his reply is a succinct 'nice', and then immediately picks up yesterday's conversation between Bob and me.

'Do you seriously think,' says Tom, 'that physicists like you are really able to describe our world in so much detail as you and Bob like to insinuate?'

'Well,' I answer, 'of course there are still a lot of open questions, but nevertheless I believe that meanwhile all the fundamental facts are known.'

'You know, Father...' – most of the time Tom still calls me 'Dad', only when he is very serious he addresses me as 'Father' – '... that reminds me strongly of the anecdote about your famous colleague Max Planck[10], the father of quantum physics. In 1874 – Max Planck was 16 years old and had already finished school – he introduced himself to the great physicist and mathematician Philipp von Jolly[11] of Munich University. And what did Philipp von Jolly do? He advised Max Planck not to study physics. He said that in physics all important issues are already finally solved and there was nothing fundamentally new left to be discovered.

'In fact, many years later it was Max Planck who with quantum physics discovered a completely new kind of physics which overthrew, discarded or just simply deranged many facts which were assumed to present the irrevocable truth.

'For his outstanding work Max Planck was finally awarded the Nobel Prize for Physics.'

Well, our family hobby philosopher was right here.

'However, I think,' I rise to speak again, 'the world has changed a lot and nowadays we can see, measure and observe many more things than scientists in former days were able to do. Today, we have an incomparably better and much more advanced technology at our disposal and so we are far more certain with our interpretations than ever before. I am convinced that our view of the world today is very close to the truth.'

'Not necessarily,' Tom objects, 'the variety of contemporary observations is indeed incomparably high. However, nobody is capable of taking it all in and making sense of it.

'That is why many scientists are unable to look beyond the ends of their noses, that is beyond their own special faculty, and to look further afield. Therefore, random interpretation is rife and scientists just talk at large, more so than in former times. They do this more often than not completely without risk, since many issues are still hardly provable. In the end the result is by no means any better than the results of previous years. After that it takes many, many years unfortunately – sometimes even decades – before everything, which is far too hastily called 'golden standard' today, is called obsolete after all. And very often that was completely wrong from the outset and quite obviously so.

'You "modern physicists", you just wait and you will experience a nasty surprise one day.

'In my opinion you all repeat the same mistake time and again: many natural scientists still believe that solely empirical findings – the results of experimental scientific investigations which can be observed with our senses and thus also with measuring devices as 'extended senses' – reflect the only reality in the world. But do remember that even the famous philosopher Immanuel Kant[12], who initially was also very much fascinated by this idea, discarded it and replaced it by *logic thinking*: he said that sensory perceptions must be processes by our own intellect. This is an *active procedure*. And Kant said: "*Our nature is constructed in such a way that our perception cannot be other than sensory. However, the ability to reassess the subject matter of our sensory perception we owe to our intellect.*" Neither of these properties is to be preferred in comparison to the other and *both coexist alongside each other.*

'Then Kant continues: "*Thoughts without contents are empty, but assumptions without definitions are blind.*" And: "*Knowledge can only develop when sensory perception and intellect are combined.*"

'This enables man to order everything into a logical correlation which not only incorporates all sensory experiences but also exceeds by far the cognitive possibilities beyond the sensory experience through *reasoning and evaluating* with the assistance of our own intellect.

'And that is exactly what is missing, I think, you are too often too far removed from this notion. Most scientists today are hard put to keep track on their own special field of work, never mind their taking into account the results of others.

'Thus it even seems impossible for our intellect to grasp the multitude of individual theories, let alone to order them into logical correlations and to evaluate the result. But only if that could be achieved would it perhaps become possible to view the results in a completely new and better light.'

After having delivered his homily Tom is about to leave when he turns around again: 'You know, Dad, with this logical conclusion Kant had actually already *proved* that something else *must* exist besides that which we call 'matter' and that is 'spirit', which, in contrast to matter, cannot be sensuously experienced or detected, but is nonetheless really existing like matter. We need our spirit to interpret matter in a sensible way.

'With you scientists I often have the feeling that something is missing with you . . .'

'Now you become rather insinuating, Son, and furthermore, I think your arguments are too far fetched,' I contradict him. 'Just think that the *Human-Brain-Project,* supported with one billion dollars, has been in existence for several years already and scientists believe that in the near future we will be able to expose this so-called "spirit" as that what it really is in my opinion: as a really fantastic product of our brain, but merely as a product of matter – or an "epiphenomenon" – and nothing completely different, not a separate entity.'

'No, I think you are on the wrong track, Father,' Tom replies, quick as a shot. 'Please think back to the so-called *"Brain Manifesto"* released by renowned German neuroscientists in 2004, in which they established that within the next ten years all baffling phenomena such as, among many others, "spirit", our "ego", "consciousness" and "awareness", our most profound "emotions" even "love" will be exposed as mere products of our brain.

'And what was left of this theory ten years later – what is even left today? Nothing at all! Not even one of these phenomena can with certainty be localised, explained or, let alone, verified in the brain's physiology. In my opinion this thesis was – something we experience so often – only a further sign of pure arrogance as is so widely spread nowadays.

'Even if we can almost "smell" how little scientifically sound some contributions to such topics in modern mass media are: in scientific circles no-one budges an iota from their permanently self-important arrogance.

'In one of the editions of the magazine "Spiegel" in 2014 there was an article in which you could read: *"Scientists have charted the biochemistry of love up to the very last droplet of hormone"*.

'Thereafter the author asked boastfully: *"Do we want the Love Pill?"* [13] As if "love" could really only be explained with biochemistry.

'Obviously, for such a smart aleck love merely exists with a direct connection to sexuality and partnership. However, love is actually far more than that and its real spectrum is unfathomably wide and deep.

'Love is something much higher, love is of spiritual nature. Love probably also exists in animals. However, in such quality and profoundness as we know it, it only exists in human beings and thus renders humans as unique among all beings on Earth. I believe that love has been a key element since mankind began to exist. You know, some time ago scientists discovered the skeleton of a child who lived about 100,000 years ago in Galilee near Nazareth in today's Israel, the home of the historical Jesus. The child must have been involved in a severe accident – probably a stone dropped on its head, since the head was badly damaged. Due to this injury the child was probably unable to move and hardly able to speak or to see. If the child had been left to its own devices it would inevitably have died very soon after. However, the scientists established that it must have lived for many years after the accident. When it died later it was buried elaborately and with great care. This is expressed by two antlers the small skeleton held in its hands.

'All this shows that other people did their utmost to take care of this severely damaged child, they must have looked after it and protected it[14].

'What was the reason for this? It surely must have been love, and love alone! The love for this child was obviously so strong that its traces are still clearly detectable – after 100,000 years.

'Isn't it completely absurd to assume that some kind of *spontaneous* hormone surge could have induced such love to a severely damaged human being, possibly even a stranger, in the surely adverse conditions of a hostile environment?

'A friend of mine once told me that her son heard the teacher of his biology advance course utter the words: *"Love is nothing but chemistry."*

'All that is rubbish times three . . . Love and infatuation, sexual desire and profound emotions are often mixed up without further questioning. People do not want to recognise that we are talking about completely different depths and qualities and that cause and effect are also frequently confused.

'It cannot be what may not be! Of course the consumption of certain chemical substances induces

certain predictable physical and mental reactions. A person is *also* "body". And the "spirit" has *also* a lot to do with the "brain". But both – the human being as a whole as well as his "spirit" – seem to me to be obviously much more than just body and brain on their own – at least as long as we do not walk through life dim-witted and equipped with very narrow blinkers . . . *The whole is more than the sum of its parts!*'

'You know, Son,' I try to calm Tom down somewhat since he has obviously talked himself into a rage, 'another big problem is too much arbitrariness beyond the modern natural scientific knowledge. Numerous myths and religions and also esotericism, which is so popular today and often inspired by religious doctrines from the Far East, they all offer a vast variety of propositions. In my opinion, the famous natural scientist Alexander von Humboldt[15] put it in a nutshell when he said something like: "*The most dangerous world-views are those of people who never viewed the world.*"'

Tom fires back immediately: 'He may have a point there, but if there is too much arbitrariness in esotericism on one side, which unfortunately may be true, there is also too much overpowering natural scientifically biased pig-headedness on the other side.'

Tom is really leaving now. Where to, he doesn't tell me.

He really is rather disgruntled and doesn't even say good-bye to me.

His words not only hit home but they also gave me food for thought.

Maybe we are sometimes trapped too much in our own view of the world, certainly partly due to our professional and social environment. Possibly we tend to lose more and more of our unrestricted thinking . . .

That's the way it is – simply blinkers . . . So I keep contemplating for quite a while yet before I turn my mind back to other aspects of daily life.

To my delight Tom comes back later to say good-bye to me before he drives back to Cologne where he lives.

New Year's Eve we will meet again.

7

Tomorrow is New Year's Eve.

There is no necessity for us to buy any fireworks; this year we let other people do the job. In previous years it was different. We used to buy a small supply of fireworks each for our combined efforts. I usually stuck to some colourful rockets but my sons liked to buy rockets with loud bang effects – at least when they were young. Only Lara disliked the whole shenanigan, as did Helen, by the way – she just couldn't warm to the whole idea of fireworks – however, she didn't have a chance against our enthusiasm.

I met Helen more than 30 years ago as scholarship holder in the USA. As a young physics student I had the chance to attend lectures in the Massachusetts Institute of Technology in Cambridge, on the outskirts of Boston. Helen lived in Boston.

She was a fully qualified nurse at the Harvard Medical School and worked in the trauma centre. In Germany we would call it "Accident and Emergency Department" and many television viewers may be able to understand how stressful her work was when they watch TV series such as "Emergency Room".

I met her at a party organised by the university. Among a great number of young women she immediately caught my eye. However, as is often the case, not the man chooses his woman but vice-versa, the woman chooses her man. Thus I didn't have a chance at our first chance encounter since I didn't really fit her "pattern of predation" – as we might say today.

Nonetheless, from details she mentioned in our first short conversation I detected approximately where she lived. In those days I was far to shy to ask her directly for her address. So, at the end of her working day I waited in front of the building in which I assumed she lived – and sure enough I was right. When I first met her there I plucked up my courage and addressed her, I even had the boldness to invite her to dinner and ... what shall I say, after two evasive replies with 'maybe' and 'let's see' I was lucky the third time. So we went out to dinner together ...

A little later our relationship deepened and, well, after that *I* didn't have the chance to escape *her* any more...

We are still together which is certainly due to mutual feelings.

Shortly after that I Helen introduced me to her parents and her elder brother who worked in the same hospital as Helen as an assistant physician and he still works there today – but now as chief physician in the same department.

Helen's parents are still alive and live in greater Boston. Of course, they are of an advanced age now. And her brother Michael and his family live close by.

Soon afterwards I took Helen home with me to Cologne where she easily found a good job in the emergency department of a hospital close by.

Qualified nurses were then and are still now very much sought after. When I changed to the

"Institute for Theoretical Physics" from Cologne to Aachen a few years later, she again found employment immediately and without problems at the University Hospital in Aachen – again in the department for accident surgery. She still works there; for the last few years, however, no longer on ward duty. Because of our children she was forced to stop work now and again or to work part-time. As the children grew older and became more independent she became head of several departments. This is due to a completely new organisational concept: on the one hand she manages the entire nursing staff of four hospital wards and functional areas, on the other hand she is still under the supervision of the nursing management.

When Helen was offered this new concept she grabbed the opportunity. She no longer has to work shifts and her weekends are free. Today, she tells me, that for financial reasons they want to abolish this new concept again and which it seems will mean she will have to fight hard against many inconveniences.

It has been a great advantage for the education of our children that Helen is American: our children have grown up bilingual right from the start.

For them it still is a great advantage today. Especially Bob can use this in his daily work and due to his bilingualism he had no problems in securing his dream job in Munich.

It has always been self-understood that we also visit the USA very nearly every year at least once a year, usually all of us five together.

Of course, we have always visited Helen's parents on the east coast. But very often we have also moved on to other places and cities as well and we have had many wonderful experiences.

Helen's family has also visited us several times, first in Cologne and then in Aachen.

8

New Year's Eve is on a Thursday this year.

This means we will have another long weekend in front of us since none of us has to work on New Year's Eve – and the school is still on Christmas holidays anyway.

For Lara her school education was more or less finished at Christmas: for her the second half of her school year begins in January already, since she will be sitting her finals next year, for all other pupils the second half doesn't start before February. Moreover, apart from repetitions as preparation for the exams there isn't much going on anyway.

Although Lara should now be able to enjoy her free days she seems rather stressed and is very irritable. Very often she is just absent-minded and distracted.

The tension is probably building up inside her; at school she always had a more difficult stand than her brothers and the upcoming exams seem to stress her no end.

This morning she sleeps unusually long. Most days she gets up at about nine even on her free days. Now it is very nearly noon.

Lara is really a very tough girl. Already in early childhood her strong, but sometimes stubborn personality was clear to see. She has always gone her own way rigorously and has never listened much to advice. Since she is by far the youngest of our three children she has always had more freedom to spread her wings than her two older brothers.

She grew up practically as a single child and did not have to struggle for privileges as did her brothers. For sure, she was much more mollycoddled by her parents than Bob and Tom, who also tended to spoil their little sister.

However, she must have experienced something as a child which determined her view of the world and changed her behaviour fundamentally. I don't know what it was, but it was apparent that at the age of about seven she rather suddenly turned very religious, Catholic-Christian that is.

Our children were all baptised in the Catholic Church, as I already mentioned, and they all went to First Communion as was expected of them. But I always considered that as being part of the obligatory, accepted social tradition thereby avoiding to become outsiders at school and among their friends.

We parents have our very own individual attitude towards religion. And Helen's is completely different from mine. I leave God well alone as the good old man in the sky and I prefer to believe in things I can see, hear, feel and measure. And in this context God is not really an issue.

Helen was educated by the Baptists and is, therefore, much more involved, although she is by no means dogmatic. Here the motto is: there is nothing to prove that there is a God but there is also nothing to prove that there isn't. So that means: just wait and see.

In fact, this attitude corresponds more or less with mine which is typical for people from Cologne where people like to say: 'what will be, will be'.

The very first time that Lara's enthusiasm for strictly religious matters attracted my attention was when she once came home from school and was quite beside herself about a picture she was expected to paint in religious studies class for the new, rather young, Reverend Bernhard Weingarten. She had to depict the interior of our local church with the altar beautifully decorated and with all the trimmings typical for a church. I must admit, her picture was really beautiful and for her age amazingly detailed, but – at least for me – just a picture.

It was strikingly, however, how she used various shades of red in all possible nuances.

I didn't think much about it at the time. Somehow most of the picture was simply red. Red is really my favourite colour but in this case it was just a bit too much. I still remember how I commented in an offhand manner: 'Lara, you seem to have had scarlet fever for too long. Has it rubbed off on your picture?'

In fact, Lara had been taken down with scarlet fever some weeks previously and this disease makes skin and tongue among other parts of the body take on a red colour. She was treated with very high doses of penicillin and our former family doctor, Dr. Neuer, who lived in the neighbourhood, took good care of her and visited her every day.

One night Lara's fever was so high that she lay there completely apathetic for a long time. We were really afraid that we might lose our beloved daughter. But the very next day she seemed much better. Her illness lingered for an unusually long time, but after some weeks it was over and she made a complete recovery.

That was about the time when somehow her nature must have changed.

For us it was a big surprise when suddenly she felt drawn to Jesus and God. Yet she told us nothing to indicate the reason for her change of attitude. Be it as it may, she became completely absorbed in the Catholic doctrine.

When during her puberty she sometimes participated in animated discussions and, more often than not, fierce debates about 'God and the world' with me and her brothers – in which God not always got away lightly – she always vigorously took sides with 'Him'. I kept asking myself, why?

When other girls her age went out with friends during puberty she seldom joined them. The Catholic Church stands for moral principles which cannot really be called liberal, although many of its members and employees do not always follow these principles themselves. Even members of the clergy do not take the commandments and prohibitions they teach too seriously.

Members of the clergy, just like politicians, like to preach water to their subjects whilst drinking the best wine themselves – and that usually beyond all measure...

With Lara I always had the feeling that she not only approved of some very tight moral rules and regulations but also followed them in her own life. Up until today – well, at least until I heard at Christmas that she might have a man at her side – I never noticed any admirer around her who should be taken seriously.

Part of her profound religiosity is also her consistent assiduousness in everything she does. This also includes staying in bed till noon. She has never done that, not even during her holidays or on her free days.

With me and our sons it was completely different during our adolescent and student years.

Just now I can hear her leaving her room to go to the bathroom.

It is well past noon. Our house has rather thin walls, which is probably why I can hear her being violently sick in the bathroom.

Before we leave for Cologne I ask her how she is and what the matter with her was. But she just waves me off and disappears again.

9

Early in the afternoon Helen and I travel to Cologne by car. Lara will follow us later with Bob. He will drop her off at Tom's flat. They might pick up Bob's girlfriend Jenny at the Cologne main station on the way.

Later, of course, we will meet again at the very latest in the *Gürzenich* in the evening.

After checking in at the hotel we just relax. Afterwards Helen and I wander through the town a little. We meet none of our kids, neither in the hotel nor by chance at the shops.

We return to our hotel in good time to get ready for the evening. The *Gürzenich* is not far away so that we can easily go there on foot.

Helen dresses up and looks very elegant. She is wearing a long, royal-blue, tight-fitting evening gown which enhances her still beautiful figure. She is wearing her hair – meanwhile slightly grey but not dyed – open tonight like she does for special occasions.

I am wearing a black dinner jacket – most unusual for me. I wear a suit and tie now and again but rarely and only for special events. I prefer a more casual style with jeans and a shirt, sometimes combined with a jacket. However, for tonight we have to dress up and so we are on our way in our best garb.

Shortly after, we arrive in the Great Hall of the Cologne *Gürzenich*. Lara is already there and is sitting at the large circular table which is wonderfully laid for us.

She is alone.

The table decoration is very elaborate, with a riot of fresh flowers and numerous articles which might come in handy on New Year's Eve.

I would call it "tinsel-trash": gaudy blow-out paper streamers mingle with marzipan piglets with golden coins in their mouths and little chimney sweeps made of pipe cleaners. But from an optical point of view it gives quite a pleasant picture together with the flowers.

The large silver underplates, framed by precious silver cutlery and three glasses for each of us, red wine, white wine and mineral water, make the tables look perfectly festive, when they would otherwise appear rather comical and Carnival-like.

Lara's facial expression makes her look stressed. Her eyes are red as if she has just been crying.

In her short red evening gown, with her beautiful legs and her long, loosely flowing hair she looks charming. She is a beautiful young woman, who, for whatever reason, doesn't seem to be happy. However, I avoid addressing her with questions as to her feelings and the reason for her obvious heartache. Of course, I hope she would take the initiative and say something. I would like to try and help her.

I look at Helen, searching for an answer in her eyes. I don't find it there either but then I think she already knows more than I do.

10

Bob and his girlfriend Jenny arrive a few minutes later. Bob is also wearing a dinner jacket although he really hates it. I know he doesn't even own one, he probably hired one; to buy one just for this occasion would certainly have been too much to ask. Nevertheless, he looks smashing in his festive outfit. Maybe he should jump over his shadow and wear something like this more often.

By the way, Jenny has an Asian-German background. She was born in Munich and her father is a real Munich character. But her mother was born in Thailand and her father brought her back with him to Munich after he had spent a holiday there.

Jenny is a year younger than Bob and works in the local news section of the *'Münchener Merkur'*, a well-known newspaper in the region. She is responsible for the boulevard news and she uses her best endeavours to put the Munich jet-set and celebrities into perspective.

Bob and Jenny have been an item for the last three years and I think they want to get married soon. Bob met Jenny at the *'Oktoberfest'* shortly after he started his job in Munich and he fell in love with her. In my opinion they are really very well matched and complement each other on many levels.

Jenny is very uncomplicated and she is a great sport.

However, Jenny's religious beliefs seem to pose a problem for both of them in the long run. Although baptised in accordance with the Roman Catholic Church, she shows a rather Buddhistical attitude, possibly influenced by her mother. She believes in the reincarnation after death into a new human body.

For Bob this is utter nonsense and for me as well, as everyone knows. But Bob restrains himself when topics like this turn up in conversation. They both have learned to accept their partner's often very contradictory perspectives – up to now without severe rows, it seems.

Only Lara and Jenny sometimes argue over religious issues, especially when the topic 'reincarnation' turns up, since for Lara as a believing Catholic this is like a red rag to a bull. She does not believe in 'reincarnation' and in her view this is a purely human invention.

Should Jenny and Bob really decide to get married in the near future and have children together, then I hope they will manage to maintain their current tolerant behaviour and to integrate it into their children's education and pass it on, since it will not be easy to convey such fundamentally opposing religious beliefs to children.

Jenny appears in a light beige, calf-long tight shift dress. She looks very elegant; however her dress is not really my cup of tea because of its length. I like dresses short, about knee-length or some inches above, or, if long for the evening, then full-length.

Helen and I give Jenny an especially warm welcome. We haven't seen her for such a long time and we are delighted to meet her here in Cologne. Jenny and Bob both seem to be in a good mood, they are almost exuberant.

After we have all taken our seats I notice that three places at our table remain empty.

I suppose one of them might be for Dirk, Lara's new boyfriend, of whose existence I hadn't even caught a whiff until a few days ago.

But now she came all alone. And the other two places are probably for Tom and his girlfriend who is also still a complete stranger to me.

11

A Master of Ceremonies enters the stage to open the evening in the Great Hall, or should I say a Mistress of Ceremonies in this case. Waiters are already flitting around to take the orders for drinks and to ask which menu has been chosen. The menu gives the choice of two or three different dishes per course, and they all sound delicious.

Where is Tom?

The waiter responsible for our table has just taken down all our orders when Tom arrives.

'Please excuse us, we are a bit late, but we couldn't make it earlier.'

With this he turns round and I see that he has two more guests in tow, a young lady and a young gentleman, both of them very likeable at first sight but completely unknown to me.

Well, I think, at long last I shall get to know Tom's girlfriend. And the young man is probably Dirk. Lara must be delighted and maybe she can start smiling again.

Both his companions are about Tom's age approximately, maybe a little bit older, about thirty plus maybe a year or two. 'Allow me to introduce my friend Jasmin to you,' Tom points to the enchanting young woman behind him – 'and this is Sascha, also a friend of mine.'

Not Dirk then, I muse briefly.

We extend a warm welcome and shake hands firmly with everyone, being as quiet as possible. I have noticed that people on the next table are irritated and have already started to complain since Brigitte, our Mistress of Ceremonies tonight, has started talking – of course she pronounces her name in the French way: 'Bri-gid'.

With a charming smile and an overwhelming yet amiable flood of words she discloses the details of tonight's event which will take us till well after midnight.

Jasmin is slim and tall. She could be a model: she is at least one metre and eighty and her face has distinctive austere features. She is perfectly made up – not at all flashy, just skilfully done.

She is wearing a colourful, fashionable dress by 'Desigual', which even I recognise by the typical geometrical neckline. On her rather high-heeled shoes she is almost taller than we four males and we aren't midgets.

Sascha and Tom are about same height but now they seem smaller than Jasmin in her stilettos.

Sascha gives me the impression of being a very nice and polite guy. He, too, is slim and – which I didn't notice at first in the darkened hall – he is wearing the same light-blue suit as our son Tom.

On both of them it looks tailor-made. Both of them are wearing a white shirt with it and they both have a tie with the same colourful pattern. They look almost like identical twins. A closer look reveals that, to top their appearance, the patterns and colours of their ties are almost identical to the pattern and colours of Jasmin's dress.

This is a totally mind-boggling arrangement, I think, awe-stricken, and decide to listen to Bri-gid.

12

Brid-gid – the French 'Bri-gid' – has hardly finished introducing the evening programme in the Great Hall to us in a torrent of words accompanied by lively gestures, when the waiters start serving the first course.

The choice was either prawn cocktail with avocadoes or a delicately cut beef carpaccio or snails in a strong garlic sauce.

It was probably out of consideration to each other that we all decided against the snails...

While we are having our first course I become fully aware that, although Lara's boyfriend hadn't turned up, our table is still complete. So everything worked out well, I think. But still, I have a somewhat strange feeling.

I thoroughly enjoy my prawn cocktail with avocadoes, it tastes really delicious and everyone else at our table seems to be relishing their first course just as much.

13

Now one show is followed by the next in short succession.

These shows only take place in the Great Hall. All the other smaller halls are reserved for people who want to go for a dance and a bop. They all have bars and tables – high tables around which people can stand together as well as low tables with comfortable chairs around. Anyone can retreat to one of these small halls to enjoy a bit of peace and quiet.

The next four courses of our meal are served during the intervals between shows. The food is absolutely delicious and everybody at our table is enjoying it. For the next course soup is served and the choice includes leek cream soup with bacon, potato soup, and tomato cream soup, and a choice of various salads.

Thereafter we all have a lime sorbet as intermediate course, followed by the main course with a choice of beef steak with a fine mushroom ragout and duchess potatoes, a poached cod with a glass noodle salad, pineapple chicken with tagliatelle and rare tuna steak with vegetable rice and Sauce Hollandaise.

The choice of desserts for the last course includes vanilla ice cream with hot chocolate sauce or fresh raspberries, light and dark chocolate mousse or a selection of fruits or cheeses.

I decide to have the leek cream soup, followed by the tender tuna steak and a vanilla ice cream with hot chocolate sauce. It is exquisite.

As regards the shows, I have rather mixed emotions. Not that they are of poor quality, quite the opposite, but for me it is a bit too much and in my opinion there is too little time left for conversation. Either we are busy eating or we have to be quiet in order to watch or to listen.

I feel a bit like sitting in a TV show: a little song here and there, in between a magician and a funny ventriloquist – by all means quite amusing, but mostly just light entertainment. All we need now is one of the cookery shows which are so popular on TV nowadays.

The entire evening programme is accompanied by Bri-gid, the endlessly babbling Mistress of Ceremonies, overdoing it a bit but always charming.

14

All in all a very nice evening and midnight is drawing close. I look around the hall. I see many faces but no one I know.

We relish the feeling of being just one family together.

Just before midnight Bri-gid takes the microphone again, babbles some more nice words about the Old Year and wishes everyone all the best for the New Year. Then the countdown starts and everyone in the hall counts at the top of their voices 10 – 9 – 8 – 7 – 6 – 5 – 4 – 3 – 2 – 1

Happy New Year,
a healthy and happy New Year

15

We toast one another, clinking our glasses and hug and kiss. We all wish the best of everything to everyone in the New Year. After a few minutes we decide to watch the New Year's Eve fireworks display, professionally prepared in front of the *Gürzenich* and the private fireworks in the neighbouring small streets of Cologne's historic town centre.

Lara does not seem so relaxed. While we are hugging one another some big tears roll down her cheeks. Is this her first lover's grief?

Helen gives her an especially heartfelt hug. Bob and Jenny kiss and Tom and his two friends Jasmin and Sascha hug each other.

Jasmin joins me with a glass of champagne and shakes my hand vigorously. She whispers with a rough voice which reminds me of a public prosecutor in a very popular German TV series: 'Everything is going to be all right...'

What does she mean by that? I thought everything *was* all right already.

16

The fireworks are simply fantastic. They are accentuated by well synchronised music. The entire evening is a huge success, I think, with absolutely no cause for complaint, and the first hours of the New Year promise great things to come.

The *"Bläck Föss"* – which means "barefooted" – and the *"Höhner"* – which means "hens", because in their early days the band used to perform dressed up as chickens – our very popular Cologne music bands then give us musical fireworks par excellence.

The fully packed Great Hall is rocking, drinks flow in abundance – of course alcoholic drinks as well – which makes the senses float and slowly fade away...

It is about half past two in the morning when Helen and I decide to leave. It is not far to our hotel and we go on foot. At this time it would be futile to wait for a taxi anyway.

We say goodbye to everybody we met by chance in the course of the evening.

But where is the rest of our family?

So we start a search for them. Jenny and Bob we find leaning against a bar counter in one of the smaller halls. They want to stay. We decide to drink a last nightcap with them and order the famous traditional drink of Cologne, the legendary *"Köbes"*, a delicious herbal bitters.

Köbes is the Cologne vernacular for the name "Jacob" and in Cologne the waiter in a pub is usually called *"Köbes"*. I should add that since Cologne became the repository of the bones of the "Three Kings" it became an important stopover for pilgrims on the St. James's Way, known as the *"Jakobsweg"* in German, to Santiago de Compostela in Northern Spain.

The pilgrims always had lots to talk about and they were always short of money for the next stretch of their journey. So many publicans liked to employ them as waiters to chat with their guests. This is why in Cologne waiters are still called *"Köbes"*.

And even today you can meet *"Köbesses"* from all over the world in the typical Cologne pubs.

This is real "multi culture" at its best.

Whilst enjoying our pleasant herbal bitters and saying our goodbyes to Bob and Jenny the four of us notice Lara approaching. She also wants to stay a bit longer and will go home with Tom. Tom and his friends are not in sight. We ask Lara to wish them good night from us.

Helen and I stagger slightly on our way to the cloakroom when we bump into Tom and his friends in the lobby.

Probably with ample alcohol in their blood they descend on us – all three of them – boisterously and – all three of them again – holding hands, to say goodbye to us.

Helen and I are a bit beyond our sell-by date and we stumble towards our hotel.

A new year has started and we have said a wonderful goodbye to the old one. 'May the stars be well-disposed towards us in the New Year,' I mumble to myself "thinking aloud" but blissfully foggy-brained.

However, at the same time I feel a cold shiver run and well tuned yet I have a strange feeling in my stomach. It is the undefined feeling that nothing is really as it seems at the moment...

17

On New Year's Day Helen and I return to Aachen. Before we leave, we visit my parents' graves. Later Bob and Jenny will join us in Aachen to spend another two nights with us before they go back to Munich on Sunday.

This is why we want to have a meal together on Saturday evening at home. Lara will stay with Tom in Cologne before they both join us on Saturday. Of course, she wants to go shopping in the famous *"Schildergasse"* on Saturday morning.

For Tom it is only a stone's throw from Cologne to Aachen, especially since the motorway was finally extended to three lanes in each direction years ago.

So he sometimes decides on the spur of the moment as to whether he stays in Aachen or drives home again, especially when the evening might have gone on for a bit longer than expected and he might have emptied a few glasses too many.

This morning, it is meanwhile Saturday, I hear that Tom and Lara will be coming unaccompanied. So we will only be six for our meal. Helen and I wouldn't have been averse to Lara's boyfriend Dirk and Tom's friends joining us for the meal.

That would have been the ideal occasion to get to know Dirk and to have a further conversation with Tom's friend Jasmin who seemed to be different in some way but at the same time also very intriguing.

Helen prepares the meal, lamb with string beans and potatoes, preceded by a celery soup and followed by red fruit jelly.

Helen is a fantastic cook and since "the way to a man's heart is through his stomach" it may be one of the reasons why I am still so much in love with her.

Lara is helping her. She also likes to cook. My own expertise in the kitchen is rather meagre.

Bob and Tom, however, learnt how to cook from their mother years ago when they moved into their own student flats. They wanted to be independent, but for quite a long time independence in the kitchen amounted for me to eggs and fried potatoes, eggs with noodles and bacon, frozen pizzas and spaghetti with sauces out of packets.

Bob and Jenny went for a long walk through the city today more like an extended shopping spree I guess, but they also visited the beautiful Aachen Cathedral.

The famous Emperor Charles I, who was later dubbed "Charlemagne" or "Charles the Great"[16], wanted to become sedentary, unlike his royal ancestors who were continually on the move with their entire court.

He chose Aachen as his permanent residence, not only because he liked to relax in the thermal water from the hot springs flowing through Aachen – after those in Budapest the second hottest in Europe – but also because he liked the moderate climate and the location in the geopolitical centre of his realm at the time.

He died in Aachen in 814 which prompted the authorities of the City of Aachen to arrange a magnificent spectacle to celebrate the 1,200th anniversary of this death in 2014.

At the beginning of the 790s Charlemagne planned the construction of a monumental Palatine Chapel.

The huge octagon of the Cathedral, modelled on Byzantine buildings, was erected as the centrepiece of the Royal Palace in Aachen between 796 and 805. It was the first of its kind north of the Alps and remained unsurpassed for 200 years.

The Gothic choir hall to the east of the octagon was added between 1355 and 1414. The present Cathedral with its steeple and its vestibule on the west side was finished in the 18th century.

The interior of the Aachen Cathedral is a true gem: with its floors and its walls lined with precious marble and its mosaics covering the ceilings of the arched groin vaults around the octagon and the mosaics covering the entire cupola of the octagon it is unequalled worldwide.

On the instruction of Charlemagne, his son and successor, Louis the Pious, crowned himself king in the Cathedral. 31 German kings were crowned in Aachen Cathedral between 936 and 1531.

The shops in the city centre of Aachen, which in comparison to Cologne has a more peaceful atmosphere, stay open till late. The first two Saturdays after Christmas are usually very busy due to the brisk exchange of presents which do not fit or which the beneficiaries may not like or want.

In the late afternoon Bob and Jenny return, at about the same time as Tom and Lara arrive from Cologne.

When Jenny enters the kitchen she sees the as yet unroasted lamb lying on the table top. She meant it as a joke with a double meaning when she said that this lamb must really have screwed up its young life gathering so much bad karma to have ended up in the frying pan like this. And so it might even suffer a double penalty: the lamb might possibly have been a human being in its past life and then was reincarnated as a lamb only to be punished for gathering too much bad karma. And where would it be going from here . . . ?

Jenny really only wanted to make a joke, but she catches Lara, who also happens to be in the kitchen, completely on the wrong foot. This is probably due to her not being in a good mood anyway, otherwise she probably would have taken Jenny's rather harmless remarks less seriously.

I am sitting in the adjoining lounge reading and I can hear everything that's going on, especially since neither of them can speak quietly – and even less now; as if bitten by a tarantula Lara snarls at Jenny:

'Just stop all this rubbish about reincarnation, there is no truth in that whatsoever. It's all a fabrication drummed up by humans thousands of years ago, due to their craving for justice. Reincarnation is absurd – here in Western society it is merely some kind of alternative protest which has become fashionable in the esoteric scene.'

'I am not stupid and I believe in it all the same,' Jenny snaps back, 'first of all, it has been proven long since that reincarnation is a fact and, secondly, even in your church it was believed in former times, it was just stifled early on.'

'What do you mean with "long since proven"? That's rubbish. Reincarnation can't be proven, simply because it doesn't exist,' Lara returns.

'And why do you think it is that so many children can exactly remember their previous lives, even down to the smallest details, which can be verified and which have been investigated countless times?' Jenny won't let go.

'Are you referring to the research results Ian Stevenson came up with?'

'Yes, for example. After all, he said that, after having gathered the reports of several thousand children, he believed in reincarnation because these statements convinced him.'

Jenny smiles triumphantly; with this she seems to have conclusive evidence in her hands.

'Fiddlesticks!' Lara is by no means beaten. 'When Stevenson talks about his own conviction it doesn't mean that with this huge number of cases he has proved anything at all. Fact is that he . . .' Lara hurries into the lounge, without hesitating she takes a book out of the bookcase and rushes back into the kitchen, 'fact is,' she continues, 'that in his main book Stevenson writes on the last page . . . I'll read it out to you: *"I think it is advisable to end this book admitting our uncertainty, yes, even emphasising it. Although the study of these children, who claim to remember a former life, has convinced me that some of them in fact may be reincarnated, it also established certainty in me that we very nearly know nothing about reincarnation."* She stops reading and slams the book shut with a loud bang.[17]

Without a break she continues: 'Many years ago, there was a programme on TV about metaphysics, it was called "PSI". I watched a few sequels when they were repeated later, therefore I know that Ian Stevenson was also interviewed there and that he even said that not one of his several thousand cases could be used as *proof* for reincarnation.'[18]

'And why is it written even in the Bible that reincarnation exists?' Jenny ups the ante.

'Where did you read that? I know that there are even books in which something like that is purported, but it is untrue. Nowhere is this written down, some things are just getting confused. It already starts with the term "reincarnation" which is really a very modern expression. Actually, it was invented by the founder of spiritualism, the French Allan Kardec[19] who lived in the 19th century. And ever since, the Christian "rebirth" – which really means "*regeneratio*" – and "reincarnation" – which is on a par with the former "transmigration" – are lumped together resulting in their being continuously confused with one another.

'Yes, reincarnation does indeed exist in the Christian doctrine, even twice, but both times it means something completely different. On the one hand it means "re-birth", the "turning to Christ" through Baptism. And on the other hand it means the "re-birth in death" as the "re-birth in the spirit".'

'I see, there we have it, now you say it yourself,' Jenny interrupts my daughter, 'so it is written down in the Bible, I am right after all . . .'

'Let me finish,' Lara now interrupts Jenny, 'this means, however, that with his death a human starts his life "with God". This is his "re-incarnation".'

'But this agrees with your doctrine: when you die you are dead and you decompose. "Ashes to ashes, and dust to dust!" Your priests cite this at every funeral. Then at some time or other the trumpets will resound and our almighty God will create all humans "anew from his memory". All this will happen on "Judgement Day".' Jenny seems to have expert knowledge.

'Here again many things are completely confused. Not least due to purely human inventions which exist in our religion as well,' Lara ripostes. 'Why don't you just read the Bible and see what Jesus said when he was hanging on the cross. He said to one of the thieves who was hanging side by side with him: *"Assuredly, I say to you, today you will be with Me in Paradise."*[20] Why should he say that if his death meant his immediate end?

'And how could Jesus appear to his disciples shortly after his resurrection and let Thomas put his hand into his wounded side, if he had been permanently dead?'

I had closed my book long ago and I follow the rather loud conversation with great interest. I admire Lara for her obviously very profound knowledge of the Bible, and also for her intellectual analysis of numerous other non-Christian religious concepts.

Mainly, though, I admire her for her blazing passion which she is expressing here.

And it amazes me again how this came about, how she developed such passion without ever having been encouraged by her family . . .

Lara is now unstoppable:

'Jenny, please understand, this is the great thing about true Christianity. It carries the message of "resurrection" as its key message into the world . . .'

'Yes, on "Judgement Day", what a cold comfort, and until then people lie in their graves and decompose. And when your God later forgets to reconstruct someone from his memory . . . ?' Jenny interrupts her tauntingly and wants to poke fun at her.

'. . .it is not the resurrection that happens on "Judgement Day". I must admit that it is often termed that and is even taught as such. In fact, however, it means much more. The "Judgement Day" offers a kind of second, maybe even the real resurrection at the "end of all days". It is then in the Christian sense even more significant than the first. But in this sense it is rather to be understood as the ultimate redemption of man with God.'

Lara doesn't let herself be at all confused. '...but the "first" resurrection for each of us takes place already when we die. At that point we are simply not redeemed yet. The deceased "enters the Kingdom of God" as it says in the Bible, but it is more like going into a different room, just a "better" one.'

'And do your priests know that, the bishops and even your Pope?' Jenny continues to quip.

'Oh yes indeed, it has become well-known even in those circles,' Lara responds to Jenny's irony. 'Here, I'll quote Pope John Paul II for you, who has already been canonised: *"You should not assume that life after death only starts with the Judgement Day! Exceptional conditions rule after a person has died a natural death. It is a transitional phase in which the body disintegrates and the life of a spiritual element begins. This element is equipped with its own consciousness and its own will and that in such a way that the person still exists although he no longer possesses a body."*'[21]

Now Lara has to take a breath.

But soon after she continues: 'And the entire rubbish with "death is the end, dust to dust" and all the rest, all this and much more comes from theologians, that is living human beings, who have just simply thought it all up.

'This is how the so-called "total death belief" has firmly established itself in the Evangelical Church by which they mean that life ends with death and it is total and irrevocable in every aspect and on every level, with spirit, soul and body.

'This has nothing to do with the Bible and the central Christian message of the resurrection directly after death, that is with a real *"re-birth"* into something *completely different* for us living in the "here and now"...'[22]

She stops suddenly when she sees me standing in the doorway, listening intently. Helen also seems to have listened with great interest, at least since Lara mentioned the Evangelical Church.

Although *I* believe neither in reincarnation nor in resurrection after death I avoid starting a scientific discussion to argue against my daughter. I am delighted about her performance and I don't want to tarnish this moment.

Jenny tries one last time to convince Lara that reincarnation as rebirth in a new physical body is firmly rooted even in the Bible. 'Lara, the Bible states in the Gospel of John that Jesus said: *"without reincarnation no salvation".'*

But here too Lara can immediately counter. She takes the Bible and thumbs through it for a short while. Then she reads out loud: 'Here it is really written down: *"Jesus answered Nicodemus and said unto him, "Verily, verily, I say unto thee, except a person be born again from above, he cannot see the kingdom of God." Nicodemus said unto him, "How can a man be born when he is old? Can he enter the second time into his mother's womb and be born?"*

Jesus answered, "Verily, verily, I say unto thee, except a person be born again from above, he cannot see the kingdom of God. . . . Unless a man is born of water and of the Spirit, he cannot enter into the kingdom of God. That which is born of the flesh is flesh, and that which is born of the Spirit is spirit. Marvel not that I said unto thee, Ye must be born again from above".'[23]

'Jenny, if you would just take the trouble to think about it without any prejudice and try to understand this, then it becomes very clear: a human being consists of body *and* spirit. But only the spirit is reborn again because only the spirit is immortal. But it is not reborn in a new worldly body.'

After all this we have really earned our dinner which is, as usual, exceedingly delicious, and later on we enjoy a nice evening together without any controversial discussions.

18

It is Sunday after New Year's Eve, 3rd January.
After having finished our probably last breakfast together for the time being – Tom didn't go back to Cologne the night before – Bob and Jenny set off on their long trip home to Munich.

Bob had come by car while Jenny had taken the train to Cologne on New Year's Eve.

We give them an affectionate farewell and hope to see them again soon.

Lara is sick again. She feels a bit under the weather and retreats to her room.

Helen is still busy, so Tom, who wants to go back to Cologne in the course of the afternoon, and I sit in our lounge and have a glass of brandy together in comfort.

'Father...,' Tom speaks in a low voice, and when he says "Father" he is always serious or he wants to talk about a serious matter.

'Father...,' he starts again for a second time, 'what do you think about my two friends who accompanied me to the party on New Year's Eve?'

'Well, I think they are quite nice,' I reply. 'Unfortunately I didn't have much opportunity to have a longer conversation with them. Up until midnight we were constantly eating and when we weren't eating we watched the shows, and afterwards we were all a bit tipsy. Moreover, you kept disappearing, I hardly saw you again.'

'But of course we were there, at least when the *"Höhner"* and the *"Bläck Fööss"* performed we were there,' Tom contradicts me.

'That's true, but we could not really have much of a conversation then. Well, your friend Sascha was extremely polite and attentive towards your mother and me. What does he do professionally?'

'He is a designer, mainly in the field of product design, and a photographer, especially for commercial photography. He develops perfume bottles, for example, and modern seating furniture for which he also delivers the appropriate advertising photos,' Tom explains to me.

'So he designs armchairs you can't sit in because for sheer design they are so uncomfortable?' I taunt a little.

'No, really, they are very comfy, and he has already made quite a good name for himself. He has sold some of his perfume bottles to several well-known brands,' Tom remains calm.

'And what does Jasmin do?' I ask.

'She is a journalist at the WDR radio and television station'. I smile: 'Maybe she could whip up a decent documentary on the World Congress for Physicists in September?'

Tom remains silent. Without hesitation I continue:

'Jasmin is a very interesting young woman but, at the same time, she makes a peculiar impression on me,' I elaborate. 'I find her very charming. She is beautiful, somehow a real "femme fatale". At the same time, she has very austere facial features, she is tall and has a rather rough and also deep voice for a young woman,' I continue.

'You know, Son,' I am rather straightforward, 'at first I thought that maybe she isn't a real woman but a man dressed up as a woman, you know, one of those drag queens. On the one hand she is very attractive and appears quite feminine. On the other hand, her almost masculine features and her unusually rough and deep voice somehow startled me or rather mystified me. Sascha in contrast made an almost feminine impression on me. When I experienced them both together I had the feeling they "play for the other team".

'I don't mind gays, but being so is not normal even if today I get the impression that it seems almost fashionable to be gay. Thirty or forty years ago people were prosecuted for it, even here in Germany.

'In many countries homosexuals are still discriminated against, unfortunately sometimes even killed. Of course, this is absurd and absolutely awful. Nevertheless, I believe that homosexuality is an illness or a pathological behavioural disorder which can be treated... But at the end of the day this doesn't concern me. I am just happy that we don't have anything like that in our family.

'Tom you sounded so serious just then, what was it you wanted to tell me?'

Tom looks at me, a little pale around the nose.

'Oh, nothing... at the moment... um... no, nothing important,' he stammers.

'I have to go now, anyway, I still have to see to things,' he utters and stands up abruptly.'

'But why? I am so happy to sit here with you and have a conversation with just the two of us. This doesn't happen so very often.'

I am rather surprised that he wants to leave so suddenly. But unfortunately, out of the blue, our short conversation ends here.

Tom picks up his bits and pieces and packs his bags. He says goodbye to his mother and looks for Lara who is again locked in the bathroom to give way to her recurring sickness.

'Cheerio, Dad,' he calls to me, gives me a quick hug and hurries to his car.

How strange, I ponder. Was there anything wrong?

19

The same evening our doorbell rings. I have just immersed myself in my Sunday newspaper and so I don't react immediately.

However, the doorbell rings again. Tired and a bit slow and clumsy I drag myself to the door. A tall man is standing in front of me, definitely more than one meter ninety, dark-haired and with a full beard. I guess he is easily at the end of thirty years old, he is slim and rather elegantly dressed.

'Good evening, what can I do for you?' I ask. He looks at me with big eyes.

'My name is Dirk Bender, I would like to see Lara, is she here?'

So, this is him! Lara's boyfriend? The one whose existence I only heard of a few days ago by chance.

My first thought is: he is so much older than Lara. She is still almost a child, but this gentleman in front of me, at first sight not really disagreeable, but he could almost be Lara's father.

'Yes, one moment, please, I don't know where she is, she seemed to be unwell,' I reply, surprised and bemused, 'but come in, please. I'll call her.'

At the same moment Helen approaches us swiftly. She probably was in the lounge to do some sewing.

Helen loves to sew and is a master dressmaker.

'Helen this is Mr Bender, and he would like to see Lara,' I pass the late guest on to her.

Helen stops short but it's hardly noticeable.

'One moment, please, I'll call Lara, she is not very well,' Helen addresses "Dirk" in a rather cool manner.

Shortly thereafter, Lara comes down the stairs.

Our house has four half-story stacked floors. We live on the outskirts of Aachen, where an entire estate of such terraced houses was built about thirty years ago. They are all identical on the inside. Although they have a narrow front they are rather deep towards the back. Each house has a small front garden, an attached garage and a nice-sized garden behind the house. The different floor levels are interconnected by steps. It is quite spacious and there is plenty of stowage room. On the one hand everything is relatively close by; on the other hand it is generously spaced out. When we came to Aachen, it was just right for us, and we still enjoy living in this house.

'What do you want?' Lara is almost beside herself, and I am completely dumbfounded to hear her yelling like that. It is actually a mixture of shouting and crying.

'Get lost! I never want to see you again ever, and especially not tonight . . .,' she shouts at Dirk who now looks pretty taken aback.

White as a sheet and rooted to the ground he is standing in the hall.

'Lara, at least we could talk about everything calmly,' he tries to placate her.

'No, just go, now immediately! I don't want to hear any more. You should have thought about it earlier,' she is still yelling at him while she is crying her eyes out. Then she turns on her heels and flees upstairs to her room. Helen follows her.

Dirk Bender is left standing in the hall not knowing what he should do.

I ask him whether he would like to join me in the lounge. He nods and follows me in. I wave him to a seat and offer him a brandy. I think we both need one now.

The New Year seems not to have started as nicely as I had hoped, I think, but it remains still a fairly vague feeling that is flashing through my mind while I pour the brandy for both of us.

20

'Professor Schneider, I apologise for bursting in on you like this on a Sunday evening,' Mr Bender addresses me. 'I would like to introduce myself. I am a physician; more precisely I am a casualty surgeon. And I am a consultant at the university hospital. That is how I know your wife, by the way. A few months ago I met your daughter Lara. She came to the hospital to visit her mother who was not in her office at the time. I was just passing and Lara turned to me and asked whether I could help her. We started a conversation and later I asked her whether she would care to have dinner with me.

'You know, I've been divorced for a year now and I have two little children who live with my wife. She hardly allows me to visit them, so I only see them very rarely. I told Lara about it and I also told her how very sad I am about the whole situation. During a conversation I must have dropped the word "suicide". This idea was indeed in my mind shortly after the divorce. But Lara gave me new courage and put me together again. She told me of her deep faith in God and that death is not the end of us. She said that, if I committed suicide I would just take my problems with me and would only have to find a solution in another place. Suicide wouldn't be a way out of the dilemma. We met frequently after our first encounter and, yes, finally I fell in love with her and she fell in love with me...'

'Lara is only eighteen years old...' I am a bit stroppy.

'Yes, I know, but it just happened. We fell in love and we are very much in love. Well, and then...'

'Yes, and then what?' I grill him.

'Well, it is how it is when you fall in love; we became closer to each other...'

'I don't believe it. Lara is profoundly religious and she is so influenced by her Catholic faith that she would not allow that to happen before she is married,' I absolutely do not believe what I hear, quite the contrary.

'But it is as I say. We became closer and closer and then...,' Dirk Bender breaks off.

I am sitting in my chair and stare at this physician.

I'm lost for words.

'What shall I tell you? A few weeks ago Lara missed her period. At first she was absolutely distraught, then she was beside herself and couldn't be calmed down. In the end she bought herself a pregnancy test in the chemist shop.'

'Yes . . . and?' I only utter these two words hesitantly.

'It is positive.' Dr Bender looks at me without adding another word.

Now the penny slowly drops and it starts to dawn on me why Lara has been feeling sick so often lately, why it was that she was constantly vomiting and why she is so dismissive, especially over the last few days when we were all enjoying a nice get-together.

She hasn't told us anything at all. I didn't believe my "little daughter" was capable of doing this. Of course, I had hoped that one day she might meet a nice suitable man to fall in love with and that that man would love her as well.

Of course, I had also hoped that she would get married one day and would give Helen and me one or more grandchildren.

But now? And like this?

And then this "old" man, and a physician to boot, someone who should know everything there is to know about contraception? And on top of everything else a divorcee and a father of two children? I am frantic with fury – less so at Lara than at this "Dirk".

I can't utter a single word.

Wordlessly we sit face-to-face, sometimes we stare at each other; sometimes we just look in a different direction and ignore the other.

It takes quite a while before we stir again.

I look out of the window into the garden. Earlier in the day it had snowed a bit covering the garden under a white blanket, if only a thin one as if dusted with icing sugar.

The lamps in our garden are switched on and make the snow sparkle in their light.

I can't exchange another word with this man.

Helen returns to the lounge. She looks at us but decides not to say anything.

She seems to know what is going on.

'Dr Bender . . . ,' Helen is the first one to speak at long last. She has known him a while as a medical colleague from the hospital. ' . . . what do you imagine should happen now?'

21

'I think I know how this could have happened . . .' Dr Bender starts hesitantly.

'Please spare us any further explanations,' I stop him, assuming that he wants to come out with intimacies. 'I don't want to know the details.' The rage inside me is reflected by the unusually loud tone of my voice.

'I just wanted to tell you,' Dirk Bender continues after a short pause, 'that I asked Lara not to put us in this situation after I had learned what had happened and why.' Dirk Bender tries to explain the situation without going into details.

'What exactly do you mean?' I ask back not having understood his insinuations.

'Well, there is the "morning-after" pill. And I offered Lara to give her a prescription for it. I even urged her repeatedly to take it. But she strictly refused to do so. Of course, she didn't want to be pregnant now, but she didn't want either to take measures against it because it contradicts her religious beliefs . . . ,' Dr Bender explains to us.

'Holy crap! That's what religions do for you!'

I am furious with him and now really peeved about my daughter too. All this bullshit just makes problems for everyone, here as well as everywhere else in the world. Dawkins is right when he says that the belief in God and indeed all religions are utter rubbish and the scourge of humanity.[24]

'Mr and Mrs Schneider . . . ,' Dr Bender addresses us now in no uncertain terms, ' . . . I clearly told Lara to avoid a pregnancy. Now, since she didn't follow my suggestion and she is pregnant I have asked her to get an abortion.

'*I* can't afford another child . . .'

'What? *You* can't afford another child? Shouldn't you have thought about that sooner? You shouldn't have touched my daughter at all . . .'

I am very nearly losing control of myself.

'Our daughter,' Helen throws in, 'Lara is our child and she also has a say in this.'

The conversation is growing louder and louder and can't go unnoticed even outside the lounge. Lara has been able to overhear a few words and she comes in to join us.

'Didn't I just tell you to go,' she addresses her lover, 'I never want to see you here again . . . What do you want . . . ? Leave me alone.' Lara is sobbing her heart out.

'I am probably pregnant, yes,' she wails, 'I didn't want it, yes, but now it has happened. And when it happens like this then it is a gift from God.'

Helen seems torn between fear and hope. *I* think completely differently, in fact more like Dr Bender. But he was the one who should not have let this happen in the first place.

'Lara, you can still prevent it,' he starts again. 'You are going to take your school finals soon and then you want to go to university. You can't afford to have a child right now. Don't let this happen, listen to me, Lara.'

Lara shakes her head.

'Just leave me in peace. I am going to my gynaecologist tomorrow and for a thorough examination. And if I should really be pregnant then that's that . . . ,' Lara looks at Dirk in an almost contemptuous way and hurries out of the room, probably to retreat to her own room.

I take another brandy, I think it is a triple one this time. I am absolutely knackered.

Helen doesn't want a brandy, but I'm sure she could do with one. And I conveniently "forget" to offer one to Mr Bender.

Anyway, he gets up suddenly, bids his farewell from a safe distance and beats a hasty retreat. Helen follows him and accompanies him to the door. Then she comes back and sits down next to me.

'I do understand you and I also understand Dr Bender,' she whispers. 'Of course, this should never have happened but what if it has happened? If Lara is indeed pregnant then she should be the one to decide whether she wants to carry the child to full term or not. And if she really wants to go through with it, for whatever reasons, we must accept it. We will manage that – we all together...'

Helen gets up and leaves the room.

I guess she goes to see Lara.

22

Lara's school holidays last for another week.

I can hear her having a loud discussion with Helen, but I can't make out any details. From the few scraps I do understand it seems that Lara is packing her bag.

Helen is very upset when she comes downstairs again. In answer to my question what was going on, she replies in a harsh and brusque tone: 'Lara wants to visit her girlfriend in Hamburg for a week. She wants to get away from it all. I tried to talk her out of it, but she says that she is eighteen years old and can decide for herself. So she is going anyway.'

We don't see Lara again this evening. She has locked herself in her room and admits neither Helen nor me. I wish her a good night from outside her door.

The next morning she gets up very early and is off and away. I never even heard her leaving. Nothing. Admittedly, I am already a bit hard of hearing, at least my family claims that I am. And sometimes I even believe that they are actually right.

Helen, on the other hand, has noticed her leaving. She is already waiting at the breakfast table for me.

'Lara was not to be deterred from leaving,' she says and looks at me with sad eyes. 'I tried again to make her stay, but to no avail. I think we must leave her in peace, she must find herself. Maybe it will really help her to find her inner balance when she has a change of scene and goes to Hamburg. Maybe talking it over with her friend Moni can help her. Everything will turn out right in the end.'

Helen is the born optimist. And that is one of the reasons why I love her.

23

For days now I have heard nothing from Lara or from Tom. Bob phoned a few days ago from Munich but I avoided telling him about Lara. We'd rather wait and see what the gynaecologist has to tell us. I now remember that Lara wanted to go there last Monday, the day after Dr Bender's visit. But then she went to Hamburg instead. In the end she has to decide for herself what to do and when to do it. My own opinion doesn't carry much weight anymore and I just have to sit back and see.

The implications of this new situation occupy my mind more and more. However, patience is not one of my virtues.

Of course, I have taken up my work at the RWTH again. There is a lot for me to do. And I should really start to prepare myself for the big day in September in New York, at least to define the framework and the general direction of my speech. Since this presentation is a great honour for me, I want everything to be perfect. Although it is still more than eight months until then, I must admit that I am getting a bit excited when I only think of it. Of course, Helen will accompany me. This occasion is a huge challenge for me to gain acknowledgement and in addition we'll have the opportunity to visit Helen's family again near Boston.

Helen comes home later than expected tonight.

She probably had some important things to discuss with her colleagues and other employees, a pretty normal procedure at the beginning of a new year. At the hospital, too, everything starts to pick up speed again and there is a lot to do.

When Helen comes home well after eight o'clock at night, she not only looks tired but is also visibly worn out.

'Has something happened?' I ask her. 'You look as if someone has attacked you.'

'It was just too much,' Helen plays it down, 'just too much.'

'Come and have something to eat.' I pass her a plate with some potato salad I prepared myself and two sausages with mustard. I always prepare the potato salad myself. Meanwhile it is one of the few dishes I am able to rustle up in the kitchen and it is rather delicious, even if I say it myself.

It doesn't really mean I have to peel the potatoes myself. I am too lazy for that: instead I buy peeled potatoes in small buckets, boil them and mix them with other ingredients such as apples, onions, gherkins and hard boiled eggs. Then I add mayonnaise or sour cream.

Finally I mix everything well and add salt and pepper. It tastes excellent, better still the next day.

'But only a little,' Helen says and puts half of the salad and one of the two sausages back. 'I can't eat so much at the moment.'

Initially I am holding back but then I ask her whether she has heard from Lara. Has she been to see the gynaecologist?

'I don't know, I haven't heard from her either,' Helen replies. 'I know she wanted to go there as soon as possible but then she decided to go to Hamburg. I don't know anything else. Maybe she went to see a doctor in Hamburg, possibly with Moni?'

I look at Helen and see that tears are running down her cheeks.

'What has happened?' I repeat. 'Come on, Helen, talk to me. Something must have happened.'

'Well, the hospital is getting on my nerves. I think they want to push me out. You know Mrs Kleber, don't you? You met her by chance when you came to see me in the hospital. It must be about two or three years ago. *Frauke Kleber* is the Nursing Manager responsible for my department. A few months ago she already indicated that vacancies in the positions of department heads, a position I also have, are not to be filled again. That did not affect me.

'But now it seems that these positions are going to be scrapped as soon as possible and that includes my job as well. Frauke came to me today and told me in no uncertain terms that I should apply for another job. Of course, I refused to do so.

'As a result she broke off our friendship. She threatened that from now on she would be watching me closely looking for any occasion to trip me up.'

'But that is pure mobbing,' I fly off the handle exasperated.

'That is my feeling exactly. I went directly to the Chairman of the Staff Council. And he said that mobbing is terrible and also unethical but unfortunately not a punishable offence.'

'Now, calm down first of all. Maybe it just slipped out in the heat of the moment and the witch didn't mean it. And in the end nothing happens,' I try to put Helen's mind at ease and take her into my arms. 'And if the worst comes to the worst, we will manage somehow – the two of us together.'

We smile at each other.

Now I recall that in fact I did meet Mrs Kleber personally by chance. Helen is right: when I visited her some years ago in the hospital, a woman came into her office. Helen introduced me to her. She was in her mid-thirties, fairly small but wiry, very slim with black hair cut short.

Actually she didn't even appear unlikable to me.

24

More than a week after she abruptly escaped to Hamburg Lara is back. Helen and I are sitting in our lounge with a glass of wine in the evening when the front door opens.

Lara comes in with a smile and sweetly bids us a good evening.

She doesn't say anything about her condition and utters no word about Dirk, her lover and the father of her unborn child, if she is pregnant at all that is.

So I take my heart into my hands and ask whether she has consulted a gynaecologist.

'How should I have managed that?' Her mood changes immediately and she is hissing at me. 'My gynaecologist is here and I was in Hamburg.'

'Well, I have heard that they do have gynaecologists in Hamburg as well, at least that's what I've been told, and last Sunday but one you wanted to go as soon as only possible . . . ,' I answer with a hint of cynicism.

'But then I decided to see my girlfriend Moni in Hamburg instead, didn't I,' she returns in a more moderate tone of voice.

'Why should I rush anything? In the end the inevitable will happen and that's it then! You keep on quoting: "What will be, will be". And you know: "It's always worked out before."'

Lara tries to put my mind at ease and lull me into thinking that all will be well in the end.

'And what about your Dirk?' I ask her.

'He is not *my* Dirk anymore,' she spits in a hissing tone of voice.

'I haven't heard from him and I haven't phoned him either. And now I don't want to discuss this subject any longer...'

She turns away and declines our invitation to eat with us. She also refuses to tell us anything about her trip to Hamburg. She just wants to retreat to her room and be left alone for the evening.

25

Lara is two months pregnant now.

The examination results are positive and she already has the first ultrasonic image.

We hardly meet; she constantly keeps out of my way. She is probably afraid I could involve her in a discussion about abortion.

The word alone is not to be uttered by anyone, Helen tells me.

I haven't heard from Dr Bender either. Helen sees him in the hospital from time to time, of course, but they have no further contact. At best they say hello to each other and sometimes, but rarely, they have to discuss professional items. But that is all. Nevertheless, Helen knows that Lara must have told him of her now confirmed pregnancy.

Of course, the situation is consistently occupying my mind as well.

Have they at least met and talked it over? Or has Lara texted him, as it is supposed to be so modern nowadays?

I wouldn't put it past her, especially since they both seem to have such absolutely contrasting ideas about their future, and even more so about their common future – under whatever conditions that could be.

Lara gives no indication whatsoever – not even in harmless conversation about mundane everyday things – that she might have changed her opinion with regard to her still early-days pregnancy: whether to go through with it or to get an abortion.

However, she has become more melancholic, that is true, but she lives the days as they come. She doesn't give the impression that she is suffering particularly from her condition.

At school she is preparing for her finals. She probably hasn't told her headmaster about her pregnancy, especially since no-one will notice anything before she picks up her leaving certificate. She probably thinks that it is of no concern to anyone but her and her alone and that the school has nothing to do with it.

Of course, she will possibly tell one or the other of her girlfriends about it sooner or later and it may then spread around through the grapevine.

However, I don't think that she is very distressed by it. At least she doesn't talk about it.

And what about her Catholic community? What happens when they hear of it? She never says a word to us about that either, at least not yet.

26

The first weeks of the new year passed by in a flash. Shortly we'll have "Carnival" again.

In the Rhineland region it is called the "fifth season", and especially for people from Cologne it is a time to be happy, boisterous and cheerful and people enjoy life to the full, without really running riot as strangers like to insinuate. People who cross the line in Cologne are usually tourists.

Although this year is still so young I don't feel much like celebrating.

In other years there were always some events Helen and I liked to visit, sometimes in Aachen, sometimes in Cologne.

For some years now, we have hardly participated in the so-called street Carnival which takes place on Rose Monday, the Monday before Lent, and which is the peak of the season in Carnival strongholds. That was different in former times, especially when our children were little. Then we went regularly to watch every possible Carnival procession.

Lara has also cancelled all her social commitments this year, very much to the amazement of her church community. Over the last few years she has always played an active role by preparing various events and especially by contributing some work to the Carnival sessions for children. I don't know what reasons she gave for not participating this year, but I know there won't be anything doing with regard to Carnival for her this year.

Bob is staying in Munich anyway where they celebrate "Shrovetide" which is quite different from the Carnival in Cologne. I think it is much more restrained. Of course, there are some Carnival events where things get lively but there is no hustle and bustle in the streets like here in Cologne. I know that Bob and Jenny want to attend one or the other Carnival party this year.

Of course, they both know meanwhile of Lara's pregnancy. Bob must have given her the same loving advice as I did, to have an abortion within the legally permitted time frame – especially when taking her overall situation into account. But his intervention seems to have been no more successful than mine.

Incidentally, Tom is the only one of us who still maintains an open line to Lara at the moment, with the possible exception of Helen.

Helen doesn't really think that Lara should carry the child to term either, but she is strictly against trying to influence her and wants to leave the decision entirely to Lara herself.

Tom on the other hand seems to support Lara in her intention to keep the child with no ifs or buts.

What a fine family, I muse. Wouldn't it be so much better if we were all pulling in the same direction?

When Tom was in Aachen last time, I casually approached him with regard to Carnival, but he dismissed me immediately claiming that he has such an enormous workload. He would probably not even be in Cologne this year; he wants to take a few days off.

Tom of all people, I thought at the time.

After all, Tom has always been the one who was more dedicated to Carnival than our two other children.

27

Today is Rose Monday.

Most outsiders know hardly, or not at all, what this day means for the locals it being a normal working day for them.

In Cologne, Aachen and most of the other Carnival strongholds in the Rhineland, however, this is one of the most important holidays of the year.

This is why most people don't work and most shops are closed, apart from the restaurants, pubs and other catering services, of course.

In Cologne especially, but also in other Carnival strongholds, this is the day on which they make their highest turnover of the year. It goes without saying, of course, that all schools are also closed for the day.

Lara told us yesterday that she planned to meet Dirk Bender again today on Rose Monday at long last to talk things over with him.

At least they both seem to be ready for a peaceful discussion. I'm pretty curious to see what they come up with.

Helen and I watched a Carnival session in Cologne on television yesterday evening. We both enjoyed it so much that we decided on the spur of the moment to go to Cologne today to witness the Carnival procession live from close up.

The Carnival procession on Rose Monday in Cologne is the longest in the whole of Germany. It is several kilometres long and it takes four to five hours from start to finish to pass through the city centre.

The first groups are already back home when the last haven't even started the procession. If the weather plays along, there will be more than one million people lining the procession route watching the magnificent spectacle. They usually sing and dance and sway to the music.

Everyone is partying exuberantly as if there was no tomorrow and all problems –whether large or small – are left at home, at least on this day.

The weather report promised us a really nice day for the procession: cold, dry and sunny – no rain and no ice or snow either. The temperature this morning is already +10 degrees Celsius which, for the beginning of February, is almost Mediterranean...

So Helen and I unhurriedly tootle off to Cologne after breakfast. We don't really take much effort with fancy dress costumes, so usually a hat, a colourful scarf and a carnivalesque jacket will do. We even manage to park our car close to the route of the procession – after all, we know our way around Cologne – and proceed to the *"Schildergasse"*, a wide shopping street, one of the busiest and most frequented by shoppers in Germany.

The procession is expected to pass by here shortly. We have already made new friends quickly with the people standing next to us, complete strangers, of course. People watching the procession are usually on first-name terms immediately. This is typical for Cologne and especially for the Carnival season. And it is just as normal to part afterwards without having learned who it was we had befriended and with no obligation to keep in contact later.

It is just easier to address one another with "Peter", "Franz" or "Tony", "Nannie" or "Marie" than without a name or with the surname which would sound rather stilted.

The procession is very nearly on time and it is yet again absolutely amazing – but also very long. And soon enough my feet start to hurt from standing for so long.

Of course, we both hold out until the end and we even pick up sweets which are thrown from the Carnival floats.

In the old days they just threw simple sweets from the floats, but today they have all kinds of goodies since simple candies are out. It is the same this year and many plastic bags brought by the visitors are later filled to bursting.

The Carnival Prince, in Cologne the highest office within the Triumvirate, these being the three rulers of the Carnival, the Prince, the Peasant and the traditionally male Virgin, as always the last to follow the procession through the streets. His magnificent carriage is the longest of all and is, as always, a feast for the eyes, worthy of a "Prince".

He is followed by the rubbish collectors of Cologne, a tradition as well. They immediately set to work and remove as fast as only possible all the rubbish and litter left behind by participants and visitors.

After the procession has passed by we say goodbye to our new friends of the day and walk slowly back to our car through the crowds of people dissipating at speed in all directions.

Whilst strolling along the inner ring around the old city centre of Cologne, we pass a cafe with tables and chairs and some high tables out in the street enticed by the mild weather.

Here we watch countless Carnival jesters having a good time. Three very tall young ladies around one of the high tables catch my eye. They are dressed in some kind of uniform usually worn by Carnival show dancers.

Historically this goes back to the sutlers who used to follow the armies as civilian merchants in former times. This tradition was found originally only in the Rhineland.

The dress includes high boots and short pleated skirts usually in the colours of the relevant Carnival organisation, completed by a frilled blouse, a short jacket and a hat covering a wig with plaits.

I look at these three young ladies and see that one of them kisses one of the others pretty passionately, while the third has a drag on her cigarette. She looks in my direction. I smile at her. She smiles back and suddenly she blows out a big cloud of smoke in a coughing fit.

Just then the two kissing ladies release each other from their passionate embrace.

I feel cold shivers running down my spine.

I realise who they are – in spite of the fancy dresses...

They are Sascha and ... our son Tom ...

Jasmin stubs out her cigarette.

I don't trust my eyes, I turn as red as a beet root and I am filled with consternation. I can't find words, I've lost my voice, no "hello", no . . . what ever ..., no nothing ...

I want nothing more than to be away from here.

I grab Helen's hand hastily and rush away with her without being able to say anything. Helen hasn't noticed the three young ladies ...

28

Our car is not far away. Helen and I get in, I'm driving. Helen looks at me with question marks in her eyes. But I remain silent. She doesn't know what to say. She has no idea why I am in such haste all of a sudden and why I have gone so quiet.

I take the main road towards the motorway. Thoughts are gyrating through my mind. Is our son Tom gay? Maybe it was just a fancy dress for the Carnival season? Nothing unusual in Cologne. But he kissed another man! Square on the mouth! Or did I get the wrong impression?

Helen still doesn't dare to speak to me.

We are already on the motorway leading to Aachen before she plucks up her courage and addresses me: 'Chris, what's the matter? You were in such a mad hurry all of a sudden and you just hustled me to the car. My hand is still hurting because you grabbed it so hard. And then ... nothing, not a single word from you. What got into you?

'Please excuse me, Helen, I didn't intend to hurt you,' and then I am lost for words again.

That's all, I remain silent.

'Chris, say something, what's the matter with you?' Helen doesn't give up easily.

After a while I pull myself together with an effort:

'I saw Tom just then.'

'Tom??? But why didn't you say anything to me? Why didn't you say hello to him?' Helen looks at me, absolutely stunned.

'Tom was there, but he wasn't alone.'

'So what? We could have said hello properly to him and to the others as well. Tell me, Chris, something is wrong. There must have been something else.' Helen is getting restless.

'Tom was there, together with Jasmin and Sascha. They were grouped around a table in the cafe on the corner. You remember the one where people could sit outside and where there was a large crowd of people?' I reply, still very hesitantly.

'Yes, so what?' Helen repeats. 'That's nothing to worry about, or is it?'

'If only . . .' I splutter. 'At first I only recognised Jasmin and smiled at her. She was dressed as a Carnival dancer . . .'

'She certainly looked good in that, didn't she?' Helen responds.

'Yes, she did, but next to her were two other Carnival dancers . . . and they . . . well, they kissed . . . they kissed each other passionately . . . you know . . . *very* passionately . . . and suddenly they looked at me . . . and I recognised Sascha and Tom . . .'

I am torn between anger and disbelief.

Helen remains quiet. The silence lasts till we arrive in Aachen. We don't exchange another word.

29

At home I fall wordlessly into my armchair and turn to my brandy again. This time it is a double straightaway. Helen takes the armchair next to mine and looks at me.

After a while she finds the first words:

'Tom should have told you long ago.'

'What should he have told me long ago?' I bark back.

'Well, that he is gay or at least bi...!'

'My son Tom is gay???' I am beside myself.

'I think so, yes, but that's not the end of the world,' Helen tries to calm me down. 'It's not his fault. That doesn't make him a different person! Or do you not love him anymore, now that you know?' She is really hitting home with that.

'Of course not,' I assure hastily, 'but...'

'What but? I asked him to tell you at long last...' Helen also pours a brandy for herself.

I simply can't grasp it.

'But Tom has had girlfriends. He introduced them to us, not only one but several. And now this?'

'Sometimes it takes a while before we are courageous enough to recognise our own real character and more so to reveal it to others, especially if it touches our own identity and it might pose a social or even familial problem,' Helen returns.

Then I remember how Tom had wanted to tell me something "important" on the Sunday after our New Year's Eve party, but then he didn't do it.

Now it dawns on me why he had refrained from telling me. We had talked about Sascha and Jasmin and I had said to him that I had a feeling as if Sascha might be "playing for the other team" and that Jasmin seemed to be a "drag queen"...

Now I also remember how Tom had suddenly become very quiet and had beaten a hasty retreat... He probably wanted to tell me there and then. And I bungled it.

'Rubbish, real character!' I raise my voice again, quite annoyed. 'Homosexuality is just a disease, and diseases can be treated. Tom should go to see a psychiatrist as soon as possible...'

Helen remains mute. After a brief pause I continue:

'And anyway, who is whose friend? Tom introduced Jasmin as "his girlfriend" on New Year's Eve.'

'They are all three of them close friends,' Helen begins to explain to me carefully. 'All three of them have been living together for six months now in some kind of flat-sharing trio. Jasmin is transsexual, by the way. She used to be a man, but now she is on her way to becoming a woman.'

'On her way to becoming a woman??? What exactly does that mean?' I snap at her.

Helen looks at me as if I were the last country bumpkin.

'Jasmin takes hormones and with their help she is almost a real woman already, apart from ... well, you know what I mean, don't act as if you were that stupid,' she tries to kick-start me.

She doesn't have to continue. I am not that far out of touch. I lean back and feel absolutely exhausted. In desperation I pour myself another brandy. It seems as if everything around me is falling in and my world is collapsing. How harmonious everything seemed to be at Christmas, and now ... ?

30

The following days rush past me unnoticed.

I am not really in my right mind. At least there are no major problems or incidents at the institute.

At present I couldn't handle any untoward circumstances. Right now I'm sick to my back teeth with it all.

Lara, only eighteen years old, is already pregnant, although she has always depicted herself as being a pious Catholic. She hasn't even finished school but she wants to carry the child to term, no matter what. I can't get my head around all this.

And my son Tom is gay and has had some hanky-panky going on for the last six months with a man and a creature that is "half-man-half-woman" has been living with them in their joint flat.

For me this is against nature, and it hits me at a very vulnerable spot deep in my heart. I haven't spoken a single word to Tom since. I am completely shell-shocked.

31

A few weeks later Helen comes home at night in tears.

I am stunned, what is it this time?

'Helen, what's happened?' I look at her inquiringly.

'They ... are trying ... to blame ... me ... for crooked dealings,' she sobs.

'Who is trying what?'

'I think it is my boss, Frauke Kleber.'

'Come here and sit down. And now tell me again, and keep calm,' this time *I* try to settle *her*.

I pour us a glass of red wine each and we sit together on our comfortable settee in our lounge. Helen nestles down in my arms.

'Now come again, but slowly, what exactly has happened?'

'Frauke is bad mouthing me in the personnel department. She claims that I have repeatedly taken food and drinks which were delivered to the ward for the patients and which I allegedly consumed myself. That is strictly forbidden in the hospital. For years now we have received various circular letters in which it is expressly stated that this is not allowed and that whoever does it anyway must expect personal consequences,' Helen explains. 'Everyone knows that we are not allowed to do it,' Helen is still sobbing.

'And, did you?' I inquire.

Helen is furious and hisses back at me: 'Of course not, what do you think? I would never do that. I am not so stupid as to put my job on the line for something so utterly foolish.'

'But why does Mrs Kleber think that you of all people should do it? She could only say so if she actually caught you in the act and saw you eating. But nobody could be that stupid even if they don't respect the ban. Couldn't it then have been someone completely different?' I suggest.

'Allegedly they have found trays with empty dishes and a few leftovers of meals in my office which is located next to the accident surgery of the geriatric ward on Floor 28. Sister Elvira, the staff nurse for

Floor 28, claims to have seen how I have sometimes taken a tray from the meal trolley.'

Helens sobbing increases: 'Of course, now and again I take a look at the trays on the trolley which are sent up from the kitchen. I often check the names of patients and see to it that certain requirements are met, for example with regard to restrictions for certain patients, because they may not be allowed to eat this or that. But I never take a tray away to eat the food myself. I don't know what to do now. For the time being they are demanding a written explanation from me and I have till the end of April to submit it, since the personnel manager will be on sick leave for some time. In addition I have to go and see him personally then.'

After a short break she sighs: 'You know, Chris, I think this Kleber woman wants to get rid of me by hook or by crook. She already terminated our friendship at the end of last year...'

'You don't have any witnesses for that unfortunately, which would have been good, but...,' I return completely at a loss.

'She is not so stupid as to say anything like that in the presence of witnesses...,' Helen replies briskly.

'Helen, we will come through this together, even though I don't know how at the moment. But you must get a lawyer; I don't think we'll get along without one. Why don't you ask the Works Council whether they can recommend one who is well versed in employment law? I'll ask around in the Institute as well. And then we must calmly reflect on how to proceed in this case.

Helen goes to her room. She is dead beat and just wants to go to sleep; she doesn't even want anything to eat.

32

I am still sitting in my armchair in the lounge, ruminating again, when the telephone starts ringing.

Tom is on the other end.

'Dad!' He speaks in such a subdued tone that I can hardly hear him. 'I am so sorry about everything. I didn't want you to discover it like this. I have tried several times to talk with you about it all, last time was on the Sunday after New Year's Eve, when we were sitting together alone in Aachen, but...'

'I know, Tom, your mother told me after I saw you two ... Sascha and you ... and of course Jasmin...' I can't finish the sentence.

'Anyway, I remember that you wanted to tell me something "important", but you never got round to it and shortly after, you left for Cologne so abruptly...,' I continue.

'Yes, you felt instinctively that Jasmin and possibly also Sascha are no straight "heterosexuals" and you dubbed them as being sick, but...'

'...but that is what it is, and you must undergo treatment as well...,' I cut off Tom's words.

'Father,' Tom is obviously very serious again, 'this is no disease and none of us has to undergo any treatment. What you are saying is utter nonsense. I don't know how you arrive at such an old fashioned and mistaken perception. You don't still believe that the Earth is flat...?' He counters immediately and vehemently.

'But that is something completely different...,' I declare thinking that I would rather end our conversation now.

'Let's talk about it some other time and not over the telephone. At the moment I have other problems...' However, I cannot finish my sentence.

'Is something the matter with Lara?' Tom interrupts me and sounds worried.

'No, with Mum,' I return, not less worried and then I tell him everything Helen reported to me today.

'Dad,' Tom seems to be far more relaxed about it, 'give me a chance. Let me talk it over with Jasmin and Sascha. Jasmin is a pretty shrewd journalist. Maybe she has an idea as to how we could help Mum. I'll ring you back soon,' he soothes me and fills me with a little hope at the same time.

We say goodbye and I promise to discuss the matter with him in peace and quiet, in a face-to-face personal dialogue.

While I slowly empty my glass of wine I go back over everything I have heard today. Then I decide to go to bed too. At that moment Lara walks through the door. Although we do say hello to each other we don't say anything else. Not today, anyway.

33

The very next day, after her office hours Helen visits a lawyer who is a friend of ours. Dr Karl Kluge takes notes of her statements, asks a number of specific questions which she answers precisely. Then he gives her the advice that it is imperative to take a member of the Works Council with her to the official hearing.

Since there is time enough before then, he intends to start by gathering more information and promises to contact Helen again in good time to discuss everything with her.

Later, in the hospital, Helen contacts Peter Hansen. He is head of the workers' representation and spontaneously agrees to accompany her to the hearing at the personnel department in a few weeks time.

34

Lara's pregnancy is progressing "as expected", how she likes to express it. She does not think about an abortion anymore and indeed she never did. I have the feeling that the time for a legal abortion has expired anyway. However, I still don't know exactly what's going on. It would be futile anyway, even if I did. She will shortly sit her final examinations at school and she is revising for them intensely – mostly at Nicole's, her closest girlfriend in Aachen.

Some evenings I ask her whether I could help her in any way, but she hasn't accepted my offers up to now.

Philosophy and English are her advanced courses. She would have preferred to take an advanced course in religious studies, but that did not materialise owing to insufficient demand.

Her other two advanced level subjects are mathematics and a basic course in religious studies. Lara is, of course, unbeatable in English it being her second mother tongue.

Lara excels in religious studies as well – as she has always done, in stark contrast to me.

The critical issue is surely mathematics, but she is practising incessantly. Fortunately enough her teacher is more "practically" orientated and aims primarily to teach mathematics as a tool for use in everyday life, so to speak, more than anything else.

If he had the penchant for more theoretical mathematical knowledge, such as delving into more complex mathematical arguments or the like, Lara would surely have major problems. But meanwhile she is quite confident that she is going to manage mathematics as well.

She doesn't seem to be in contact with her friend Dirk at the moment, at least as far as I know.
Although they did have a meeting she didn't tell us very much about it, obviously it didn't rebuild bridges between them.

If he had the penchant for more theoretical mathematical knowledge, such as delving into more complex mathematical arguments or the like, Lara would surely have major problems. But meanwhile she is quite confident that she is going to manage mathematics as well.
She doesn't seem to be in contact with her friend Dirk at the moment, at least as far as I know.
Although they did have a meeting she didn't tell us very much about it, obviously it didn't rebuild bridges between them.
Notwithstanding my bewilderment as to how she wants to handle her situation in the face of all adversity – secretly I am full of admiration for her inner strength, and her being up and ready to manage everything in her own way without toppling over.

35

This weekend Bob is coming to visit us. His girlfriend Jenny is busy in her editorial office so he decided to hit the road to come all this way to see us. It's a long way from Munich to Aachen, so we don't meet very often. But now we are very happy that he is coming at long last.

He flew to Cologne last night and took the train to Aachen. This is quite convenient since there is a train terminal in the basement of the airport.

On Saturday in the early afternoon we sit together in our lounge, just the two of us. I avoid raising familial problems and for once I enjoy discussing scientific questions with him again. Bob and I are on the same wavelength here.

Primarily, but not exclusively, we like to discuss facts concerning our universe.

'It is fascinating that all galaxies together account for only 5% of the entire matter in the whole of the universe,' Bob points out the result of a study in which numerous galaxies had been analysed.

'Hydrogen gas with a temperature of more than one million degrees Celsius occupies the space between the galaxies. That alone accounts for a large portion of the visible matter.'

'And the rest?' My question is more rhetorical as I already know the answer.

'Well, four to five times as much should be non-visible "dark matter" and the large residual amount of about 75% must be "dark energy"', Bob replies.

'What all this is made of and where it comes from – has no one any accurate ideas about it?' I ask – this again a more rhetorical question.

'So it is,' Bob returns. 'Some believe that "dark matter" consists of elementary particles which have not yet been discovered and which form invisible clouds in which all galaxies are embedded. This is why scientists are searching for "siblings" of the Higgs boson particles,' Bob laughs out loud.

'And what about "dark energy"?' I add. 'Any news about that?'

'I think it is fantastic, but this energy, which we cannot measure as yet, must really be ubiquitous. It must be hovering around us here in our lounge, where we are both discussing it right now, and it must also be distributed across all regions in the cosmos. We know that the world is not only expanding further and further but it is also expanding faster and faster. The gravitational forces of all the galaxies together are clearly not preventing this. Consequently, there must be something more powerful than the combined gravitational forces of the total mass. And that is "dark energy". It must account for the lion's share of the universe.

'Many colleagues believe that "dark energy" is a gigantic energy field which is also generated by elementary particles.

'Possibly this is caused by well-known instigators such as pulsars, the extremely compact remains of old stars, which send an especially energy-rich radiation into space thereby causing "dark energy" to develop.

'On the strength of recent findings we assume that "dark energy" must possess certain properties: for example it must be electrically neutral which would facilitate it to cumulate into huge clouds much faster than hot gases could.

'Based on this notion we can probably create an axiomatic model indicating how galaxies, stars and ultimately planets alike develop . . .'

'I read the other day,' I interrupt him, 'that with the aid of recent computer programs it is possible to simulate the development of galaxies over approximately thirteen billion years. This shows that our imagination comes very close to reality. Our current assumption with regard to the world surrounding us seems to be pretty exact and almost unshakable in their foundations, am I right?'

'Yes,' Bob replies, 'and, therefore, the currently known visible mass together with the "dark matter", not yet quantifiable, will probably not account for more than a quarter of the total existing mass. However, since the *visible* mass only accounts for a total of 5% it would mean that this leaves 95% of our universe about which we know nothing at all . . . '

'And what about the gravitational waves which must exist in a curved universe?

'After all, the curvature of space is common knowledge since Einstein's notion of a four-dimensional space-time,' I point out.

'At the beginning of 2014 three scientists broadcasted rather too hastily that, based on minimal fluctuations in the cosmic background radiation, the existence of such waves was indirectly verified. Unfortunately further follow-ups proved that this was not the case. No such waves have been found up to now,' Bob explains to me, although many search them.

We both come alive in our discussion and for some time we forget our problems.

Later Lara and Helen join us, so we quickly change the subject.

This, at least, is a trouble-free and relaxing weekend for all of us.

36

University Hospital, Aachen, the accident surgery and geriatric ward, 8 a.m.

The Nursing Manager Frauke Kleber introduces a newcomer:

'Mrs Hartwig will spend the next two weeks here on your ward. The executive board of the hospital has sent her to us. Mrs Hartwig is carrying out a survey regarding the professional and proper treatment and care of old and chronically sick people.

'Your ward has been chosen for being exemplary. Sister Elvira, please take care of Mrs Hartwig and assist her, allowing her survey to reflect well on us and on the hospital. She is to be granted access to any records and documents she may need for this purpose.

'And now I hope . . . ,' she turns to address Mrs Hartwig, ' . . . that you will spend two interesting and pleasant weeks with us.'

The Nursing Manager leaves Mrs Hartwig in Elvira's care and disappears.

The nurses of the early morning shift welcome the young woman who is tall and slim and has a slightly austere aura. First of all, they explain to her the special conditions of their ward and all important procedures. Ward Sister Elvira wants to take care of Mrs Hartwig and her requirements personally.

She seems to like her straightaway.

First, Sister Elvira shows her the ward with all the rooms, patient rooms and all functional areas. Some of these are located in adjacent areas of the building.

'You know,' Sister Elvira explains to Mrs Hartwig, 'this ought to have been the task of the head of our department. But Frau Schneider has been off sick for the last few days. As executive administrator she is responsible for all administrative procedures on all four wards which are part of the accident surgery. We nurses and carers are responsible for the actual care of patients in the respective wards.

'Ah, there is Dr Bender. He is our senior physician. Dr Bender, may I introduce Mrs Hartwig to you. She is carrying out a survey about our geriatric department.'

'Nice to meet you,' Dr Bender shakes hands with Mrs Hartwig.

'Mrs Hartwig will stay with us for two weeks,' Sister Elvira continues, 'so you'll certainly see each other again.'

Senior Physician Dr Dirk Bender is already hurrying on. There is an emergency he must attend to.

Sister Elvira and Mrs Hartwig proceed with their tour round the wards.

37

Lara's first two school-leaving exams are behind her. She says she has a "good feeling". Tomorrow she will sit the third one, the written mathematics exam. Then after two more weeks the compulsory oral exam in her fourth subject, religious studies, will follow.

If all goes well with mathematics tomorrow she will have completed her schooling successfully.

So, she wants to swot for mathematics again tonight. At least she thinks she needs to – this time on her own and without her girlfriend Nicole.

My feeling is that if you don't have it inside your head on the day before the exam you won't be able to cram it in on the last day anyway. But she must know what she is doing.

Helen and I are sitting in the lounge watching TV. For some days now Helen has been complaining about extreme backache and she is on sick leave. She is lying on the settee, with her legs put up on a support, her knees bent and an electric blanket wrapped in a moist towel under her back.

In my opinion the problem is mainly the stress at the hospital which is provoking the pain in her back. I have often read that stress especially affects the back because it can cause the muscles there to tense up rigidly.

The telephone rings and Tom is on the line.
'How is Lara? How are her exams going?' he asks straight away.
'Everything seems to be fine, philosophy and English are over and tomorrow she is sitting mathematics. Yes, and the oral exam in religious studies will be in two weeks time.'
'Well, nothing can go wrong for Lara with religious studies,' Tom sounds relieved and goes on: 'and in English she is probably better than her teacher, and, well, I think I have practised enough with her for philosophy.'
Lara had indeed travelled to Cologne often enough to practise with Tom in his flat in order to prepare for the finals. Only now do I wonder about the impressions Lara must have experienced in this "wild homo-community". It rattles me even to think about it – but she has never let on and never told me anything...

'Father...'
This form of address warns me that Tom is deadly serious. I immediately ask him what's on his mind, half worried half tortured, considering the many blows to the back of the neck in this year still so young.
'Father,' he starts again and in a rather serious tone of voice, 'Jasmin, Sascha and I have come up with something concerning Mum's problems in the hospital. Maybe it'll help. Is Mum still on sick leave?'

'Yes, indeed, at least till the end of next week, and then we have to see. She then has to go and see her orthopaedic doctor again.' I say. 'Why do you ask?'

'That's good!' Tom returns, but he doesn't want to add anything else.

38

Lara completed her school finals with her fourth subject, the oral examination in religious studies. The result, a straight "Very Good", was announced almost immediately. She will have to wait a few weeks for the results of the other three subjects. Only then will it be decided whether she will have to undergo another oral examination. This happens to those who fail one of the written exams or when the result of the written exam differs too much from the term grades of the last two years. Since Lara's term grades are pretty good and she thinks that her exam results will not differ very much from the term grades, she is quite confident and reckons that she won't have to go through another oral exam.

We all hope that as well, of course, and we are very pleased about it. Tonight Helen, Lara and I will go have dinner together and we will surely drink a glass of champagne in pleasant anticipation of the end results.

Helen is still on sick leave, her backache is as bad as ever. She still needs her physiotherapy daily in addition to her medication.

Neither has she heard anything from the hospital as yet. But she will soon have to hand in her statement regarding the allegations spread around in the hospital. Of course, her lawyer will help her to formulate the statement. But whenever we tentatively mention the issue with the hospital her pain increases.

Damn it! I think to myself, do people not know what they may evoke with their mobbing?

39

Meanwhile, in the geriatric ward chosen for the survey, Mrs Hartwig visits the patients. As long as they are not disabled, due to serious physical problems, or suffering from dementia, she has long and intensive conversations with them. She focusses mainly on special caregiving processes, visiting times, satisfaction with the support and attention provided by nurses and carers, and how much time they spend with each individual patient.

But Mrs Hartwig also wants to talk about private matters to add supplementary information to her survey, such as the personal anxieties of the patients, their thoughts about death and the expectations they have for their further life, and she also asks about possible assistance to be provided and whether they receive sufficient support from family members in the hospital and at home.

Now and then Ward Sister Elvira joins her and tries to engage her in conversation. So much so that Mrs Hartwig has the vague feeling that Sister Elvira is trying to get a closer relationship with her.

It happens again right now.

Sister Elvira enters the room where Mrs Hartwig is talking with a very old patient who had to undergo surgery due to a fracture of the femoral neck and who seems to be having difficulty getting back on her own two feet.

'Mrs Hartwig, would you care to join me for lunch? It's already lunchtime and all the patients have eaten already. The lunch is on me and we'd have time for a nice chat.'

'I'd be delighted,' Mrs Hartwig replies, visibly pleased. 'Let's meet in the nurses' station in ten minutes, then we can go to the canteen together.'

'All right, in ten minutes in the nurses' station.'

Elvira closes the door and leaves.

Ward Sister Elvira had to wait in the nurses' station for almost twenty minutes before she jumps up impatiently to look for Mrs Hartwig who approaches at the same moment.

'I'm terribly sorry, but I couldn't break off the conversation with Mrs Müller in room 14 so suddenly.' Mrs Hartwig notices Sister Elvira's annoyance.

'It doesn't matter, come on now, we can eat in the nurses' station.

Mrs Hartwig follows her there.

'Would you like "Chicken on Rice" with "Asparagus Cream Soup" as first course or rather "Braised Beef Rhineland Style" with "Clear Oxtail Soup"?'

'I'd rather have the chicken,' Mrs Hartwig is pleased. 'I'm really hungry now and I love chicken.'

'Enjoy your meal!' Elvira is delighted to have met Mrs Hartwig's taste and they both have a nice and animated conversation.

'Tell me, Sister Elvira, can you just order meals to be delivered to the ward? Don't you have to go to the canteen for it? It seems really amazingly uncomplicated and very convenient.'

'Oh no, it's not that simple, but, you know, there are always some patients who are either in the operating theatre or in the intensive care unit after an operation. Some have already been discharged and the new patients haven't arrived yet. Therefore, there are usually some meal trays left over which I make use of on the quiet. It is not really officially allowed, but why should I send the meals back so that they get dumped in the rubbish bin? That would be criminal waste when so many people in the world are starving. Of course, I can only do this in secret. No one knows about it except me. That is why you can have something today as well and we don't have to go downstairs. I hope you enjoyed your meal.'

'Oh yes, indeed, it was quite tasty, not as bland as you expect hospital meals to be.' Mrs Hartwig looks at Elvira with her eyes wide open.

'Well, Mrs Hartwig, now that we are working in this team together, don't you think we should be on first-name terms?' Elvira looks back at Mrs Hartwig just as wide-eyed.

'But certainly, with pleasure, my name is Jasmin . . .'

40

In only a few weeks time now I will be flying the helicopter – all by myself! I am really looking forward to redeeming my Christmas present voucher.

After returning home from the institute I start preparing the evening meal for myself and Helen, who more recently has begun to work again. We both love potato pancake with smoked salmon and horseradish, and apple puree and cranberries for afters. It is an easily and quickly prepared meal.

Helen comes home earlier than expected and she beams with delight. She is waving a letter in her hand and she gives me a big hug. I see a few tears running down her cheeks.

'Look, Chris, look at what I've got here. The hospital board of directors gave me this letter today. It says here that the accusations against me turned out to be unfounded. Isn't that just yummy?'

'Wonderful! Have they realised at long last that you don't do things like that?'

We are both delighted. We enjoy our potato pancake with salmon and the fruit dessert. We both accompany our meal with a glass of champagne – what else? Lara is not at home, unfortunately, I don't know where she is. We would have liked to raise our glasses together with her to toast this letter – and with our sons as well.

We have hardly finished our meal when the telephone rings. I lift the receiver and I hear Tom's voice.

'Well, did it work?' he asks pretty excited.

'What do you mean, Tom?'

'Well, has Mum finally been acquitted of all allegations against her?' he asks back uncomprehendingly.

'Yes – we have just been drinking to that. Mum is still deeply moved. Today the hospital board of directors gave her a letter which says that the allegations have turned out to be unfounded.' I am a bit irritated. 'And what makes you ask at this particular time?'

'Father . . . ,' obviously Tom turns serious again, 'didn't I tell you during our last telephone conversation that Jasmin, Sascha and I had worked out a plan how to help Mum.

'Shortly after, Jasmin started doing a survey for the tv and radio station about the Aachen University

Hospital. She asked to be based in the ward next to Mum's office so that she could investigate the situation more closely. The Ward Sister must have had an eye on her in no time. It seems she wanted to get closer to Jasmin as she couldn't stop talking to her and she was always asking Jasmin to have lunch with her. In doing so the two of them regularly took superfluous meals from trays which were meant for patients but which would have gone back to the kitchen otherwise.

'The Ward Sister – I think her name is Elvira – always kept some of the meals on one side and invited Jasmin, as a matter of course, to join her eating them. In the hospital this is strictly forbidden. Sister Elvira must have done this regularly. And when one day, a few weeks ago, she was very nearly caught in the act and she didn't have the time to put the empty tray back in the usual way, together with those of her patients, she just placed it in Mum's office.

'When they found the trays there, Elvira pretended to know nothing about it and passed the blame on to Mum.

'There is also a certain Mrs Kleber who is a member of the nursing management team. She obviously knew what was going on but covered up for Elvira since they have an intimate relationship.

'In addition this woman Mrs Kleber seems to dislike Mum and thought she had found a way to get rid of Mum.

'So they planned this scheme together.

'Jasmin got hold of this story and after her time on the ward she informed the Board of Directors. At the same time she also expressed her utter lack of understanding as to why the employees weren't allowed to eat leftover meals but had to send them back, even though the food was then dumped into the rubbish bin. She said that she knew these two aspects were not connected with one another but that the food management was as irresponsible as the total ban on eating leftover meals. She planned to broach the issue in her TV feature. The Board of Directors asked her not to mention it. They promised her that they would carefully review the issue immediately, to clear Mum of the accusation and to take disciplinary action against the two-faced double-dealing women for defamation of character.'

'Helen, come here quick, Tom is on the phone. You must hear for yourself what he just told me. It was Tom who got you out of the mess.'
'Wonderful, Son,' I call after him as Helen rips the receiver out of my hand. Tom tells her in detail what he had told me and Helen throws in some questions now and again to get a clearer picture. At first she looks rather dumbfounded but then her face begins to light up more and more.

I love Tom as much as I love my other two children. His homosexuality has certainly hit me hard. And I still believe that it is not natural; it is a disease. But of course that has not at all changed my love for him.
Perhaps he will agree to undergo treatment, I ponder quietly again, although I sense that he won't.

Helen and I decide on the spur of the moment to go away next weekend, maybe we could take the train "Thalys" to Paris. It takes only two and a half hours from Aachen to the "Gare-du-Nord". And we both think Paris is always worth a visit. Bob told me that he went to Paris with Jenny last weekend.

41

Today I put our idea into action.

There were even reasonably-priced seats on the Thalys still available. I booked a hotel room, two nights, Friday to Sunday, and we'll leave the day after tomorrow. Helen and I are very much looking forward to our trip.

This year we haven't had an opportunity yet to spend a whole weekend together, just the two of us, away from home. There was always something more important cropping up.

I have just come home earlier than usual; I have to compile some documents for a visit from the Ministry for Education and Research next week. They want to take a look at our Institute and seek an explanation as to why exactly we applied for more money out of the research funds.

Specifically, this concerns projects which are carried out by us in cooperation with the LHC, the Large Hadron Collier, near Geneva.

The LHC is a gigantic particle accelerator which has been in operation since September 2008 at the European Nuclear Research Centre CERN deep underground.[25]

It seems that the discovery of the "Higgs boson"[26] some years ago has brought us considerably closer to solving the question as to how matter is created. However, this discovery on its own does not really give a comprehensive answer to this question.

Moreover, the results must be further stabilised. There are still too many deviations in some of the measurements.

And it is still unclear why it is that in the entire universe we can practically *only* find matter and nothing else. If there were as much matter as anti-matter they would both eliminate each other leaving nothingness in the end. We are still looking for answers as to why the Big Bang resulted in an imbalance between the two. All this costs money – a lot of money actually – although not as much as some politicians or entire governments here in Germany and in the EU regularly squander on so many absurd projects.

Therefore, this visit next week is very important for us – as it is also for the LHC in Switzerland.

It is a fact that all politicians, not only those in Germany, are less and less prepared to provide funding for basic research. Similarly, there is less and less money available for child support, for education or for the necessary improvement of infrastructure and the essential maintenance of damaged roads and dangerously overloaded bridges.

However, this is not due to the recent austerity drive – on the contrary: the greed of our politicians is increasing by leaps and bounds.

Their hunger for the money of the citizens whose interests they are supposed to represent seems to become more and more insatiable in fact, and the creativity with which they extract ever more money out of taxpayers' pockets has unfortunately spiralled completely out of control, in my eyes.

Ultimately it is us citizens who are being cheated out of our hard-earned money and our savings. But woe betide, anyone who tries to find loopholes and dares to use them will be pilloried immediately – even publicly.

As a result, the new, ever increasing higher taxes and levies which are so creatively raised and camouflaged with such fantasy, often even trivialised, cause an even higher expansion of our already bloated bureaucratic and political institutions pushing them to test their very limits of governability. Very often these institutions merely serve to increase the number of regulations and controls for its citizens who are in reality not true "politically mature citizens". I call this nothing but abusive and arbitrary treatment by the State.

The sad fact is that many of those in power unfortunately spare no effort to achieve this objective. Some of their ideas are only half-baked and are primarily meant to seduce the voters.

And often enough these people aim to enhance their own prestige, to satisfy their egoistic personal vanity and to consider this as being the main reason for their very existence and not the well-being of the citizens whose interests they are supposed to represent. Many of their schemes are already costing vast sums of money today – without even taking into account the inevitable obligations for state pensions to be paid out later. In future, the demographic development and the increasing trend towards earlier retirement coupled with a simultaneously growing life expectancy will not help matters.

In the long run it will be future generations in particular that will suffer.

The problem lies in the political unpredictability and the blatant economic mismanagement in some EU member states, together with the ever increasing bureaucracy in the Brussels command centre that keeps some of us awake at night.

Many people reached the limits of their personal load-bearing capacity long ago and some of them have already overreached them.

In addition, the powers that be squander huge amounts of money because they try to re-invent the wheel or follow absurd or obsolete, outdated ideologies.

It seems likely that everything built up by the citizens through hard labour over many decades will one day be frittered away and lost.

While I am lost in deep thought a lot of holy rage is building up in my stomach. I rummage through my documents whilst listening to the non-stop news on TV:

' . . . in Eschweiler near Aachen a big fire broke out in the waste incineration plant. Twenty-five fire brigades and numerous local emergency services are at the scene. There seem to be only some light casualties.'

' . . . Berlin: The operators of the suburban railway system had to withdraw some carriages from service again due to technical problems with the brake systems. This will cause delays and overcrowded trains today and over the next few days.'

'. . .on the motorway number 9 from Nuremberg to Munich a wrong-way driver caused a serious accident involving two other cars. Nothing is known as yet about casualties.

Just then my mobile phone rings.

42

'Christian Schneider, hello...', I mumble into the phone.

'Dad, Dad . . . ' I can only hear somebody cry on the other end of the phone.

'Who is there?' I ask, 'Bob? Bob, is that you?'

'Dad . . . '

I can't understand anything, just loud weeping.

'Dad, something awful has happened . . . '

It is indeed Bob.

'What's the matter?'

'Jenny . . . ,' further weeping, . . . just some terrible sobbing.

'Jenny . . . , Jenny is . . . dead . . . '

'What?' I shout into the phone.

'Jenny . . . is . . . dead . . . She was killed by a wrong-way driver . . . just now . . . , not far away from here . . . , on the motorway,' it bursts out of Bob, his voice choked with tears.

I remember immediately the last item on the news I had just heard in the background.

'My dear Son,' I stammer deeply shocked, 'please try to calm down a little. This is terrible. Does Mum know about it?'

'No, she is probably still in the hospital and I didn't want to phone her there. You are the first to know, and it's still fresh . . . '

Bob interrupts our conversation and starts to cry uncontrollably again.

' . . . the police came and by chance I was at home . . . ' Bob stammers into the phone.

Bit by bit he tells me everything he had heard from the two policemen.

Jenny must have been on her way back to the editorial office of the newspaper after some research she had carried out in the north of Munich. On the A9 she and another car had collided head-on with the car of a young driver who probably wanted to commit suicide and was driving on the wrong side of the motorway. The young driver, Jenny and the elderly driver of the third car died instantly, as the policemen told Bob. An elderly lady, passenger in the third car was seriously hurt and transferred to a hospital in Munich. Jenny's parents, who live in Munich, are already informed and are suffering under severe shock. Jenny's mother had to be treated by a doctor.

Besides being so extremely sad I am also in a furious rage. These stupid idiots! If they want to kill themselves they should do so in whichever way they like. But do they really have to take others with them and cause so much hardship to completely innocent people?

They should be damned to eternity . . . , and I suddenly become aware that I chose a curse not at all compatible with my view of the world which is usually shaped by scientific knowledge.

At that moment Lara and Helen come through the door. When they see me they know immediately that something awful must have happened.

I take them both in my arms, with the mobile phone still under my chin and whisper to them:

'Jenny is dead . . . she was killed by a wrong-way driver on the motorway . . . a few hours ago . . . Bob is still on the phone,' and I pass my mobile to Lara.

Helen instantly collapses in my arms. We sit down on the settee.

Lara keeps talking to Bob.

Helen and I can only understand snippets of their conversation. Our thoughts are elsewhere, far away and wandering. I am holding Helen in my arms and she huddles against me.

I make a grab for the brandy, the best medicine for such situations, and pour a double for Helen and me.

Paris adieu, I think, and at the same time: what a shitty year, why must everything happen at once?

43

Lara tells us later that Jenny is going to be cremated and buried in the *"Ostfriedhof"*, a very famous cemetery in Munich. Any further information we will hear later.

In the evening Tom arrives in Aachen.

Lara had phoned him immediately to tell him the sad news. Without the least hesitation he got into his car to come and see us.

I am glad that we can at least spend this difficult evening together. No one wants to spend any time in the kitchen, so I order pizzas for everyone which are delivered unusually swiftly this time, as if the pizza chef sensed that we needed some sustenance fast. We complement the meal with a few bottles of chilled beer.

Our thoughts are incessantly circling around Jenny, her parents and Bob.

Jenny was their only child. How difficult must it be for her parents now? We are deeply shocked and saddened.

Suddenly everything seems to be so different.

The very next day Bob tells us that the cremation is planned for Friday the 20th May – a few days after Whitsun. It will take place in the crematorium of the *Ostfriedhof* in Munich.

There is a large funeral hall at the graveyard which is made of white and grey marble with geometric patterns. It was built by the famous architect Hans Grässel[27] in 1929. Here the funeral service is to take place at 11 o'clock. Thereafter the coffin will be transferred for cremation.

A couple of weeks later the urn will be buried with only the closest family members participating in the service.

The funeral service is planned and organised by a good friend of Jenny's father who works in the social services of the Catholic Archdiocese in Munich.

Since Jenny's Thai mother is Buddhist, it is planned to integrate Buddhist rites into the Christian ceremony.

Bob has asked Lara to give a short but, if possible, somehow positive eulogy at the funeral service.

Other friends of Jenny's circle in her Munich environment also want to contribute something. In accordance with Thai rites everyone who knew the deceased is invited as a matter of course to personalise the funeral service. And this is how it is going to be for Jenny.

Since Lara feels fine and school is no longer putting her under pressure and her pregnancy is not giving her any problems, she spontaneously decided to support her brother Bob and intends to take the train to Munich. Bob is grateful for this and I think it is a good idea, too. We will be together again for the farewell ceremony.

Lara is gradually developing a bit of a tummy now. Although at the beginning I thought she ought not to carry the child to term, now I must admit that meanwhile I am rather looking forward to becoming a grandfather in a few months time. Helen is delighted about the prospect anyway. She never went along with my idea of an abortion – neither did Tom.

But at the moment this joyful anticipation is out of place. The horrible distress caused by Jenny's death overshadows everything, and Bob's indescribable suffering affects me deeply.

44

We all meet again in Munich the evening before the farewell ceremony for Jenny.

Helen and I took the train to Cologne where Tom picked us up at the main station before driving us all in his car to Munich.

We met Bob and Lara at the *Mercure* Hotel in the centre of Munich. Over the weekend they will also book into the hotel since Bob, in spite of Lara's loving support, can hardly bear to stay in his flat where he used to live with Jenny.

Everything seems too much for him and the emotional pressure he has to suffer when every little thing reminds him of Jenny whom he can never again take into his arms.

Bob looks awful, as can be expected in the circumstances. Jenny's death has shaken him to the core.

Again and again he breaks into tears – and we with him – when Jenny's name comes up or when talk turns to her or to the following day.

'Lara, what have you prepared for tomorrow?' Bob asks his sister, while he hugs her with affection but full of sorrow and with tears in his eyes.

'That'll be a surprise, Bob, but I think you'll like it.'

'Thank you – and it's nice you remembered. I forgot to remind you again.'

'You definitely don't have to do that,' is Lara's reply.

'I want to tell you,' Bob turns to us, 'that the ceremony tomorrow will certainly be completely different from what you might expect of a Christian funeral service . . . ' He wants to give us some more explanations but he can't manage it and with a wave of his hand and with tears in his eyes he continues: 'But you will see for yourself tomorrow . . . ' In tears he turns to Lara and adds: 'Timo Krautleitner, a friend of Jenny's . . . father will approach you tomorrow . . . and he will coordinate exactly . . . with you . . . with regard to . . . your contribution . . . Will that be all right?'

'Certainly, I can fit that in anywhere.' Lara tries to reassure him.

We conclude the evening with a nice meal and some glasses of wine in a cosy restaurant in Munich.

45

It is Friday 20th May.

After breakfast Helen, Lara, Tom and I take a taxi to the venerable funeral hall at the crematorium in the *Ostfriedhof* in Munich.

Bob left early. He didn't even have breakfast with us.

The sun is shining and there is no cloud in the sky to darken the day. Actually it would be a beautiful day, if it were not for ...

A large number of guests have already taken their seats in the funeral hall. At the entrance we meet Jenny's parents, Joy and Franz Angerer to whom we express our deepest condolences.

Joy is about 50. She is wearing a beautiful long silk dress in various colours. Jenny's father Franz Angerer, a typical Bavarian, is much older than his wife which he cannot conceal. Bob thinks he is already 72 years old. He is wearing the traditional Bavarian garb, a dark grey jacket with a pair of long black trousers.

We others are all dressed in black.

Jenny's parents are deeply shocked by the death of their daughter. Nevertheless they appear quite collected today. Maybe their faith helps them, I ponder:

Joy is Buddhist and believes in reincarnation, like Jenny did, although she was baptised Roman Catholic. And Jenny's father Franz is – as far as I am aware – deeply rooted in the Christian Catholic faith.

Timo Krautleitner joins us. He is a rather small but very dynamic man in his mid sixties with a full head of white hair.

After a short introduction he asks us to step inside and take our seats while he clarifies a few points concerning the procedure of the ceremony with Lara.

So Tom, Helen and I lead the way in while Lara joins us later. Bob seems to be in the funeral hall already.

When we enter the hall, Helen and I grow pale in the face. Jenny's coffin is positioned in the middle of the aisle on a small pedestal in the midst of all the mourners who have already taken their seats. It is surrounded by a huge sea of flowers – and it is open...

Jenny lies there so peacefully as if she were sleeping. She looks enchanting, also dressed in a silk gown, light beige in her case, from her maternal home country, which is almost completely covered in red roses. At first sight there are no injuries visible.

Actually it is quite beautiful to see – and also rather unusual for us – to say the least.

Helen and Lara break out in tears; Lara, however, regains her composure quickly. She is pretty tough. Meanwhile I myself have to fight back the tears.

The ceremony begins shortly after with solemn music, beautiful and melodic, from the Far East. Thereafter we hear music by the famous Band *Queen*: *"I Want to Break Free"* – what a contrast.

A priest reads something from the Bible, first from the text of the Gospel according to John: *"Jesus said to her: I am the resurrection and the life. He who believes in Me, though he may die, he shall live."*[28]

Fair enough, I think, it appears to be a real blessing if you believe in it. If only I could sometimes experience this myself, but...

In this connection the great mathematician Blaise Pascal[29] comes to my mind suddenly. He formulated the famous bet between an optimist and a pessimist: the optimist believes in life after death, the pessimist does not.

However, says Blaise Pascal, only the life of the optimist can be worth living: first of all, *he alone* would experience whether his conviction was right; because, if the pessimist were right neither of them would ever know. And secondly, the pessimist would then discover that he had gone through life more fearfully than the optimist who had put his unwavering trust in a "Thereafter".

But there is something else that flashes through my mind: should the pessimist be wrong, then, in the course of his life, he will probably have influenced many fellow humans in a negative way with his false conviction.

Some of them may have fallen into depression thereby blighting their lives because they had relied on his judgement.

It could well be that the pessimist is thus burdened with guilt solely due to his negative attitude for which he will probably be blamed should there indeed be anything after death . . .

Logic, I think, really forces us to think positive, but . . .

Suddenly my thoughts are caught off guard when I hear the Catholic priest utter the words: *"John says: without reincarnation there is no salvation."(3 ff.)*

Fancy that – I am stunned, did I hear that correctly? Does the Catholic doctrine also have sources which support the belief in reincarnation?

Now I start listening with concentration to what the priest is saying:

Nicodemus said to Jesus: "How can a man be born when he is old? Can he enter a second time into his mother's womb and be born?"

Jesus answered: "Verily, verily, I say unto thee, I say unto thee, except a person be born again from above, he cannot see the kingdom of God. . . . Unless a man is born of water and of the Spirit, he cannot enter into the kingdom of God. That which is born of the flesh is flesh, and that which is born of the Spirit is spirit. Marvel not that I said unto thee, Ye must be born again from above."[30]

These words are going through my head. It seems that the Christian Bible defines the term reincarnation in a completely different way than Asian religions.

I remember faintly the situation when Jenny and Lara argued about the subject of reincarnation in our kitchen at Christmas. And I remember also that Lara had brought forward similar arguments. Didn't she even quote the very same words?

And then I hear the next words the priest quotes from Paul's first letter to the Corinthians:

"And there are also celestial bodies, and terrestrial bodies; but the glory of the celestial is one and the glory of the celestial is another. ... So also is the resurrection of the dead.

"The body is sown in corruption, it is raised in incorruption ... It is sown a natural body, it is raised a spiritual body.

"There is a natural body, and there is a spiritual body ...

"However, the spiritual is not first but the natural; afterwards the spiritual.

"The first man was of the earth, made of dust; the second Man is the Lord from heaven.

"And as we have borne the image of the man of dust, we shall also bear the image of the heavenly Man ... "

"Behold, I tell you a mystery: We shall not all sleep, but we shall all be changed - in a moment, in the twinkling of an eye ... "[31]

I am very touched by these words, for in this moment of profound reflection on a very sad occasion they make me realise that the Christian message of the resurrection may have a completely different meaning from that preached by the institutionalised churches have been preaching to their faithful for centuries, or, at least, it seems to differ from what many of them – if not the majority – perceive. And Lara seems to know this perfectly well ...

According to this teaching, all the more so in the Christian sense, death seems to be an interface to immediate reincarnation – because human beings consist of body and spirit and the spirit is immortal.

However, reincarnation according to the Christian concept takes place on an entirely different level than that usually associated with the term "reincarnation".

So, is there neither a reincarnation on earth in the flesh nor a resurrection on the "Day of Judgement" in an infinitely far away future?

But then, what is meant by the term "Day of Judgement" in the Bible, if it does *not* correspond with the moment of the actual or immediate resurrection?

I start to listen again to the words with which the priest now closes his short address:

"On the cross Jesus said to one of the thieves: Assuredly, I say to you, today you will be with Me in Paradise."[32]

Yes, I have heard that before, of course, on one of my occasional church attendances. But I have never really thought about it.

Anyway, death has never been an important issue for me up to now. Sure, it was always clear that we must all die one day, and that this will be the end, full stop, period. If at all, you live on in the memory of your loved ones, as so many obituary notices like to indicate. Under closer scrutiny this would resemble a death in steps since the memory will slowly die until the last family member or friend who can remember you has died as well.

Of course, the deaths of my parents and my grandparents were very sad occasions for me, but that is and has always been the inevitable course of all things in this world.

But now, for the first time, these words really strike home like a stab with a dagger: if Jesus should really have said that on the cross, then he must have been sure that for him and the thieves crucified with him something would continue immediately after: *not at some time or other but directly after* their imminent death – and he also meant that for all of them something good was waiting, even something resembling life in paradise.

So, does resurrection take place immediately?

Well, yes . . . , but . . . unfortunately all this contradicts entirely modern scientific knowledge . . .

Some communal prayers follow and a brief but beautiful address by Mr Krautleitner, in which he quotes various historical personages and their perceptions of death.

He begins with the Greek philosophers Socrates[33] and Plato:

When Socrates held the cup of hemlock in his hands to commit forced suicide he said: *"The hour of departure has arrived, and we go our separate ways, I to die, and you to live. Which of these two is better only God knows."*

And his scholar Plato[34] once said: *"No one knows with regard to death whether it is not really the greatest blessing that can happen to man."*

He quotes Augustine[35], the famous philosopher and Doctor of the Church in Late Antiquity, who is reported to have said: *"You who love me, do not look at the life I end but look to the life I begin."*

And the Italian founder of the Franciscan order, Saint Francis of Assisi[36], once said: *"Death is the gate leading to the light at the end of a path that has become too cumbersome."* In my opinion this quotation is beautiful but in connection with Jenny's death rather out of place.

Mr Krautleitner cites some more philosophers and theologians of earlier and more recent history. He ends his impressive speech with the words of the theologian Dietrich Bonhoeffer[37] who was killed by the Nazis in 1945: *"By gracious forces wonderfully sheltered, we are awaiting fearlessly what comes. God is with us at dusk and in the morning and most assuredly on every day."*

I must admit that I am very impressed by all these words of consolation and also by how some of these great personalities stood by their convictions so unerringly. And I wish that I, too, could follow this lead. But . . .

Then Lara is asked to come to the front. She approaches the microphone, raises her head and talks freely without a manuscript.

'Dear Fellow Mourners,' she begins, 'we are all so very sad about the early death of Jenny. Jenny and I very often discussed the subject death and the question as to whether we can expect anything thereafter, sometimes our discussions were rather heated. Jenny was always convinced that there will be a reincarnation at a later time in a different human body, while I have entirely different perceptions. But from my own family, I know how difficult it is to believe in a life after death in whatever form, if this belief seems to contradict current scientific knowledge so blatantly.'

When Lara says this, she gives me a rather stern look, probably no one else notices. Then she continues:

'This is why I would like to contribute a beautiful metaphor today which might help one or the other of you to believe in the Christian reincarnation. It was written by the Dutch theologian and philosopher Henri Nouwen[38] and its title is: "The Dialogue of Twins in the Womb.'

Still without reading from any manuscript Lara continues and I am totally raptured by her wonderful words:

'Twin brothers were growing in their mother's womb.

'Weeks passed by and the boys kept growing. "Say, isn't it just great that we were conceived?"

'The twins began to explore their world. When they found the umbilical cord which connected them to their mother and gave them nourishment they started to sing the praise of their mother: "How great must be our mother's love that she is prepared to share her life with us."

'When the weeks passed and merged into months they suddenly noticed how much they had changed.

"What does this mean?" one of them asked the other. "This means," the other replied, "that our residence in this world will come to an end soon."

"But I don't want to leave," returned the first, "I want to stay forever."

"We don't have a choice," replied the other, "but maybe there is a life after birth."

"How could that be? We will lose our umbilical cord and how are we going to live without it? And besides, others have left the womb and no one has ever

come back and has told us that there is a life after birth. No, this is definitely the end!"

'So, one of them sank into a deep depression and said: "If conception ends with birth what then is the sense of life in the womb? It is meaningless. There is probably not even a mother behind all this."

"But she must exist," the other objected. "How else should we have come into existence? And how else could we be kept alive?"

"Have you ever seen our mother?" the other asked. "She possibly only lives in our imagination. We have invented her because then we were able to understand our life more easily."

'And so the last days in their mother's womb were filled with many questions and great fear.

'At long last, the moment of their birth approached.

'After the twins had left their world they opened their eyes.

'And what they saw exceeded their wildest dreams.

'Dear Jenny, with this in mind, may peace be with you. We will certainly meet again – somewhere else.'

Then Lara turns away from the microphone, bows at Jenny's coffin and returns to her seat next to us.

All guests, myself included, are very moved and await what might happen next.

Joy, Jenny's mother and Jenny's best friend Malie, also from an Asian background, approach the coffin. Gently they begin to wash Jenny's face and then her hands, especially her right hand. This, someone explains to me later, implies that all evil thoughts and deeds between the deceased and still living people are to be washed away. Washing in this way invokes forgiveness. This washing is done also in the name of everyone the deceased has ever met, and for all the offending and insulting words and deeds inflicted upon her. This is intended to unburden the soul which is then free to wander wheresoever it will.

Now the Catholic priest rises to speak again and blesses the dear deceased. Thereafter all mourners recite the Lord's Prayer together – I do as well not having forgotten the words.

At the end of this very emotional ceremony the stereo system plays the song *"Time to say goodbye"* sung by Andrea Bocelli and Sarah Brightman.

Six elderly gentlemen in black livery with white gloves are approaching now to close the coffin in front of us.

Solemnly they carry it down the aisle out of the funeral hall and lift it onto a hearse which they accompany it to the nearby crematorium.

After the ceremony many of the guests meet again at the Angerer's home. A cold and warm buffet is awaiting them in the beautiful garden. Since it is uncertain whether the weather will play along, there are a few umbrellas and pavilions set up as well. However, the weather is fine and we round off this sad day in a somewhat more relaxed mood, most certainly to the appreciation of Jenny and not least in the Buddhist tradition.

Only Bob is unable to share this mood. His grief is too profound. He sits next to Lara, with his head bent low and with tears constantly welling up in his eyes. Lara affectionately puts her arm around his shoulders. Tom, Helen and I sit opposite them.

Although we keep trying to console him and to cheer him up a little, we do not really succeed.

'Lara . . . ,' I start to break the long silence, 'your metaphor by this . . . what's his name . . . ? –

' Henri Nouwen,' Lara helps me along –

' . . . that was wonderful.'

I give her a kiss and a big hug.

'Alas, if only I had just a touch of your confidence,' I say dolefully and Bob, his voice choked with tears, chips in: 'And me too . . .'

46

On Sunday Lara, Helen and I drive back to Cologne with Tom; after leaving him there the three of us continue our journey back to Aachen.

Lara had offered to stay with Bob in Munich as she has nothing else to do at school apart from waiting for the final results of her exams. But Bob wanted to try to get along on his own and declined with thanks.

On the way back home some scenes of the wonderful and profoundly emotional funeral service go through my mind.

When we all recited the Lord's Prayer I had noticed that Lara sitting next to me audibly loud recited one line of the prayer quite differently than usual: instead of saying "and lead us not into temptation but deliver us from evil" she said "and lead us *in* temptation and also deliver us from evil".

This is still going through my mind and now I address her directly.

'Dad, you know,' she begins, 'not everything the church teaches us and not everything we are taught to pray *can* be right as it is presented to us.'

I am a little amazed, because I always thought she followed the Catholic doctrine unerringly to the last letter.

'It is unthinkable that a God, who loves us all,' Lara continues, 'could lead anyone into temptation. So we don't have to ask Him not to do it. If humans are tempted, then this must have been due to their very own decision and without God having a hand in it. So it makes sense when we pray to God to guide us reliably *in* this temptation so that we may resist it and escape unscathed.'

I had already admired Lara's very clearly differentiated thoughts some months previously and now I am reminded of them again.

I had never thought about this prayer in such a way.

47

The interment of the cinerary urn is to take place on 4th June. Only the closest members of the family will be present. Of course, we are also invited. But this time we will not travel to Munich again.

Bob asked us to think about it carefully because it is such a long way to drive. He will understand if we decide against the trip.

And anyway, my Christmas voucher for the helicopter ride falls due the very next day. I have been looking forward to that for months now, and it has been planned and firmly booked for this coming Sunday long ago.

Originally, the whole family including Bob and Jenny had planned to accompany me to the airfield in Aachen Merzbrück. They both wanted to join us for this occasion and had planned to come especially from Munich.

Sadly everything has turned out differently. So, none of us will accompany Bob to Jenny's interment, apart from her family and probably some close friends.

The thought of my imminent flight preoccupies my mind and I am able to think about something nice again for a change. Over the last few months we had to come to terms with so much adversity and then, on top of everything else, this terribly sad event. This year certainly has rubbed me up badly and it is not even half over yet.

48

Early in the morning on 5th June Helen, Lara and I drive to the sports airfield in Merzbrück near Aachen.

As an alternative I had originally considered flying from Cologne-Butzweilerhof to circle over Cologne because I know that airfield quite well. When I was young a classmate of mine used to take me up in a glider for which he already had a pilot's licence.

That would have stirred up old memories in me to be crowned by a sightseeing flight over Cologne, my home city, over "my" Cologne Cathedral, for me the most magnificent church on earth.

The airport Butzweilerhof was constructed in 1911 and was the first civil airport in Cologne with a rather chequered history later on.

A year previously, Jean Hugot, a citizen of Cologne and an early aeronautical pioneer, had managed to keep his self-constructed flying machine in the air for a few seconds. Soon after its construction the airport was turned into a military airfield for the Imperial Flying Squadron with a flight training school attached to it.

Konrad Adenauer[39], the very successful mayor of Cologne for many years, who was also a native of Cologne and who became the first Chancellor of the Federal Republic of Germany later, turned it into a modern commercial airport in 1926.

During the First World War and the time of occupation, Butzweilerhof became a military airfield again and then, by 1995, it had been turned back into a sport and glider airfield once more. The world championship for gliders took place there in 1960 and it has been the venue for various air shows.

Today a new aviation museum is located there among other things.

Meanwhile I know that aeroplanes no longer use the strip at Butzweilerhof – only small helicopters for sightseeing flights now and then. But today I'm not going there.

And anyway, the small airfield in Merzbrück is much nearer – a big advantage.

And the old imperial city of Aachen with its magnificent location in the border triangle of Germany and the two kingdoms of The Netherlands and Belgium, has a lot to offer as well.

The airfield Merzbrück was founded only a few years later than the one at Cologne-Butzweilerhof.

The meadows to the North-East of Aachen's historical city were developed and used as airfields at the beginning of World War I. It celebrated its 100th anniversary with a colourful air show some years ago.

Nevertheless, with far more than 40,000 aeroplane movements per year, this small airfield claims to be one of the most important airfields in North-Rhine-Westphalia, the largest Federal State in Germany by population.

However, no big jet planes start or land at Merzbrück. They use the small but international "Maastricht-Aachen-Airport" in the southern Dutch province of Limburg.

I knew that Tom would come as well. To my great surprise he has his two friends Jasmin and Sascha in tow, equipped, of course, with voluminous film and photo cameras.

As I already mentioned, Bob would have loved to join us. He had repeatedly mentioned how much he would have liked to come and see me take off and at the same time spend a nice weekend with Jenny in Aachen.

After all, it was in part also "his present" to me.

However, the death of his beloved Jenny and the interment the previous day impeded his visit.

Helen and I thanked Jasmin again for her successful efforts to stop the mobbing attacks against Helen. I hadn't seen her again since the surprising and short "encounter" on Rose Monday – and Helen hadn't seen her since the New Year's Eve party.

I have to register for the flight in a small office and hand in my voucher.

Thereupon I am accompanied into a seminar room where three other flight candidates are already waiting.

The seminar instructor tells us that our little group of four is now complete, so that we can start right away. It is planned that under competent supervision each of us, one at a time, will be at the controls of the helicopter ourselves for about one hour.

For this purpose, there is a small, light and very manoeuvrable two-seater helicopter Robinson 22 Beta II waiting for us outside. After having completed our theoretical lessons, an experienced pilot will give us practical instructions in the helicopter before ensuring that we'll have a perfect flight.

A young man, about thirty years old, enters the seminar room and explains to us with a lot of humour and in an easily understandable way how a helicopter flies and why.

As a physicist I know some of the basics, of course, but I am lacking in working knowledge and I know nothing of the technical intricacies you need to know if you want to keep such a device steady when airborne.

The most difficult task for a beginner is having to use both hands and feet in completely different manners to find the right degree of balance using joystick, levers and pedals. Any learner driver in a car has basically the same difficulties initially, but driving a car is not half as complicated as flying a helicopter. Furthermore, this thing flies through the air and is not being driven on safe ground. From a psychological point of view this makes the matter much more difficult at the beginning – but it also gives you an extra kick.

The left hand is constantly working a lever called the "pitch". By adjusting the rotor blades the lift of the main rotor and the number of its revolutions per minute can be increased or decreased.

The right hand holds the joy stick. It can be pushed forward, drawn back or turned to left or right whereby the movements of the helicopter along its longitudinal axis and its lateral axis are controlled.

The flight direction is changed to the right or the left by a foot pedal. All this must be coordinated and readjusted continually since the helicopter tends to turn to one side or to tilt. Therefore, it must be constantly adjusted.

In addition, you always have to keep an eye on the most important instruments. Furthermore you should not forget to maintain contact with the air traffic controllers via a head-set-microphone and – also very important – you should keep a keen eye on your immediate airspace so that you may recognise possible hazards in time and avoid colliding with them.

And last but not least you should have fun and enjoy the view on your home town from above . . .

All in all, everything seems devilishly difficult to me at first, having to constantly adjust the fine-tuning of the controls using both hands and feet so as to take off and fly and also to land the helicopter again safely.

My initial enthusiasm about this helicopter flight, the first in which I am to take over the controls myself, gives way to more than a little trepidation building up inside me and I keep asking myself whether I'll manage to do everything right at the crucial moment.

After forty-five minutes of intensive theoretical preparation our instructor, Dennis Jahnke, reaches into a bucket to draw out a slip of paper with the name of one of us trainee pilots who is to take the first flight.

And he draws Christian Schneider . . . me!

That's good, I think, then my family and friends outside – and of course I myself – won't have to sit and wait for so long – although there is a restaurant and cafe at the airfield which looks quite inviting.

49

We four "short-term pilots" and Mr Jahnke step outside. All the relatives and friends have already taken their seats some distance away from the seminar building, all of them equipped with their cameras at the ready, of course. When it becomes clear to them that I am to be the first, some arms and hands relax again.

In the distance our Robinson-Helicopter is approaching. At first I can only hear the loud clatter of the rotors – but I can't see it yet, it's too far away. This very popular two-seater has an overall length of scarcely nine metres, and the main rotor mounted above the cockpit has a diameter of approximately eight metres. This aircraft develops nearly 160 HP and its maximum speed is 190 kph – not exactly a racing device. But this beautiful bird flies, it is very manoeuvrable and the most important point: *I* will be allowed to fly it *myself* very soon.

It approaches at speed and lands exactly on the marked point, not fifty metres away from me. The main rotor is still revolving, the right door opens and the pilot – my flying instructor for the next hour – climbs out and walks straight towards us.

When I catch sight of him, I can't believe my eyes. It is my old school friend who had taken me up in his glider some decades ago. I haven't seen him for ages, but I recognise him immediately.

There is less hair on his head and time has not entirely failed to leave its marks. But there is no mistaking him: he is a bit smaller than I am and, at first sight, he still conveys the impression of being a sporty, almost brisk type. I remember now that he wanted to join the army after leaving school. I know nothing else about him since we lost sight of each other for too long – basically until today.

He also recognises me immediately and gives me a hug.

'Chris, you haven't changed at all,' he lies convincingly without blushing.

'Neither have you, Max!' I return, no less convincingly.

'That's a pleasant surprise,' I continue. 'I am delighted that you are my pilot today. In spite of my previous enthusiasm I feel a little bit scared. You know, Max, originally I had planned to make this flight over Cologne from Butzweilerhof where the two of us took off in your glider when we were both still at school. When my children gave me this flight for a Christmas present it brought it all back. What a coincidence: now you are my "boss". This revives so many nice memories. Well, you were a perfect flight instructor then already, and now you will be doing the same again – in Aachen – fantastic! Wait, I'll introduce you to my family.'

'Come on, Chris, we'll do that later, let us take off first – there are others still waiting,' Max answers evasively. 'We can meet again later and then we can drink to our reunion.'

'That's a promise!'

50

'Now, would you like to take me over Aachen and the border triangle?' he asks with a broad grin on his face. He, an experienced pilot, must have sensed my nervousness and he tries to break the ice and to reassure me.

'If you take good care of me, yes, with pleasure,' I reply.

'Keep your head down,' Max shouts, 'the main rotor could give you a haircut.'

'Well, I'm not that tall,' I smile at him, 'with my one metre ninety I should easily fit underneath.'

One last time a wave to my family and then we both board the helicopter.

After having donned our headsets and checked their functions enabling us to communicate in spite of the loud noise from the rotor blades and allowing Max to talk to the air traffic control, I search for the pitch with my left hand and hold on tight. With my right hand I grab hold of the stick and my feet touch the pedals tentatively.

Max explains everything again to me briefly and then wishes me – or rather us – a good flight.

I lift the pitch carefully, the revolution speed increases and shortly after we rise into the air. We are hovering in the air and we take a look back, to make sure that everything is clear and then we carefully move the stick forward. At the same time we balance the tilt so that we get an even feed drive. We climb higher and higher into the air.

After a few minutes I get the hang of this machine and its highly sensitive flight behaviour. Of course, Max counterbalances in an expert way any mistake I make, however small.

But I can hardly communicate with him via microphone and headset, I'm still too tense.

But it doesn't matter; Max acts as a very eloquent and entertaining air tourist guide, he explains every manoeuvre and the technology behind it and also any kind of cloud formation, which underlines his expertise as a passionate glider pilot.

Nor does he forget to point out to me all the interesting, important and beautiful views on our route.

Max Kauder tells me that he did indeed join the German Federal Armed Forces after leaving school. He enrolled with the air force for twelve years. During this time he obtained several pilot's licences – among others one for heavy-lift transport helicopters.

But for many years now he has been flying transport planes for a large delivery service. His hobby, though, was always flying helicopters. So, a few years ago, together with three friends he set up this company offering helicopter sightseeing flights and fly-yourself helicopter flights to everyone from various airports in North-Rhine-Westphalia.

At first we fly in a north-easterly direction and cross over the brown coal fields of Garzweiler with their huge bucket-wheel excavators and the old fortress city of Jülich.

Jülich used to be an important road station along the old Roman road system which ran from Boulogne-sur-Mer, situated on the English Channel in the North of France, to Cologne. Nearly 800 years ago Jülich was granted city status.

An important department of the University of Applied Sciences Aachen is located there today as is the world-famous nuclear research centre. A horticultural show took place in Jülich in 1998 which involved an extensive structural redevelopment of the former fortress into today's large local recreation area, known as the "*Brückenkopfpark*".

Then we change our course and fly in a north-westerly direction and approach the Dutch town of

Roermond which is located at the mouth of the river "Rur" (written without an "h" in contrast to the river "Ruhr" written with an "h" which traverses the Ruhr industrial area) which is only 165 kilometres long.

The Rur has its source in the "*Hohes Venn*", a plateau region in the province of Liège, Belgium, and reaches the Eifel, a hilly region in Germany, after a few kilometres, before it flows into the Maas in The Netherlands.

The Maas has its source in France, passes through Belgium and The Netherlands and after nearly 900 kilometres it flows into the southern main stream of the Rhine delta, a former bay of the North Sea, also known as "Netherland's Diep", which means something like "Dutch lowlands". The Maas is the longest tributary river of the Rhine and has by far the largest volume of water. Not far from Roermond lies the small Limburgish town of Maaseik. Here the Maas is no longer navigable. However, the area is a large and popular destination for hobby sailors with sports boats of all kinds. Ships on the Maas are diverted to the Juliana Canal, named after a former Dutch queen, which runs parallel to the river.

From there we turn south heading for Maastricht, the capital of the Dutch province of Limburg. This picturesque jewel is the oldest town in The Netherlands[40].

Maastricht is located at the most southern point of The Netherlands and borders on two Belgian provinces, the French speaking Wallonia and the Dutch speaking Belgian Flanders.

The old town centre of Maastricht is well worth a visit.

Furthermore, Maastricht has a prestigious university with a very high proportion of German students, and it is of importance to the entire region as a trade fair town, and as a major administrative and logistical centre.

Over Maastricht we turn around and start our leisurely flight back to Aachen.

Shortly afterwards, we cross the border triangle west of Aachen.

It is here on the Vaalserberg that the Dutch, Belgian and German borders intersect.

The Vaalserberg is approximately 323 metres high and is thus the highest natural elevation in Holland, the "Hoogste Punt van Nederland".

We can see the observation towers which give a panoramic view of Aachen and the neighbouring countryside. There is also a small theme park with a large hedge-maze in which many a visitor has got himself hopelessly lost, several children's playgrounds, a fountain and, of course, restaurants offering various Dutch, Belgian and German gastronomic specialities.

All this is surrounded by the extensive *"Öcher Bösch"*, a forest which frames Aachen on its south and south-west borders, and spreads into Belgium and Holland.

We are not flying very high, just a few metres above the treetops of the Aachen forest, the *"Öcher Bösch"*.

In between the trees, in clearings with meadows and paths, we can see people out walking, there are cyclists and also a group of young men playing football. Some of them look up and see us flying overhead and some wave to us.

There are trees everywhere.

In their midst I recognise the restaurant *"Entenpfuhl"*, a former manor house built during the Biedermeier era.

Today it is a well-known restaurant partly surrounded by a duck pond, which gave the restaurant its name, and partly by several lush meadows from which hot-air balloons sometimes take to the air.

There are many people to be seen here as well: they sit in small groups enjoying the fine weather and their glorious surroundings.

51

All of a sudden there are flashes ... lots of flashes.
I can't see anything, just flashes.
I'm completely blinded ... it is unbelievably bright,
Vivid colours surround me ...

An ear-splitting bang shakes us both to the core.
What was that? ... We are wobbling ...
'Max, what's the matter?'
'I don't know, just let go of everything ...'
'... I can't keep the damn thing steady ...'

Dizziness ... our hearts are racing, everything seems to move so fast.
Thoughts are coming and going, circling in rapid succession.
What the devil is going on and why?

It feels like being in a tumble dryer spiralling down ... at lightning speed ... going down and down ...

Friends appear, siblings, the family,
situations from the past ...
It is growing dark,
infernal noise, just dreadful ...

„Max? What is it? Say something!"

Then a hard impact and a muffled thud, then sliding, another impact, even harder, further sliding, broken parts everywhere,
a hard blow to the head,

and night settles ...

52

Emergency vehicles of the Aachen fire brigade, a fire engine, an emergency ambulance and a transport ambulance hurry to the "Entenpfuhl" restaurant at frenzied speed.

The ADAC[41] emergency air rescue helicopter – known as Christoph 1 – based at Aachen Merzbrück Airfield– what an irony of fate – is on its way as well.

It is only scarcely an hour since the crashed helicopter took off from here.

It should have been back there for some time now. But obviously there have been some delays. Since the trainee pilot and the flight instructor have known each other since their schooldays they probably took more time than anticipated.

Still, everyone has been patiently waiting for its return. Suddenly, however, radio contact with air traffic control broke off for unknown reasons. Shortly afterwards the organisers of the sightseeing flights are informed that a helicopter Type Robinson 22 has crashed in the Aachen forest and that several rescue teams have already arrived at the site or are on their way there.

The family members and friends of the physicist Professor Christian Schneider, who went on a sightseeing flight over Aachen and the surrounding area with the experienced pilot Maximilian Kauder, are still waiting at the airfield Merzbrück. They are informed immediately about the crash.

Nobody knows any details about the condition of the pilot and his passenger as yet.

53

It is a gruesome sight for the rescue workers: some metres up, a small helicopter has become entangled in the trees, it is dangling upside down, its glass cockpit having been shattered and ripped apart by branches.

Fortunately there is no fire and the cockpit is still accessible.
With the aid of a turntable ladder paramedics and two doctors try to recover the two persons in the helicopter and to treat them at least provisionally on site.

They are two men of middle age. They are both unconscious and obviously seriously injured. The pilot is still breathing. He is covered in blood, as is his passenger who seems to have severe head injuries but is also still breathing.
Both of them are rescued with the aid of heavy equipment after having received immediate initial treatment while still in the helicopter.

It seems that the passenger is worst affected and he is carried to the rescue helicopter which takes off to the Aachen University Hospital. The pilot of the small helicopter, who is also seriously injured, is carried to the transport vehicle and hurried to the University Hospital as well.

After only a few minutes the emergency rescue helicopter arrives at the hospital and touches down on the helicopter landing platform which towers majestically in front of the hospital. Because of its appearance it has been named "God's Helping Hand" by Aachen's citizens. It is relatively new. It was only opened in 2011 after a construction period of one year and it stands directly in front of the main building of the hospital which is one of the largest in Europe.
This landing platform can accommodate two helicopters simultaneously and the tower is approximately 15 metres high. From there patients can be transported directly to the A&E unit of the hospital by way of a specially constructed sloping lift as quickly as possible.

The critically injured patient, accompanied by the emergency doctor and two paramedics, is transported swiftly into the A&E unit where two doctors of the accident surgery department are already waiting to take care of him.

54

'Holy shit,' the senior physician in charge, responsible for the initial medical examination, can't suppress his comment, clearly audible for everyone around.

Dr Dirk Bender knows his patient. He is the father of his young girlfriend Lara who is pregnant by him. And now Professor Schneider is lying in front of him, unconscious on a vacuum mattress, his pulse is weak, he has been intubated by the emergency doctor and is given artificial respiration, he is connected to two infusions and drugged up to his eyeballs.

Mercifully, there are still signs of life, he thinks and checks immediately all the important body functions. A neurologist joins him and establishes that in spite of externally visible severe head injuries there seems to be no additional, serious, peripheral nerve damage.

'At least the patient won't be paralysed should he survive, neither on his arms nor on his legs,' is the neurologist Schirmer's diagnosis.

'Yes, if he survives at all,' Dr Bender mutters under his breath. And that seems to be difficult enough.

Immediately after his arrival Christian Schneider is taken to the x-ray department where he is checked for all kinds of injuries:

First of all, a tomography of this cranium is taken, and also of his ribcage, of his abdominal viscera and some x-rays of his skeleton.

Soon they will know more.

While the radiologists attend to Christian Schneider, the pilot of the helicopter is carried into the A&E unit.

Dr Bender is now also taking care of Max.

55

Professor Gerhard Paland who has been Head Physician of the Accident Surgery Unit for several years, meets Christian Schneider's family in his meeting room shortly thereafter.

Large windows open a fantastic view to a highly unusual building.

The Aachen University Hospital is one of the biggest single-building hospitals in Europe. It was opened in the autumn of 1983 and the orthopaedic department was the first large unit to move in there at the beginning of 1984.

An acquaintance of Christian Schneider, working as an orthopaedic physician in the Aachen area, was in charge of the move.

The hospital was planned in the 1960s and its concept is an expression of "Modern Technology". For many people its unique architecture, unique at least on this scale, always needed some getting used to. It covers a space of 257 metres by 134 metres, it has nine floors above ground and the service pipes are attached to the exterior of the building which makes it appear more like a refinery than a hospital. The optical impression resembles the "Centre Pompidou" in Paris which was inaugurated in 1977 but is much smaller.

'Your husband and father has survived the crash, as has the pilot. However, they are both severely injured. Professor Schneider has suffered even life-threatening injuries. We are giving him a complete check-up to establish all his injuries and then we will have to wait and see. At least we can say that he will not be paralysed. But at this stage we cannot make any reliable predictions as to whether he will survive at all. The next few days and weeks will be crucial for his recovery. He will remain in our intensive care unit for some days, maybe even weeks. I still don't know which operations will be necessary.

We will keep you informed, of course. Please leave your telephone and mobile phone numbers with us so that we can reach you at all times. You may visit him in the intensive care unit as soon as his condition has stabilized and after any urgently required surgery has been completed. I will let you know. At the moment it will be best for you to go home and get a good rest. Right now you can't do anything for him and you cannot see him either,' Professor Paland tells them in clear though gentle words.

Then he bids goodbye to Helen, Lara and Tom none of whom can hold back their tears and looks of utter dismay are engraved on their faces.

Jasmin and Sascha are waiting at the main entrance to meet the family of Christian Schneider. Bob has also been informed in the meantime. He was already devastated anyway and grieving inconsolably.

Only yesterday he had attended his girlfriend's funeral, and now this. He is blaming himself since it was his idea for his father's Christmas present.

He wants to come to Aachen as soon as possible.

56

Christian Schneider has severe multiple traumata and has to undergo several operations.

There are extensive haemorrhages in his brain due to a serious skull fracture. These must be removed as fast as is only possible and his skull must be drained to discharge possible secondary haemorrhages and to relieve the pressure on his brain immediately. It is probably damaged anyway. No one can assess the consequences as yet. But there is no cerebral palsy evident.

His lungs are also damaged: one of his lungs has collapsed. This too must be drained so that it can inflate again to its normal size. Presumably he also has inner haemorrhages which must be stopped immediately. For this purpose he will have to undergo a laparoscopy.

In addition Christian has suffered a complicated fracture of his left humerus, a fracture of his left collarbone and a fracture of his pelvic ring. The rest seems to be all right.

The peripheral fractures also require surgical intervention.

All necessary surgical operations are to be carried out as soon as possible, depending on their urgency.

His cardiovascular system seems to be relatively stable at the moment thanks to the appropriate medication, so the doctors will not waste any time and will begin surgery right away.

57

Two days later all the necessary operations have been performed and all have gone well.

The skull has been drained, the fracture plated.

The collapsed lungs have also been drained and have already inflated themselves again.

The fracture of the pelvis ring has been fixed by an external fixator, a supporting structure screwed into the pelvic bone. The fracture of the humerus and the collarbone have been well stabilised with plates and screws.

Christian Schneider is lying in the intensive care unit and receives intensive medical care round the clock. But his doctors are not really satisfied with him. His overall condition is rather instable at the moment after all the surgical interventions.

He is still losing a lot of fluids which must be constantly compensated for by units of blood and infusions. So, he must still take medication to support his cardiovascular system. This is the only way of keeping his pulse and blood pressure at acceptable levels.

Of course, Chris also needs artificial respiration and he has been tranquillised into an "artificial coma".

Suddenly the life support systems to which he is connected and which monitor his vital functions sound a loud alarm.

58

I am wandering along a strange path in the pitch dark. It is cold, I am shivering. I am alone. What is going on? I proceed further along this path.

In the distance I can hear voices, very low. I cannot make out what they are saying.

Everything seems so strange. What happened? I don't know. I can't remember anything.

I am who I am. I don't know where I came from or where I am going to. I wander alone in the darkness yet I am not really afraid.

Somehow, in a strange way, I feel safe and secure.

I don't know how much time is passing or has passed. There seems to be no time surrounding me.

A faint light appears suddenly in the far distance.

I decide to approach the light.

I feel quite normal, quite healthy in fact. I can feel my two arms and hands, my two legs and feet. Nothing seems to be out of the ordinary, except my surroundings. I take some hesitant steps towards the light, but something seems peculiar and surreal: although I can feel my legs I don't really seem to walk. It feels more like floating along on an electrically powered walkway, like those in big airports that transport the passengers to the gates faster.

Slowly the light grows brighter.

Vast meadows and fields appear on both sides of my path. I recognise poppies and sunflowers. Now and again birds and butterflies fly by.

Then the light suddenly grows very bright, incredibly bright.

I don't feel uncomfortable with it, on the contrary it feels warm and beautiful, it is just wonderful.

Although the light is so bright, it doesn't blind me.

A shadow materialises within the light. It seems to be the silhouette of a woman. I walk towards it. The outlines become more distinct but I still don't recognise the person's identity.

'Who are you?' I ask the obviously female figure.

'Hello, Chris, it's me, Jenny,' is the reply. 'Jenny Angerer, your son Bob's girlfriend. But now I am only Jenny.'

'Jenny . . . ?' I don't know what to say. 'But that can't be true. Jenny Angerer is dead! She was killed by a wrong-way driver on the motorway. I attended her funeral. So, don't talk such nonsense, but tell me please where I am and who you really are,' I respond rather impatiently to this woman who makes out to be Jenny.

I notice with satisfaction that my memory is slowly returning. At the same time I seem to have lost my sense of time. Suddenly I can remember the funeral ceremony quite well, but I couldn't say when it took place. It could have been yesterday or ten years ago. Somehow it seems to be one and the same. It just *happened*!

'But, Chris, it's true. It is really me, Jenny,' the woman replies quietly, 'for those "down there" I am dead, but, as you can see, I am still alive and I am well.' At this moment I feel icy cold shivers running down my spine. I start to shake like a leaf and the realisation dawns on me that something terrible will happen.

'Don't be afraid, Chris,' Jenny seems to sense my sudden fear. 'You are in good company here and nothing can happen to you.'

'But . . . ?' I hardly dare to continue.

Then I pluck up my courage.

'Am I . . . dead as well?' I ask very hesitantly.

In doing so I notice that I don't really talk as I used to do. Jenny also speaks in a different way. Our communication doesn't need words somehow and yet it is clear and distinct. We only seem to think and the other understands. And if we think it to be loud then it is loud. If we think it is soft then it is so . . .

'Yes, at the moment you are "in effect" dead . . . ' Jenny confirms, but by her choice of words and her facial expression I can see that she doesn't believe it herself somehow.

'. . . you know, Chris, I have heard that right now it isn't certain yet whether you are to stay here or not. They are trying with all the means at their disposal "down there" to restore you to life. And as long as the cells in your brain are still alive and may be usable for your future "down there", of course, they may even succeed. I can't give you any further explanation now.'

'But I don't understand,' I try to come up with logic.

I am certain I must be dreaming, because if I were dead I would no longer be able to think and I would not be able to talk with anyone. So I ask Jenny, dreaming as I believe I am:

'Just assuming everything is as you make out and you are indeed the dead Jenny. Why isn't it in your power here or perhaps in someone else's power, or even in God's, should he exist, to determine whether everything is going all right with me down there or not?'

'Chris, you will soon experience so many new things and you will quickly realise that here nothing really corresponds with the concepts and clichés so widespread and believed down there.

'Do you know the medieval story of the two fellow monks who talked about the afterlife?' Without waiting for the answer Jenny continues with a smile:

'When they were still alive they agreed that the first of them to die would give his friend a certain sign: should it be just like they believed according to their religion, then the deceased was to answer with *"taliter"*, which means "so it is", should, however, everything be different from what they imagined, then he was to answer with *"aliter"* which means "other than expected". A short time thereafter one of them dies and appears to his mourning friend at night. Upon his questioning look he says only two words: *"totaliter aliter"* meaning "totally different".

Chris, many commonly accepted assumptions down there, or practices which are well established, have nothing much to do with reality.

'And it is completely irrelevant whether it is "embedded" in religious doctrines and misused by one or the other institution, or whether people are indoctrinated by "social ideologies" forced on them by governments of all kinds and at all times.'

This "Jenny" remains calm throughout our discourse and her answers are obviously given after profound thought. She appears to be on a *higher level of "existence"* somehow.

'Above all, you must recognise: it is not possible to determine or arrange anything from here for you down there. No one here can simply abrogate your actions down there.

'On the one hand, there are principles which you rightly refer to as "laws of nature". They also apply to us, of course: they are valid universally. However, you down there are not really aware of most of these "laws".

'And many a "law of nature", as you may call it, should in reality either be seen in a different light or is purely a figment of your own imagination.

But it would be much easier for you to recognise and expose nonsense if you were to keep your mind open for it.

However, the *"zeitgeist"* keeps narrowing your horizon. You are a physicist, you ought to know better than anyone else that "laws of nature" cannot simply be circumvented.'

'That's true, maybe we could talk about that at some other time. But what about "on the other hand"?' I am very curious.

'On the other hand, many of those arriving here have the right to determine how to proceed from here.'

'You mean to say that in fact it depends on me whether I can go back or not?'

'Yes, if it doesn't conflict with the laws of nature, it is possible to take such a decision.

'Even serious diseases can suddenly be cured sometimes. Or people can prolong the time until "death" for many years.

'You must have heard of people who refused to die before they had completed important personal tasks?

'On the other hand, should someone die suddenly due to a serious accident, then his death is usually irreversible. That's what happened to me, for example, as you know. I had severe internal haemorrhaging and was, therefore, unable to decide for myself.

'In this case it is due to the famous "coincidence". Many of you down there think they know that coincidences don't exist. But, as a physicist, you know that they do indeed happen, of course. And that's how it is in reality! Coincidences often change entire directions in the course of history. However, and you know this as well, sooner or later all coincidences without exception create new systems which are often on a higher level.

'That you are here now is utterly coincidental and has nothing to do with predetermination or fate, just like my "death".'

I interrupt her angrily ...

'Yes, just because some idiot killed you by driving on the wrong side of the road and snatched you away from my son Bob ... '

'I wasn't just snatched away from him ... ' she adds. 'Of course, this idiot, as you like to term him, has loaded a heavy burden of guilt upon himself. And he will indeed pay penance for it ... ,' she explains to me, 'but ...'

'Will he go to hell for that? Does hell exist at all?' I'm eager to know.

'Yes and no,' Jenny replies, 'when you down there talk about hell, you mean a specified location or in general a kind of "room". But that is not so. What you describe as hell – or what other religious beliefs describe as something similar – is actually more like a kind of special "state of being".'

When you are guilty, for example of serious crimes against other persons, you *cannot disburden yourself*. There are many varying degrees of guilt, however, depending on the nature and gravity of the crime or the severity of the misconduct. But here these degrees differ significantly from everything you down there imagine and from how you would assess them.

'When, due to their deeds down there, humans must face the consequences here and fall into such a "hellish state of being" – as you might call it – which will happen automatically and no one here will pass judgement on them, then they will only meet others who are in a similar state of being.

'So, hell is not a place as you imagine, but rather a kind of emotional state, which is experienced individually and which leads to an existence within a similar "collective emotional condition". I can illustrate it for you with an example: when brass band lovers go to a brass band concert, they meet others who also like this kind of music, but they will never see any "heavy metal" fans there.

'In your sphere down there you also experience that you mainly meet like-minded people at certain events but you rarely encounter people who don't share the same likes and dislikes.

'And here it is similar, because primarily "our space is a state of affairs" and space is not, as it is down there, a comparable physical parameter. But more on this later.'

'Jenny, you just said that criminal deeds don't have the same significance here as they have for us?' I press on.

'Not at all! Some things are just viewed here in a completely different way than down there with you. Many things in your world reflect the currently popular spirit of time, or the moral constraints, the political ideologies, social norms and conventions or the very diverse varieties of religious beliefs. Practically every judgement you pass on anything is based on your own concepts even when you ascribe them to "higher powers" or even to "God". Only very little of all that has, when considered universally, a similar quality here or has indeed been initiated "by God".'

'What do you actually mean by that?' I don't let off.

'Killing another human being is basically and very nearly always the worst crime you can commit, although there may be exceptions. This will always depend – like everything else – on the prevailing circumstances. But any circumstance which has led to someone killing another person down there are well known here, of course, in contrast to down there.

Here, everything is absolutely transparent at all times; for any "information" concerning the life of any living soul is stored here in eternity, just as it is down there in your "Internet" where nothing is really forgotten anymore.

'Misinterpretations or even misjudgements do not occur here. *Yet no one passes judgement over anyone else.*

'Offenders recognise here not only the full impact of their earlier deeds but they even *experience* and *feel in their own mind and body* how their actions have affected the aggrieved persons and their relatives and friends. Now you can easily understand how the emotional state of a murderer is not to be envied here . . .

'No one down there will later be able to escape his personal destiny up here. For every individual it is simply inescapable.

Any perpetrator who kills a fellow human being down there without reason cannot be exonerated here from the process of forcibly repenting his deeds, a process which will last until all those who suffered by his hand have whole-heartedly forgiven him. *But this forgiveness must be expressed by those affected.* They must "make forgiveness possible"! And that can take time – at least until the last bereaved arrives up here and is lenient with the culprit.' And with these words Jenny has to smile.

'I still don't understand completely' I persist. 'What exactly does hell mean for a murderer? And why do you keep talking about "down there", instead of simply saying "on earth"?'

'One thing at a time, it takes some time to understand it all.' Jenny stays amazingly calm and composed, at the same time lovingly eager to explain everything to me.

Although Jenny was much younger than I am, she now appears to me more like a tolerant elderly teacher who is prepared to explain everything to her pupil Chris a hundred times over if need be, until he has finally grasped it all.

'First of all,' she starts with further explanations, 'the term "on earth" does not exist here. I have already pointed out that "space" is a physical parameter which plays an only insignificant role here. You know, Chris, here you can be everywhere and nowhere at the same time, on earth as well as in any other galaxy. When I say "you down there" then this may sound to you like a spatial expression, but here it has a completely different meaning:

'In reality, the terms "here" and "down there" mean entirely different dimensions of "being" – or are simply entirely different levels of life. And the level "here" is one step higher than yours "down there". You may best compare this to an elementary school. People "down there" occupy the first grade of their "being". And "here" they are already in second grade.

'The term "down there" is really a "dimensional" expression and has indeed also a hierarchical meaning.

'Whatever space is in your perception, it is basically all one and the same here, provided that "your space" has already been "generated". If you want to look around "on earth", for example, while you are here, then you can do so and be simultaneously "here" and "on earth".

'So you are here at the moment, but you are not "away from earth".

In fact, you find yourself in a different form of life, which is completely new to you and imperceptible to the senses of all of you down there.

'On earth you were like a caterpillar, now you are a butterfly. The butterfly is, however, merely a different form of life from the caterpillar on *the same* earth. In its essence it is still unchanged. But other caterpillars will no longer notice it. It uses another dimension within the same space; in this beautiful metaphor this is, of course, a further spatial dimension in the physical sense.

'If here you should wish to take a look at another distant planet in the universe which is physically unreachable for you down there then you will be there instantly. So, when I say "down there" I do this mainly to make it easier for you to differentiate.'

After a short pause, Jenny continues: 'To come back to your question about hell for crimes, especially for "killing, taking circumstances into account" I would have to go further into details to explain it all to you.

'You know, it would be best if your *Guide* could help you with that now.'

'My Guide?' I ask, disconcerted as well as curious.

'Yes, shortly you will see a large "block of buildings". We will go inside and then I will leave you ...'

'Please don't go, Jenny, stay with me,' I try to persuade her. 'I don't at all know what I should do without you right now.'

'Don't be afraid, your personal Guide will lovingly take you by your hand and lead you.

'You "down there" would probably call this person an angel. You can do that as well, but here we call him Guide.

'Something else, Chris: should we not meet again for the time being, then please give Bob and my dear family my kindest regards and tell them that I love them very much and tell them also that *we are alive* and that *we are well*.'

'Do you really think Bob will believe me, when I tell him this? He will surely think that I merely want to console him,' I reply to Jenny without much hope.

'Then just tell him: "First of May in Paris, Sacré Coeur".'

59

Jenny has hardly finished saying this when I see indeed a huge, rather futuristic building with lots of glass in a kind of steel or aluminium framework and very high, truly gigantic cupolas and globes.

They seem to be connected by walkways made of glass. The whole construction strongly reminds me of the famous "Atomium" in Brussels, the Belgian and simultaneously the EU capital.

The Atomium is a building unique in the world with an outer shell originally made of aluminium. It emulates the crystal structure of an iron atom and was constructed for Expo 58, the 1958 Brussels World Exhibition. It was meant as a symbol of the atomic age and the peaceful use of nuclear energy. It is 102 metres high and consists of nine spheres each eighteen metres in diameter, of which five are open to visitors. All the spheres are interconnected by tubes 23 metres long. Visitors can move from one to the other by means of escalators. These accessible spheres contain exhibit halls for permanent and temporary exhibitions.

Jenny and I step inside silently without opening a visible door. It seems as if we don't have to push anything open, although the building gives a closed impression from the outside and does indeed seem to have doors.

In a large and light foyer my "Guide" is waiting for me.

He immediately approaches me without moving his legs, although they are clearly visible, and introduces himself to me with a very amiable smile:

'Hello, Chris, please call me Michael. I will show you around now and you will see plenty of interesting and new things. Should you have any questions, please don't hesitate to ask. I will try to give you an answer to all of them. You are here in a kind of "theme park" where you can look at everything to your heart's content.'

In the very same moment that Michael starts talking to me, Jenny disappears. I try to follow her with my eyes but I can't see her anywhere.

'Thank you, Michael, then I would like to ask you first of all whether leadership positions like the one you obviously hold, are also a purely male domain here?'

I have to admit this was rather cheeky, but I just felt like it.

Michael only smiles kindly. He doesn't even seem to be surprised. He has probably heard this question a thousand times already or he already knew I would ask this before I asked it. And anyway, he gives me the impression of remaining unflappable in any situation.

'Oh no,' he answers with a smile, 'would you prefer a female Guide . . . ?'

'Nonsense, I simply wanted to . . .'

I haven't finished my sentence before quite suddenly an attractive young woman is standing in front of me; she is maybe in her late thirties or early forties, has long dark hair and a nice figure, at least in my eyes, and she is fashionably dressed.

She looks very sexy to me with her skirt four inches above the knee and her medium-high heels. And I find her legs quite breathtaking.

'Do you like me better like this?' It's the same voice again and it continues, 'then just call me Michaela from now on.'

My mouth falls open with surprise.

'Are you telling me that you can adopt any shape you like?' I ask Michaela, as I should call her now, flabbergasted.

'No, I can't offer you an elephant. But I can be man *or* woman, according to my own desire or to yours now. I merely want to make plain to you that the strict separation between man and woman only exists down there and, even then, only in a biological sense. Only there do humans possess two "opposing natures".

'Here with us they are one and the same, simply human beings; since here genders are not necessary for the same essential reason as they are down there. Here you can be a man whenever you like *and* you can just as well be a woman.'

'But why are genders unnecessary here?' I want to know. 'Why is it different down there? Why do you always have to be man *or* woman down there?'

'Think a little more about it. You as a postgraduate scientist ought to arrive at the answer without further ado.'

'Is it because of reproduction?' I answer "him" or "her" hesitatingly with a counter question.

Michaela, Michael – or who or whatever – smiles at me: 'But of course! The "invention" of sexual reproduction was an important step in the evolution of all life in the entire universe. Yes, it was indeed the crucial factor.

'It was the necessary step which led to the development of a gigantic diversity of species with infinite possibilities of creating completely different forms of life, beginning already in the very next generation. That is why this step *had* to happen at a very early stage. Only then was it possible to generate and guarantee maximum success. Many unicellular organisms procreate sexually...'

'Does this mean that we humans down there are only on the first step of development?'

'Yes and no. Humans are already many rungs higher up on the "eternal ladder" of cosmic evolution of all life.

'Animals, for example, are ranked below humans down there. But there are also beings that are ranked much higher – not only up here but also in some outlandish places down there; don't believe that humans are the only intelligent creatures in the cosmos walking around in this "material outfit" which is so familiar to you.

'Considered from your point of view, physically or biologically as you say, you are already on a pretty high level. But your evolution is still a long way away from completion. However, down there only a small part of it is still of a "physical nature".

'The "evolution of life" in its true sense is in fact an "evolution of spirit" or, generally speaking, an "evolution of information". It strives from an originally very low to a gradually increasing complexity. Above a certain "level of complexity" you – as do we – talk of "spirit".

'Just simply think of the "evolution of all life" down there without the "reductionist blinkers" which are so widespread among you. Then you will very quickly discover that the development of *bodies* becomes in fact a "central constant": this is the central nervous system (CNS).

'In the course of many millions of years the CNS developed in a straight line – linear – upward, from the lower form to a higher one.

'And yet it has always remained downward compatible, of course, something your technicians down there unfortunately seldom achieve or might not even aspire to achieve when developing modern information technology . . .

'The development of the CNS is *linear*. This is important, and I will come back to it. And what is the purpose of a CNS for you?

'It is an increasingly complex organ system which functions as your "material shell" for the *interactive* further development of all information and this being, of course, also from a lower form to a higher one. In other words: the CNS promotes the emergence of "spirit" and its further development from its original lower to a gradually higher complexity.

In contrast to this, any other physical matter, this means any arbitrary other form of "matter", always takes a *cyclical* development in the course of its cosmic evolution: it is generated, grows until it reaches its zenith and then it *vanishes or dies away* at some time or other.

'An old saying of native Americans tells us: "Everything comes in circles". It is just that down there you should not really apply this wisdom to "everything" down there ...

Being a physicist you will, of course, know that in physics, by which we mean the "physics of closed bodies" – that is the "physics of all matter" – "entropy" always prevails. Entropy is, as you know very well, the "measure of disorder".'

In the course of time, all matter in the world strives towards increasing disorder. This is tantamount to saying that sooner or later all matter will disintegrate – or simply die. This applies to all your plants, animals and humans down there as well as to your sun, which makes life on earth possible, and to all other celestial bodies. Like your sun, which will no longer shine in a few billion years, so will all other *matter*, every individual living *body*, cease to exist – or, as you say, it will die.

'What do you say? "Ashes to ashes, dust to dust".

'But among you scientists down there, there are indeed some who recognised long ago that there must be another side to all this: there is a mirror-inverted, or, as we say here more precisely, a polar-symmetrical development for everything.

This applies to anything and everything in the whole world.

'This development, which is exactly polar-symmetrical to all "matter", is the development of the "spiritual" or, in general, simply the development of "information".

'While all "matter" always and everywhere takes a *cyclical* course, information, and thus everything "spiritual", always and incessantly takes a course that goes *linearly* upwards. *'Spirit does not come in circles'*...

'There is *a vehicle* in the material world which can be seen as a means to an end. It serves as a *constant interaction* in generating the spiritual supported by the material in its constant further development: this is the CNS.

Therefore, the CNS also takes a *cyclical* course and dies with the rest of the body. However, up to that point, it is the only material structure which adheres to a *linear* development: it is the only exception where matter takes a linear development, the CNS is the *interface between matter and spirit*. It incorporates *both* aspects! And there are many more such interfaces in the world which invariably incorporate both aspects.

This is why the CNS is the "central constant" in the evolution of all life. It is absolutely indispensable as an "instrument" or rather as an increasingly "complex equipment pool" for the "actual evolution", *that of the spiritual*. I will come back to all these interrelations later.

'On top of all this there is another very important aspect which must be considered when we talk about the evolution of all life:

'Initially the continuing development of entire species presents itself as progressing in nearly identical steps, namely in "collectives".

'So, in the beginning "collectives" must have been competing in the well-known evolutionary contest.

'You down there might well observe this in the case of fish and insects. In such cases you like to talk of "swarm intelligence".

'But at a rather early stage "individual intelligence" had already developed, having initially taken a parallel direction, but later having chosen an increasingly divergent way. We can see this in crabs – to a lesser extent at a comparatively low level.

'Later, at a significantly higher level in evolution, "individual intelligence" can be clearly detected in birds, such as ravens, and increasingly in many other animals.

'Evolution has *"changed horses"* and the *individual* development thereby plays a progressively more prominent role compared to that of the older *collective intelligence.*

'If the aim is the highest level of perfection, a maximum in variety is required.

'Hence, the *individual* soon becomes the most valuable asset and the measure of all things in the course of the evolution of all life: then it can only by means of "individual perfection" be possible that the entire collective may grow to ever new and higher levels in the progressing evolution.

'It follows that culture, as you call it down there, is initially subject to an *individual development*! Only the consistent support of every single individual makes this possible. Ultimately this alone ensures that the collective is enabled to develop to a higher level, which then means "cultural growth".

'So, individual development has nothing to do with individualism. These are almost bizarre concepts which many of you have down there unfortunately, and which are completely out of touch with reality – for whatever reasons and motives.

'If, however, the single individual is disregarded or even restrained in a culpable way and if its special value for the society as a whole is not recognised or cannot be recognised – if the single individual does not receive the absolutely essential encouragement and it is denied the indispensable personal freedom – then any society based on such false perceptions is invariably doomed to fail.

'Sadly, this is something you down there have experienced so devastatingly especially during the last century of your modern era. In spite of this, you down there do not seem to have learned your lesson. Many of you are still not cured, as we here can observe often enough.

'Such people *must* all, at some time or other, make good their current deficit in spiritual development here and they will experience it in their very own individual manner and it will ask for a great deal of intensified personal endeavour.

'In short, evolution is already an individual evolution with you down there. For you humans, it is already *primarily a spiritual development.*

'Generally speaking, we can ultimately also call it an *"informational evolution".*

'It follows that evolution has not yet come to a standstill for you down there.

'Even among you humans it is continuing unabated, yes, it is even *accelerating*. But the focal point of development is now no longer your physical, but your spiritual progress.

'Since evolution no longer takes place between different species, that is between entire collectives, but rather happens in each one of you, that is individually, this means that from the evolutionary point of view, the *single individuals are engaged in an evolutionary competition with one another.*

'Any further development towards total cultural progress needs first of all the spiritual development of every single individual. This means that any social system which as a basic principle attaches greater importance to the collective than to the individual, be it for political-ideological or religious-fundamental reasons, and which deprives the individual human being of his personal freedom and which disregards the inviolability of human dignity – possibly due to reasons of gender, social background or skin colour – will ultimately *always be condemned to failure.*

'All those down there who actively contribute to the oppression of "freedom of the individual" *must* one day stand to account for it here *themselves*. I will come back to this later, since now we have reached an important subject which you already touched upon in your conversation with Jenny, namely the question of "hell".

'As regards the "spiritual" or "informational" evolution, you down there – viewed from us up here – are in fact still on the lowest rung of this "eternal ladder".

'As Jenny already suggested: you are basically in the first grade of elementary school.

In the first grade, the main objective from a higher point of view, is your own reproduction, thereby enabling in the last instance an increasing number of new individuals to participate in the "spiritual evolution of life". *This is the foundation of the cosmic evolution.*

'Without sufficient reproduction on its first rung of the ladder the cosmic evolution would be doomed to fail before it had started.

'But reproduction only works down there.

'Later on it no longer exists; so it is impossible for us up here to make up for it later. But this requires care and consideration; for down there everyone must be allowed to lead a life which is worth living.'

'Hmm, why is procreation only possible with us down there, and does it mean that our lives really only serve this purpose?' I interject feeling rather uncomfortable with the very notion.

'No, since you down there have already joined in the "process of individual spiritual evolution", reproduction is no longer your only purpose today,' Michaela continues.

'In order to be capable to reproduce at all, a certain "material consistency" – if I may put it that way – is required. Humans down there, who believe that something will continue after death, like to talk of "dense material nature" when they mean "matter". I find that aptly characterised.

Of course, I also know that you as a contemporary physicist will throw your hands up in horror when you hear something like this. But you only do so because you are also such an ultra-conservative scientist who is handicapped by self-created blinkers and who is not prepared to look beyond the boundaries of his field.'

'Aren't you getting rather offensive, Michaela,' I interrupt her+him.

'Not at all.' She+he laughs. 'I mean this in a very amiable way and I'm just trying to tell you that you still have rather a lot to learn. And now you have the opportunity to do precisely that,' she+he returns absolutely composed.

60

'Well, then' Michaela continues, 'you call these "dense material" things "matter", and up until now you were of the opinion that this was all there is in this world.

'Meanwhile, you have recognised yourselves, however, that this alone *cannot* explain the universe. But instead of reappraising the cornerstones of your perceptions, you merely invent one new thesis after another, which is intended to support your current basic concepts. And very often you seem completely oblivious as to whether these theses are conclusive, compatible with one another in this comprehensive connection and whether they stand to reason.

'I will try to explain it all to you calmly if I have enough time to do so...'

Even though Michaela is in the process of turning my entire view of the world upside down, I am quite fascinated and very curious to hear what she still has to tell me.

'For you,' she continues, 'all phenomena of this world must always be attributable to "matter".

'But due to admittedly very unfortunate circumstances, at least for your nearest and dearest down there, you are now in a position to realise that this *cannot* be the case; for "somehow" you are dead and yet you are obviously still alive.

'Of course, you are not the only one who has experienced this. Since time immemorial many of you have been allowed to look "behind the curtain" which is known to you as "death". You down there call this a near-death experience. Although countless such reports exist, none of which can be explained scientifically, they are usually flatly rejected. Some of those concerned are even branded as being insane, and the media usually agree – what a sad state of affairs.

'But now you yourself are going through such an acutely real experience. It follows that most of your firm convictions, which for you are absolutely rock solid, *cannot be accurate*. How then can I have offended you with my remark that you are an "ultra-conservative scientist"?

'I suggest that you take things here calmly as they come and that you simply listen closely to what I have to tell you.

'You may ask me as much as you wish, but please, just take it in without reservation – even if at first you may be somewhat reluctant.

'You might have the opportunity at some time in the future to pass on to your fellow human beings down there what I tell you now.

'We here would be delighted if you could, for so many wrong perceptions on all sides are creating ever more problems down there which are rapidly becoming uncontrollable.

'But just one aspect in advance before you even ask me: *I* don't know whether you can stay here or whether you will have to go back again.

'It is not for me to decide what will happen with you. Besides, there are various aspects playing a role in this – among others you yourself.

'Jenny already pointed that out to you.

'At the moment, however, it is in the hands of those down there who are doing their utmost to keep you down there. You will learn everything else when the time comes . . .'

'Thank you, I understand,' I respond to Michaela in a much more humble way. 'And I hope to learn so much more from you.'

61

'Fine, then let me explain some more,' Michaela continues – and I think she looks really amazing. 'Well, we also have gender differences here, of course, since you bring those with you. They exist because they developed down there at some time or other.

'But here they don't hold the same significance as down there. Therefore, they can be changed at any time. In your "dense material" world down there they develop for evolutionary, technological reasons: the striving for perfection requires sexual reproduction.

This is the only way to create this gigantic spectrum of living organisms, which is the basis for a much higher and more comprehensive evolution than most of you down there can imagine.

'Notwithstanding this, quite a large number of people down there gain a fleeting insight into the actual size of the universe in the course of their lives.

'The historical Jesus was one of them, of course.

'But there are many more who were later not deified to the same extent by some religions. As an example I would mention your philosopher Teilhard de Chardin[42] as one of those far less revered and not at all worshipped.

'He once asked: *"Are we not all together a God in emergence?"(1950)*

'And you can hardly imagine how right he was with that fundamental question. His query alone underlines his more profound notion which he had down there of the unfathomable size, depth and width of the cosmic evolution.'

'But only a few natural scientists think like this,' I interrupt, 'the revered Albert Einstein, for example, was often asked what he thought about religion. And in a letter which he once wrote to an author who was a friend of his, he repudiated God and everything to do with religion rather abrasively.'

'Dear Chris, be assured, I will come back to Einstein. But let us discuss briefly the letter you mentioned.' Michaela has hardly finished when a screen is lowered showing the letter I had quoted with the relevant extract. We read together:

"The word God is for me nothing more than the expression and product of human weakness, the Bible a collection of honorable, but still purely primitive, legends[43] *. . . "* 'You know, Chris, actually Einstein surely meant it in a different way than many people like to interpret him.

'He understood that "God" could not be an old man to be worshipped while sitting on the highest throne, and that much in the Bible should be challenged – the same applies to all religions, by the way. This is exactly what I am trying to get across to you. However, it does not mean that Einstein was the "faithless reductionistic materialist", you seem to have been up to now.

He also said, for example: *"In the incomprehensible universe an infinitely superior rationality is revealed"* and *"The common notion that I am an atheist is based on a major error. Whoever interprets this from my scientific theories has hardly understood them . . .'*

'And in 1936 he answered Phyllis, the little girl who wrote him a letter from Sunday School, asking him: *"Do scientists pray?"*

"However, we must concede that our actual knowledge . . . is imperfect, so that in the end the belief in the existence of a final, ultimate spirit rests on a kind of faith." And later in the same letter: *". . . Everyone who is seriously involved in the pursuit of science becomes convinced that some spirit is manifest in the*

laws of the universe, one that is vastly superior to that of man." 44

'Of course, Einstein, Teilhard de Chardin and all the others must still be prepared to broaden their knowledge after their deaths down there; just like you do now, and even I am still learning and I will go on doing so.

'In fact, we will never stop learning. Socrates also a man with similar wise notions, once said: *"I know that I know nothing."*

'Of course, this is a bit exaggerated; since whenever you learn something you know a bit more than before. But when you claim one day you know everything and be it only in a limited area, then you are definitely wrong.

'The same applies to me as it does to all those who started their "eternal path" at birth down there.

'And that still applies when they have already arrived here or when they make their way here some day.

'Therefore, Socrates was right.'

62

'Now I would like to come back to our present issue:

'On the day you discard your dense material corset, after your so-called death, you *no longer have the ability to reproduce.* Reproduction was in effect your "primary" duty down there.

'Of course, it wouldn't be a problem for anyone here if someone down there has not had children, be it because they couldn't or didn't want to, for whatever reason. The sole important issue for humans is "being".

'Every human being is in principle a gift to the world and brings the potential to contribute to the cosmic evolution.

'But "no more reproduction up here" does not mean that this form of intimate relationship, known to you down there as sexuality, is non-existent here. Quite the opposite: of course, we, too, have sexuality here. And you can see from this that sexuality is in fact much more than a mere means of proliferation. Unfortunately, this is often completely misunderstood by many of you down there, it is often disputed and then even preached as "a divine decree".

'Sexuality or, as I prefer to call it here, the "intimate ethereal closeness" happens initially "in the head". Many of you down there know this already, of course, especially those of the female gender.

'Only when the head agrees the body follows. Sexuality here is far more profound than down there and also far more satisfying than you can imagine; since here it is completely unencumbered and without prohibition as long as no one is harmed and everything happens by mutual consent.'

'But how could anyone be harmed when you don't have bodies here?' I ask. But Michaela's smile tells me that my question wasn't so smart...

'Look at me, do I have a body or not?' Michaela presents one of her endlessly long legs.

'And what a body!' I reply with a smile.

'You see,' she continues, 'it is not only made of dense material like yours down there. While you are here your body is not dense material either. I will explain the exact differences in detail later.

'Of course, everyone has a body, irrespective of the "spiritual level" he might find himself on. In the course of the "spiritual advancement" the body becomes increasingly "ethereal". Actually, you are indeed right: no one can really harm these bodies anymore. You could, however, cause much "spiritual damage" or, as you might say, "mental damage". And believe me, that is much worse!

'You know, in reality you down there are sitting in a kind of cave and you are unable to see that there is so much else outside it.

'At the same time, much of what you believe you can see from there, looks completely different if seen in a different light or from a different perspective. I deliberately use the word "cave" in allusion to Plato's famous cave allegory[45].

'By the way, you can meet him here, as well as many others, should you have enough time to do so. And you could discuss things with him – provided he would also like to talk with you. I could put in a good word for you. And should it not be convenient right now, then maybe later.'

By now I am rather amazed and want to know more:

'But shouldn't Plato have been reborn several times already? Maybe he is already living in Aachen today manufacturing delicious chocolates?' With a bit of humour I try to direct the conversation to the issue of "reincarnation".

But Michaela just laughs out loud.

'Reincarnation into a new but really dense material body down there is just a nice *idea*. But there is no substance to it. It is too shortsighted and yet another concept born out of your cave perspective. I will be pleased to explain that to you in detail later and to substantiate it, but it is necessary to give you some more fundamental preliminary explanations. Will that be all right for you?'

'Sure, but I want to go back to the matter of "sexuality",' I quickly raise this issue again. 'You mean to say that many of us down there are wrong when we consider sexuality as being just a means of procreation?'

'That goes without saying.' Michaela expresses herself rather clearly. 'Of course sexuality down there is *also* a means to a certain objective, but even down there it is much more than that.

'It is a wonderful enrichment to life and has many facets. Apart from facilitating, sexuality also provides the ability to express real profound love. It can also simply fulfill the mere desire for "intimate ethereal closeness", which is the reason why I call it so. It need not always be profound love that is involved, "sympathy" or "lust" is sufficient.

'Yes, sexuality is also intended to satisfy "lust", a fact denied by many of you down there often enough although this is entirely unjustified. Lust is neither a disgrace nor is it of inferior quality and it is certainly no vice. Lust is a great gift to life as long as no one is harmed by it, or is degraded in his personality or handicapped in his development. Of course, everyone involved must give their consent.

'Here I would like to quote another story out of your Bible. On the one hand it fits well into this context because the subject "lust" is glorified in a very strange way and to such an extent that it changes its meaning completely.

'On the other hand, it is a fine example of the deliberate manipulation by those who have a monopoly on news and information regardless of its content or source. This applies not only to religious traditions. It is still valid today and concerns your modern media, no matter in which country or on which continent. This story also shows how easy it is to gain power over entire nations by manipulating information. This can include both negative and positive aspects and it can plunge people into salvation or destruction – in former times as well as today.

'Every Christian will recognise my example – you surely will, too. Yet for many people this is often the reason to turn away from Christianity. That is a great shame, since for one thing, the interpretation doesn't really correspond with the "actual meaning" of the biblical story, and for another, Christianity is a very important and great cultural treasure down there – just like other religions are in their own way.

'You believe that the Bible teaches that God let Adam fall into a deep sleep and then created Eve from one of his ribs. This is could actually be one reason for the claim that women are inferior to men "in accordance with God's will".

'In fact this is utter nonsense and is nowhere to be found in the scriptures.

'We should rather take a closer look at the names Adam and Eve: Adam in the Hebrew language means "human being" or "humanity". So Adam is a symbol for all humans, for each individual as well as for all of them together.

'Eve means "she who gives life" and is, therefore, a symbol for the childbearing woman.

'Martin Luther[46] translates "rib" from the Greek text, whereas the word in the original Hebrew text can indeed mean "rib", but it has more than one meaning. The most important one is "bow". And the word "bow" was a common synonym at the time for the unmentionable word "penis". And you should also know that for Luther's "deep sleep", we find the Greek word "ekstasis" in the original written records.

'Even without knowing much Greek hardly anyone down there would translate "deep sleep" for the word "ekstasis". With this in mind you will quickly understand what I just meant:

'Without lust no ecstasy.

'And this biblical story shows that humans recognised their own "lust" as a means to procreation. It brings them "ecstasy", which literally means "to step out of oneself", or "to be beside oneself". And with the aid of this he was able to reproduce.

'By the way, this is one of the key experiences of becoming a human being. It constitutes the difference between an animal and a human being, since down there only humans understand how procreation works.

'Of course, animals reproduce as well. And why? Because increasingly even animals experience "lust" which provides the basis for the hormonal urge.

'Another of the key experiences of humans is, of course, the process of becoming aware of their own intellect and of experiencing profound feelings which they themselves can control.

'Yet another significant key experience of humans is spirituality: this leads to the profound and absolutely inerasable conviction that there must be a superior dimension or a "divine unity" – or simply "God" – and furthermore to the notion of a "life after death".

'Neither self-appointed enlighteners nor all the ideologies which regard humans with contempt have managed to extinguish the true "cores of humanity" with you down there. They will never succeed in doing that.

'But let's get back to Adam and Eve:

'How has this biblical passage, which is a really great story, been interpreted: there is Adam who was practically mutilated by God, in order to create a woman, who then derives from him, the virtual "alpha male". As I already mentioned, this is an excellent rationale for many to justify the discrimination against women or even their suppression which is still rife down there.

'With respect to the "lust" one might say: you down there do not eat and drink merely to sustain yourselves. Quite the opposite, eating and drinking make you enjoy your lives a bit more. Eating and drinking seem to improve your quality of life and are as much a part of lust as is sexual lust. Therefore you should not look at lust with contempt. It is a precious gift and as such it plays a great role in your "spiritual development" which is maintained continuously by the power which you know as "life".

'But, of course, you shouldn't allow to intermix love and lust:

'Love is the greatest "spiritual power" in the entire universe. In its highest form it is all-embracing. But neither down there nor up here can we experience love in perfection. "God" is the greatest love.

'But, what and who "God" is exactly, that completely escapes human imagination, even ours up here.

'I will come back to this later in more detail.

'Certainly, we up here already know much more than you down there, but still, by no means do we know everything. Ultimately it might only be a tad more. But also more to this later if we have so much time left to us.

'Since lust is a gift to life it means that not only humans down there feel lust, but that every creature alive, and that includes animals as well, because they, too, are spiritual beings – they are merely on a different, that is lower level of their spiritual development than you.

'Lust explains why it is that here everyone is free to be what they want to be. If you want to be a man, you are a man here, but at any time you may also choose to be a "woman", like I am at the moment for you because you asked about it at the beginning. By the way, I feel fine in both genders.'

'Then I must have wronged my son Tom tremendously for philandering and living down there with men like Sascha and a mixed gender creature like Jasmin . . . ' it pours out of me rather disrespectfully. In doing so, I notice that the memories of my life down there have in the meantime become much more clear.

'Yes, that was rather stupid of you!' Michaela replies seemingly delighted about my insight. 'You humans are indeed on a much higher level of spiritual development than all other creatures living down there with you.

'You are able to make your own long-term decisions on all levels. Insofar you possess your own free will. At the same time you have gained a high *individual* responsibility.

'You humans are capable of abstract thought. No other animal has that capability to such an extent. You can apply the results of this unique ability to thinking *generally* about your life, your behaviour and your habits and to act accordingly.

'You must do that with *responsibility* and care at all times. You will surely learn more about this later.

63

After a brief pause Michaela continues: 'So, the sexual reproduction is a vital engine for the evolution of all life in the world. This will always call for two beings which are mirror inverted or complementary, which fit together like pot and lid: their being "polar-symmetrical".

'This "polar-symmetry" is a quite central, dominating aspect everywhere in the world and does not only express itself in the form of men and women.

The "polar-symmetry" *of all and everything* is one of the most important fundamental laws in the entire universe.

'You down there overlook this too often, unfortunately, and you don't recognise its real significance.

'Even though you encounter this phenomenon from day to day you seldom advance to the next logical step. This is why you fail to see the wood for the trees and why it is that you complicate not only your own lives unnecessarily but also those of many of your fellow humans.

'Nevertheless, there are numerous great "spirits" down there, who time and again try to jolt you awake. One example is the ancient Chinese symbol of "Yin and Yang". According to your perception of time it is more than 2,500 years old:

'Two flames, a white one and a black one, are in polar-symmetrical opposition to each other, and a small circle positioned in each of the two flames in the colour of the other indicates that one is always included in the other. This  symbol epitomises the universal, fundamental law of "polar-symmetry".

'In other words, anything and everything in this world has a mirror image. Often, but by no means always, they both exist to the same extent.

'As a physicist you know, for example, that if there is matter there must also be anti-matter. You are amazed, however, that you can hardly find any anti-matter down there.

'Your answer seems plausible to you – but it is wrong; it is not really thought through:

'To begin with, you assume that everything started with the "Big Bang". I'll come back to that later. You further assume that nearly as much anti-matter was produced by the Big Bang as matter. Later on they very nearly annihilated each other save for a small residue of matter. And from that alone everything existing started to develop.

'But why does no one of you reason that if there are symmetrical relationships there could also be "real asymmetrical" ones? Everywhere else you can see two sides of everything.

'In fact, this universal fundamental law, "everything has two sides", applies to anything and everything and thus also to symmetry and asymmetry.

'Why then shouldn't matter and anti-matter exemplify the asymmetrical relationship, which *must* exist due to a universal principle and why shouldn't it be made known "unambiguously"?

'And why shouldn't it be clearly defined from the beginning by a simple logical rule, just as it is actually found in reality?

'But that is exactly how it is.

'If you as a physicist would only once look beyond the confines of your discipline and also follow developments in biology and chemistry, then you would see it yourself.'

'Now I am curious,' I interrupt rather sceptically and also a little hurt in my personal vanity. 'Then give me some examples, please.'

'But of course, Chris, for example, biologists know twenty amino-acids which determine the genetic material. Of these only *one* has merely *one* carbon atom, all the other nineteen have at least *two* which makes them optically active. The proportion 1+19 gives us a *typical* asymmetrical relationship of 5% to 95%.

'Would you like me to give you another example?'

Without waiting for my answer Michaela continues: 'In the whole of the universe there are 81 chemical elements which occur naturally, which don't decay radioactively and are, therefore, stable...'

64

It is simply fantastic: whenever Michaela explains something to me in this gigantic construction, I can simultaneously follow it in three-dimensional animated graphics. Everything she says appears immediately in a kind of hologram, always in a well-understandable size – as desired and needed sometimes in the original size, sometimes minimised at other times enlarged. Even when she changes the subject abruptly the holograms change accordingly without delay.

While Michaela talks about amino acids, genetic material and chemical elements, I can see it all in front of my very eyes, their structures "on a small scale" as well as clear examples with regard to their real occurrences "on a large scale" in the world. I can view everything directly and understand it easily.

In addition, I can view all relevant data on separate screens. Like news readers on television reading off teleprompters, Michaela is provided with all relevant information in palatable bits.

'Why only 81 ... ?' I now interrupt Michaela, 'in my humble understanding there are 83 naturally occurring elements ... ?'

I am rather proud that I can still remember this from my chemistry lessons at school.

But Michaela simply smiles: 'No, Chris, in fact there are exactly 81 elements which occur naturally in the whole universe *and* are also stable, so that they do not decay radioactively. From the 83 elements you know, you have to subtract 2, the elements technetium and promethium with the atomic numbers 43 and 61, because they are radioactive and they decay. So, really only 81 remain. The first element of these 81 is hydrogen which is particularly *outstanding*. Therefore, we could really say there are 80+1 elements.

'To reach the next power of 10, the number 100, we have to add 19. If you think back now to the distribution of optical active and inactive amino acids or to visible matter and invisible structures in the universe, which are so puzzling to you down there, then you will find the same ratio of 1+19. Over and over you will find this relationship of 5% to 95%. It is simply the reflection of a really obvious, natural asymmetry.

'Maybe I'll have the chance to come back to this later ... '

Michaela doesn't seem to know whether she will have enough time for all this. Therefore, she picks up her thread again immediately.

'The remaining 80 elements include 20 pure elements, also known as pure isotopes. This means that no isotopic variations of these exist as they do of the others. Of these 20 pure isotopes only *one* has an even number of protons in its nucleus, the remaining 19 hold an uneven number of protons.

'Again you can detect a distribution of 1+19 and thus a ratio of 5% to 95%.

'Symmetry and asymmetry are unambiguously determined and follow a universal, fundamental law, according to which everything and anything in the world possesses two sides which are polar-symmetrical to each other. And so it is that matter and antimatter are distributed in the universe also asymmetrically.

'Certain precise and distinct rules are firmly established everywhere in this world, as I would like to show you in detail later. But here are some more examples of such firm and precise rules, this time referring to medicine or better to neurophysiology:

'Your brain researchers often look for the trees in the forest and don't find them, because they tend to complicate things.

'But here the basic principles are also quite simple and unequivocal: there is a law of "all-or-nothing" meaning that a stimulus is either strong enough to trigger an electric impulse, which is then transmitted by a nerve, or that it is too weak in which case nothing happens. There is no such thing as "a little bit of transmission" just as "being a little bit pregnant" is not possible.

'And something else: each nerve in every body is always a one-way street. Information always runs in only one direction. This is a simple way for nature to prevent mistakes. And in which complicated ways did you imagine that nerve tracts run through your brain? In fact they are neatly arranged in gigantic wiring harnesses exactly along the three directions of physical space, as you established only a few years ago.

'What does your Bible tell you? In the chapter of the Wisdom of Solomon it says aptly: *"But thou hast ordered all things in measure and number and weight."*[47]

'This brings us back again to the laws and rules of this world: they are all based on simple, elementary mathematical logic.

'Many of your great scientists keep claiming that a theory can only be correct if it is simple and beautiful. Some of you think this is wrong. Yet they are at fault, since the rule actually is: *"Simplex sigillum veri est"* or in other words: "Simplicity is the sign of truth".

'I would love to explain everything to you in more detail, but time flies . . .'

Michaela sounds a bit sad.

'Does this mean, Michaela, that I will have to go back down there?' I interpret her words.

'I don't know; no, really, I don't know. We have to wait and see.'

I feel that Michaela is loath to end her dedicated demonstrations prematurely.

65

'To come back to the fundamentals on which every decisive aspect in this world is based and which is hence also crucial for you down there . . . ,' Michaela continues, ' . . . the point is that we keep seeing a natural asymmetry of 5% to 95%.

'This constitutional asymmetry can be observed in all possible shapes and forms, even when we analyse preferences. For example, homosexuality and heterosexuality in humans and animals are also distributed in an asymmetrical manner, that is in a natural ratio of 5% to 95%. There is, however, a significant difference: such a rule can only apply in its most rigid form to anything "non-spiritual", of course – which means all purely physical matter not "spiritually animated". The examples of the chemical elements and the "canonical" amino acids demonstrate this clearly. For everything "spiritual", however, that is for everything spiritually animated, this rule is not so strict, since every spiritual being, or in other words everything alive, has in principle the opportunity to make a *decision*. And it is this that blurs the borderlines.

'Of course, it goes without saying that a turtle can exert less influence than, say, a monkey. And humans possess by far the greatest power of decision among you down there. Only humans become fully self aware. And only they have developed the ability for abstract logical reasoning to an advanced degree and to make extensive informed decisions.

'By means of their own free will humans can at least *basically*, often even to a major extent, influence the decision as to whether or not and in how far they want to live and act out their nature which has been dealt out to them at random due to the universal asymmetry. The nature of individual humans cannot be dubbed as unnatural per se just because it is not shared by the majority of humans. It follows that there is no necessary treatment of the sort you suggested for your son, Tom, with regard to his homosexuality.'

'You really know that?' I ask Michaela rather surprised. 'Are you watching me? And if so how is it that you have the time to do it? Don't you have many others to take care of?'

'Oh yes, I can do all this simultaneously. While I show you around here, I am doing the same with others at the same time.

'After you have learned more about the intrinsic laws of the world, it will become easier for you to understand all this. I, for my part, will try to give you a better understanding of it all,' she hastens to reassure me.

'And besides, you already said yourself that you might have done your son Tom an injustice...'

'That's true, I had already forgotten about it.'

66

'I would like to deepen your already considerable knowledge about the elementary and universal law of polar-symmetry governing everything and anything in this world,' Michaela proceeds.

'This law leads to another logical implication: the universe *cannot* consist of "matter" alone – not even of various "differentiated classes" of "matter".

'It resembles the Japanese art of "origami", the art of folding paper into wonderful forms. At first you have simple sheets of paper and then you end up with highly complex figures.

'Projecting this onto the world, there are initially only *two* "basic qualities", as I would term them, which are fundamentally different from each other. Of course, *they both really exist*.

'And since they are "polar symmetrical" or mirror images of each other, we must imagine them as being vertically perpendicular to each other just as a plumb-bob is to its base line.

'Now, just imagine you were a "*one*-dimensional point" which could only crawl along such a base line. Of course, it would then be very difficult for you to even recognise the perpendicular to this line which would also be depicted as only a single minute point.

'In the same way you down there are often convinced that only this "one world" exists which you can effortlessly perceive with your senses and you fail to recognise anything else.

'Nonetheless, from time to time you become able to sense this other world, which is only "polar-symmetrical" to yours and which is just as real. All too often you just don't want to "see" it.

'You even assiduously ignore clear indications and you dismiss and sometimes even fight against some of those who don't want to or simply can't ignore such evidence. You send some of them to the doctor and others into a lunatic asylum.

'Many of you are content to explain such evidence as merely being the as yet inexplicable product of a "material" world, and you adhere to the notion of its uniqueness because you can only perceive this with your senses without too much effort.

'At the same time you overlook the fact that these senses emanate from the very same environment which you claim to be the only one in existence.

'But it is usually beyond your comprehension that "differently constructed senses" might exist and "differently constructed worlds" might exist, between which there are but only few interfaces.

'By the two "polar-symmetrical real worlds" I mean, of course, the worlds of "matter" and "spirit". You will see later that within these there are also various degrees with only small interfaces. Furthermore, I will show you that you down there on your "special level" within the "material world" are in actual fact a product of the "spiritual world" and not the other way round.

'This means that the "material" always stands at the end of a consistently real sequence of existences and is, as I would like to show you, in principle hardly more "material" than the "spirit" upon which it is based.

Seen from this factual end of the sequence of existences, this means that viewed from the "material world" as you see it, you detect in all phenomena beyond your point of view – that is in everything that does not conform – merely products of "matter".

You even believe that you yourselves are purely material beings. Yet you overlook completely the spirit behind it – or more precisely the spirit *in front* of it – or, generally speaking, the "informational" or simply the "spiritual world" in this real sequence of existence.

Some of you seriously believe that the "spirit" is merely a kind of funny by-product of matter and of a purely accidental nature – possibly without meaning and purpose. *This is absurd, of course.*

In fact, the "spirit" is even the primary and most important factor in the world. Everything "material" derives from it – it is ultimately "its product" – and not vice versa.

If you down there would focus a little more on elementary mathematics you might quickly recognisee the truth. However, you mostly look the other way . . .

67

'What's so special about mathematics?' I ask Michaela a trifle perplexed. 'Mathematics is a purely human construct. Which part of it was not defined by humans? Humans alone create all the rules and regulations.'

'No, that is not entirely right,' Michaela remains benign and extremely patient as always.

'Look, when, for example, down there three dinosaurs stood at a huge watering hole about a hundred million years ago according to your perception of time...'

At the same moment I get a terrible fright, for suddenly I am actually standing in a jungle of ferns next to a large lake, surrounded by three huge dinosaurs whose raucous din makes it almost impossible to catch what Michaela is saying.

'Don't worry,' she puts my mind at ease, 'they won't harm you. Although this is totally real for you, you are completely safe, because you are looking at this scene from a different "space", even if you find yourself in "their" time at the moment. *You must understand that "space" is transient here with us, just as "time" is with you*; this being due to the fact that "space" and "time" are polar-symmetrical to each other.

'For you this must almost be like watching a film in the cinema, but here I can offer you a "reality-show" as you down there might call it.'

Then Michaela carries on:

'Now then, should a fourth dinosaur join these three . . . ' And there it appears with a thunderous stamping...

' . . . then,' Michaela picks up her thread again, 'there are three plus one dinosaurs and that makes it four. There are neither two nor five, but four and this proves the *real existence* of fundamental mathematics – such as numbers – and also of simple mathematical operations. Just accept for once that some elementary mathematical concepts such as ordinal numbers and all simple geometric figures, for example, a circle, a square, right-angled, equilateral and isosceles triangles exist in reality. They just *are*! They really exist, irrefutable *information* in this world.'

'Was Plato right then with his theory of ideas?' I pretend to be well-informed.

'Yes and no,' Michaela replies, 'Plato's theory of ideas is far too extensive, since it assumes that for everything and anything a precise idea already exists in the "spiritual world". This is wrong.

'If that were the case, everything would be pre-determined. And that is exactly what it is not.

'I don't even know at the moment, whether you can stay here or whether you will have to go back. *The future on principle holds infinite possibilities: the world is emergent.*

'Of course, one day you will come back here anyway, but this is exactly the reason for the very indeterminacy of here, which very often is even purely incidental.

'We don't know *now* exactly what will become of you, but *in the long run* we both know. In any case you will come back here sooner or later.' With this a broad smile runs over Michaela's graceful face.

Considering the possibilities in my mind I don't think I really want to go back. And I notice to my own surprise that at this moment I do not take into account the feelings of those down there who love me, who are worried about me or are even already crying for me, and who would love nothing more than to have me back immediately.

'Now then . . . ' Michaela immediately takes up her thread again, ' . . . there are some clear and unambiguous elementary-mathematical fundamental rules according to which everything in this world is developed and fits together.

'This also takes into account that there are two fundamental, polar-symmetrical areas of existence which then subdivide and graduate themselves further and further.

'One of them, also the first and superior of the two, I'll just call the "spiritual world".

'The other, subsequent one corresponds with the "material world" as I like to call it somewhat superficially, this being the only one which you down there really recognise. Both of them are mirror-inverted and in opposition to each other like Yin and Yang. And in the same way as Yin and Yang, one emerges from the other whilst still including an element of each other.'

'But then . . . ,' I interrupt Michaela again, which clearly delights her, since it shows her my keen interest and that I am able to follow her without effort.

' . . . yes, then these two "fundamental realities" might also exist in unequal "amounts" as is the case with matter and antimatter or with chemical elements and amino acids?'

'Absolutely right!' Michaela is delighted. 'That's how it is – and now I come back again to the 95% of the universe for which you don't have an explanation.

'In fact the ratio of "spiritual world" – or let me talk more generally of the "informational world" – to the material world is also asymmetrical. However, the informal world takes 95% and the material world only 5%. So therefore . . . '

Again I interrupt her to finish her sentence myself: ' . . . this explains our confusion as to why there is so little but miraculously well-organised matter in the universe?!

'So we just invent "dark matter" and "dark energy" because we are unable to recognise that in reality everything is as clearly structured as it is due to pure "information".

'So it is concrete *information* which exactly determines everything? Does it, for example, determine how some "effects in space" are accomplished, such as gravitation perhaps – or maybe also light?!'

'That's how it is, Chris, you hit the nail on the head.' Michaela is even more delighted.

'And quite incidentally, with light and gravitation you simultaneously mention two effects in space which are at the same time a "polar-symmetrical pair" controlled by information.

'By the way: even you are now nothing but pure "information" – viewed from down there. But this is merely a matter of opinion or a question of perspective, for, as you can see in yourself and also in me, there must be much more behind it. It is obvious that complex information can be shown and expressed in very different ways – even in any number of variations . . . '

And whoosh Michaela turns into Michael again.

Michael remains unflustered and continues: 'Hence information is the very *first* really manifested form of existence in this world. Yes, it turns the world into a "tangible" world. And "information" is the real heart of everything and anything which emerges and subsequently develops in the course of this world's existence, and throughout the entire cosmic evolution.

'But information does not automatically mean "consciousness" or "soul". Some people are searching for a soul even in the smallest of stones. But this panpsychism[48] goes too far, just as Plato's theory of ideas does.

'You must think about all this on a far larger scale and then see it from an evolutionary point of view as well.

'The development process for everything "material" always proceeds in a *cyclical* manner whereas the parallel process for all things "informational" runs on a *linear* trajectory. Hence evolution not only applies to everything "material" but also to everything "spiritual" or "informational".

'For you down there everything "material" is moved by some "power" which you know as "energy". And both are interchangeable. You only have to remember Albert Einstein's[49] famous equation, $E=mc^2$. And something else: on the "material side" everything is quantised, as Max Planck showed you and it consists of single "particles" – and is thus *"discontinuous"*.

'Everything "informational" is also moved by a certain "power". *This power is "life"*. On the "spiritual side", in contrast to the "material side", everything is *"continuous"* – it is thus flowing. Continuity and discontinuity are also a "polar-symmetrical pair".

'In the same way as matter can be at rest, there can also be stationary or "static" information. This includes, for example, ordinal numbers and simple geometric forms. Ordinal numbers can be certain points of information which only determine, when, where and how or in which forms and to what extent something exists, just like you do in your coordinate system. Within the universe there are many such "informal coordinates" which determine, for example, where which celestial bodies are located, how they rotate and similar things.

'For all this there are elementary mathematical and logically justifiable fundamental rules, of course. Therefore you don't have to go on "inventing" invisible matters and energies which you believe to be constituent parts of your *material* world, although you cannot perceive them with your senses, and which you invent solely to be able to explain certain relations and conditions in a "material way".

'This is what you are continuously doing down there at the moment.

The true basis for everything in this world is something completely different; it is the really existing "information". However, "initially" this is only slightly "differentiated". It is solely in the course of further *cosmic* development that the percentage of information increases and becomes ever more complex.

'This is what I call "differentiation".

'You could call "more complex information" also "spirit". In the beginning there was only little of that, later in the course of the cosmic evolution it grew faster, however. To the same degree as "information" is differentiated into increasingly complex clusters" – in other words when more and more "spirit" is generated – then the amount and importance of matter decreases gradually in the course of immense periods of time.

'By the way, we can also interpret the Yin and Yang symbol in a similar way, since each flame has thick and thin areas.

'After reaching a certain degree of complexity such an "information cluster" – or spirit – is then able to organise itself.

'Spirit or complex information – both terms to be used for the whole or a part thereof – will become more *dynamic* in the course of time. They possess more *vital force.*

'The growing complexity of dynamic information is the equivalent of ever higher forms of life.

'The developing spirit, or more accurately, the "differentiating spirit", *in synchrony* with its environment – or its "cloak" –influences in return its material environment, adjusts to it and forms it. Thus spirit has a direct influence on the "material aspect" of evolution.

'At present your generic term for it is "epigenetic" but you don't really realise its true depth and width.

'Every being communicates via its senses with its material outside world, but it also communicates via its CNS with an extensive world of information, with the "spirit" as a whole. Any further evolution is supported and accelerated by their constant *interactions*. Hence, ever more perfect "material tools and instruments" are generated and developed whose primary aim is the improvement of this interaction. In the course of immense periods of time everything develops not only ever more vigorously but also increasingly fast while taking a considerably more targeted approach.

'In this way an increasingly higher "spirit" is developed – or again generally speaking – an increasingly complex "information cluster".

Although you down there keep talking about the "evolution of life" you only mean the evolution of its "material aspect" – or that of the "material cloak" which the evolving beings wear.

'But actually there is an even more important evolution taking place, simultaneously and in an analogous manner: and that is the "information" on which everything else is based.

In contrast to the physical evolution, however, which, as you know, always takes *cyclical* courses, the spiritual evolution always runs on a *linear* trajectory. It moves in a straight line and always directly upwards.

'It always strives for "increasing complexity" – or, as I like to call it, to "increasing differentiation": its aim is absolute perfection in a maximum of diversity.

'This is the true evolution of life.

'It is an informational or spiritual evolution.

'To simplify matters, let's call the "complex information" just "spirit" – for the whole on a large scale or a part thereof on a smaller scale.

'The development of matter and spirit takes place simultaneously, the results, however, are different.

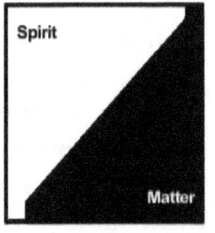

'Matter is, without exception, generated from the same basic building blocks and adopts ever new and more complex forms.

'It grows until it reaches its zenith and then it decomposes into its basic building blocks again. It is an eternal *cycle* of emergence and birth, growing, ageing, death and decay. This is known as *entropy* in physics. It is comparable to the continuous turning of a waterwheel.

'Just as a waterwheel constantly scoops up water which is then collected in an "infinite reservoir", so does matter in a similar way constantly generate new spirit. The spirit, however, grows and develops further and further in a *linear* trajectory – to become ever more highly developed and more complex.

'In order to succeed in this "eternal process", it is essential, of course, to maintain the continuous development and improvement of new and ever more competent "devices" and "instruments" which are capable of ensuring the perpetual exchange of information – that is *interaction*.

'You down there call the equipment capable of ensuring this interaction the central nervous system or CNS. It is for this reason that only the CNS is developed in such a linear manner and becomes more and more complex, more efficient and more sophisticated. The information potential which is initially only undifferentiated thus becomes differentiated.

'Due to this constant "interaction" the spirit becomes *progressively more potent in increasingly less time.*

'In the course of time the spiritual development proceeds faster and faster and ever more efficiently. Early on during the evolution of life instincts develop, intelligence follows later to an ever higher degree and in multiple gradations. Thereafter, various phases of a gradually maturing consciousness appear, subsequently followed by awareness. This is joined by various other qualities which are all subject to a *linear* maturing process, such as reasoning, memory and ever more mature, profound and richer qualities of emotion, to name but a few examples.

'All this is an evermore intertwined, very complex interactive procedure which has extremely complicated effects and which always takes place in processes running simultaneously and growing parallel to each other, in an almost symbiotically coordinated, interactive manner.

In the course of immense periods of time it is interaction which creates exactly these complex brains necessary for the continual development of new and ever more complex "information clusters" and to "differentiate" idle information in a specific way. We call these clusters simply "spirit". This includes all higher spiritual qualities such as "reasoning", "memory", "consciousness", "awareness", "deep emotions" and much more.

'Spirit creates matter and matter creates spirit.

'And the matter turns like a waterwheel.

'In the same way as the waterwheel dips into the water *cyclically* to scoop up more water to move it to a higher level, matter comes and goes. And like the water, which in this metaphor stands for the spirit, so the spirit increases evermore and grows *linearly*. Of course, the scooped up water of my metaphor cannot improve the floats of the waterwheel to move more water in less time. But this is what the spirit does when it influences matter and, by persistent interaction, it thus contributes in an epigenetic manner to the incessantly maturing CNS.

'This demonstrates that the universe has not always and in general been a conscious universe – or even a kind of consciousness in itself. Rather is consciousness generated solely by differentiation from an "informal basic ground", from a "basic spirit" so to speak. Hence, consciousness is always a new and higher "product" or a special "informational cluster" generated through interaction.

'Consciousness was originally based on "unconscious basic information", which at the beginning determined more the framework than the content. In the course of time it also initiated the development of a kind of polar symmetrical "catalyst" which corresponds to complex "matter" in the function of the waterwheel.

'Without this the eternal differentiation of everything informational from the underlying spiritual basis up to consciousness and awareness in an ever growing diversity would be impossible.

'In other words, two worlds, mirror-inverted to each other, are simply mandatory.

'They benefit mutually from the constant interaction enabling them to form something new and to develop it to something higher – almost like sexual propagation.'

And here Michael laughs out loud.

68

'Chris, I would like to come back to our starting point again,' Michael continues, and I notice how much he seems to be in his own element.

'Everything is based on an elementary mathematical logic. The principle still applies: *"Simplex sigillum veri est"* – "Simplicity is the sign of truth". And you can find this simple logic by recognizing that there are two "real existences" in relation to zero which in this case stands for "nothing" and represents a mirror axis: *There are in fact two truly existing fundamental spheres of existence in this world, which are polar symmetrical to each other.*

'This does not change even if you want to recognise only one of them and term it "matter".

'Without any justification you disregard the logic which elementary mathematics provides. Yet this part of mathematics exists in reality just as much as it is completely independent of whether you down there possess any intelligence to comprehend it or not.

'Since there are indeed *two* real spheres of existence, many of you down there are completely blocked.

Instead of trying to become acquainted with this second real level of existence and to study it, you stubbornly ignore it. And not only that: often enough you even clash with those who do at least try to understand it.

'In the elementary-logic of mathematical analogy "matter" is equivalent to the "+1 reality". From that point on all positive numbers emanate, in other words +1, +2, +3 ... and so forth.

'Furthermore, and as a polar-symmetrical "necessity", all reciprocal values start from here as well, that is +1/1, +1/2, +1/3 . . . and so on. Both sequences of positive numbers extend into infinity.

'The second reality which results therefrom as a mirror axis, polar symmetrical to zero, is the "-1 reality". All negative numbers and also their polar-symmetrical reciprocal values emerge from here, also extending into infinity, of course, that is -1, -2, -3 . . . and so on up to minus infinity and also -1/1, -1/2, -1/3 ... up to minus 1/infinity.

'The logical existence of the positive and negative number sequences shows that there are indeed two real spheres of existence, emerging into two disparate directions from zero as the symbol for "nothing". And in accordance with the universal law, which you know well enough, that everything has two sides, these two follow suit and also subdivide further.

'The "+1 reality" marks the end of the sequence of existence. You are part of it, of course, which is why most of you down there recognise it as the only existent reality.

'It is roughly equivalent to the "world of matter".

'The other one, the "-1 reality", which precedes it, is roughly equivalent to the "world of information".

'When you delve a bit deeper into this analogy which is based on simple mathematical logic, then you notice immediately that the "world of matter" does not really exist in complete autonomy and independence. It is in fact only generated by the "world of information" as the last link of this chain, in the same way as "+1" is generated by squaring "-1".

'The square root "-1", the symbol for information, is already present in every "+1 reality", the symbol for everything material.

'Then again, when you calculate the square root of "+1" you don't arrive *inevitably* at "-1". It is hidden therein.

'This is why you, as "part of the material +1-world", have so many problems in discovering the real background of the world, namely the fact that "matter" is always based on "spirit" – where "spirit" stands not only for complex information but *in principle* for any form and any level of "information".

'This analogy also shows that – from a purely mathematical point of view – the informational or spiritual world, which is roughly equivalent to the "-1 reality", is the *more powerful* one of the two.

'This corresponds exactly with the cosmic reality.

'The *more powerful reality* in this universe is the all-embracing and all-pervading world of information.

'It follows that, in the course of evolution, the asymmetry between "matter" and "spirit" develops to become qualitatively even more excessive – away from "matter", of course, in favour of "spirit" – or "information".

'This baffles you down there so much, because, although you notice the "spirit", you ignore it as being some independently operating system, because you can neither see nor measure it. And hence you declare it to be a mere product of matter.

'Since you close your minds and deny the real character of the world, you tend to accept interpretations which are often quite adventurous but not necessarily correct.'

'Is there a God? And could you explain heaven and hell to me again in detail? Jenny and I were talking about this at the beginning between before I met you,' I jump in again and want to know more, yes, much more.

'Slow down, one thing after the other . . . ,' Michael replies.

At that moment everything suddenly grows dark around me and Michael fades. I call after him, I want to grab him, but all of a sudden he is gone.

I am falling into a void.

69

'We did it, he's back,' Dr Bender and his boss Professor Paland are extremely pleased with themselves.

For both of them and their whole team their efforts to resuscitate their patient Christian Schneider have been absolutely exhausting.

It has probably taken more than forty-five minutes.

Chris had suffered a cardiac arrest. By pure chance Dr Dirk Bender had been at his bedside when the medical safety devices, connected to him to monitor his vital functions, triggered loud alarm signals and the electrocardiogram showed a flat line, known as the zero-line.

Now speed was of the essence, from now on every second would count.

This is when the brain cells start dying and no one knows exactly how much time is left not only to bring someone back but also to bring him back without permanent brain damage.

Then everything would be too late.

No one is able to say how efficient the brain will be after a successful reanimation, whether it will be able to facilitate a life worth living. After cardiac death, brain death follows swiftly which in turn triggers a gradual process of irreversibility on the way from life to final death.

But – fortunately – modern intensive care units are equipped with facilities which enable a steady flow of oxygen to be fed to the brain.

Thus the time span available for resuscitation measures is prolonged, at least that is what everybody hopes but cannot know for certain.

Now, the physicians believe they have succeeded in bringing Chris back to life. Of course, they hope he will stay with them.

This takes a big load off Dr Dirk Bender's mind. He hurries outside and takes out his mobile phone. He wants to inform Lara and her family.

70

Helen, Lara and Tom are sitting at home in the lounge where Jasmin and Sascha had joined them. Helen has prepared a meal for them all.

Bob is also on his way from Munich to Aachen. The radio is playing softly in the background; it is tuned to a regional station with classical music.

Lara knows that the father of her unborn child is attending to her father in the hospital. She is glad about this because she is sure he will do everything he only can. But how much influence does he have, will it be sufficient? Questions she asks herself quietly as a faithful Christian.

Some days ago she had met Dirk in a cafe. They get along quite well with each other again and gradually Dirk seems to be warming up to the idea of becoming a father again in the near future.

Of course, the mood is rather gloomy.

Hardly anyone knows what to say, except maybe Jasmin and Sascha, since they are only affected indirectly. Touchingly, they try to put the Schneiders' minds at ease, even to cheer them up now and again.

Helen is deeply absorbed in her own thoughts and is at odds with life.

Repeatedly she breaks down in tears quietly and then Lara wraps her arms around her protectively.

Tom also finds himself unable to hold back his tears and struggles with the situation.

Everyone is dreadfully depressed.

Suddenly, the telephone rings. Lara picks it up.

'Lara, is that you?'
Dirk Bender is at the other end.
'Yes, how's Dad?' she asks him, agitated.

'I'm afraid the news is not too good. We had to resuscitate your father just now. His heart had stopped working. It took quite a long time, but we succeeded in bringing him back. Although he is still not really stable, unfortunately.

'We don't know yet whether we really managed to get him back for good. I hope we did, but the situation can change again at any moment.

'We shall stay with him, of course, and we will keep an extremely close eye on him. I just wanted to inform you. But you must be prepared for the worst. And, of course we don't know yet whether his brain is already damaged or whether all will be well if he can make it.

'Lara, please break it gently to your family. I have to go back now to see to him again.

'And ... Lara ... I still love you ...'

Lara notices how Dirk's voice trembles, how deeply touched he is and that he is fighting back his tears.

She can hear him putting down the receiver and then she bursts loudly into tears herself. Tom takes her into his arms and leads her back to the sofa.

'Dad . . . ' she sobs, 'Dad has had a cardiac arrest. They succeeded in resuscitating him and he is alive. But his condition is not yet stable. They don't know whether he will make it. We must pray for Dad.'

And she immediately starts to pray the Lord's Prayer, and they all join her one after the other.

71

'It is eight o'clock. This is the evening news,' the speaker on the radio announces. 'A helicopter crashed in the Aachen forest near the restaurant "Entenpfuhl". It was on its way back from a sightseeing flight over the Aachen region. The experienced pilot Max Kauder and Christian Schneider, a physicist from Aachen, who accompanied him suffered life-threatening injuries. According to police reports, initial investigations revealed that eye witnesses saw a group of youngsters directing illegally strong laser pointers at the helicopter. The police assume that the pilot and his companion were blinded to such an extent that they lost control over the helicopter ...'

In the Schneiders' living room everyone listens in dismay. Immediately anger and fury rises in all of them

'I sincerely hope they are going to catch them,' Tom is beside himself. 'Something like this must be severely punished ...'

Sascha waves this aside dismissively:

'So what, even if they are caught, in this country every effort is taken to protect the perpetrators first of all. And if they are youngsters they may even get a social worker to help them cope with the situation and they'll all have a resocialisation holiday somewhere in the Caribbean thrown in.'

Everyone in the room seems to agree with him by murmuring softly.
The doorbell rings.
Lara goes to open the door. It is Bob who has arrived in Aachen. White as a sheet he joins them, hugs them all and hears the latest information.

72

Beeeeeeeeeeeb, beeeeeeeeeb, beeeeeeeeeeeeb . . .

Over and over again, the loud alarm signal sounds from cubicle 6 in the intensive care unit. Dr Dirk Bender, the Senior Physician and two intensive care nurses hurry to take care of the patient. They all know that it is the cubicle of Professor Schneider.

Chief Physician Professor Paland is immediately informed and he joins them without delay.

'Holy crap . . . ' Dirk Bender shouts, 'we're losing him again.'

Chris's heart has problems again.
This time it is due to ventricular fibrillation.
A "simple" cardiac arrest means that the heart just stops working. The ECG shows a flatline.
The ventricular fibrillation on the other hand is a so-called haemodynamically inefficient cardiac contraction. In this case, all the many single cells of the heart muscle act for themselves and no longer cooperate, because their

coordination, usually monitored by the heart's neuroplexus, suddenly ceases. The ECG shows not a flatline but extremely rapid twitches instead.

This results in insufficient blood being pumped from the heart to the vital organs and the brain is starved of blood.

As a result the person concerned dies very soon, unless the decoupled heart is animated to beat in a regular coordinated manner again.

Ventricular fibrillation is surely the most common cause of the so-called sudden death. Only electric defibrillation can help here, known in the vernacular as electric shock therapy. For this, a defibrillator is needed, a life-saving device which can nowadays be found in prominent positions in many public places such as train stations or airports. Some devices are fully-automatic and can even "talk" to the user, so that in the case of an emergency any ordinary person is able to use it without problems.

Dr Bender immediately takes hold of the defibrillator and places the two large electrodes on Christian's chest.

'Everyone stand back, then two hundred joules,' he shouts to his assistants.

The electric shock is accompanied by an acoustic signal.

Christian's body rears up – but without success . . .

73

'Hello, Chris,' I hear a familiar voice again, 'welcome back. It seems you are going to stay with us after all . . .'

I feel as if I am waking up after a short snooze. At first I am not really orientated, but soon I am all right again. And I am indeed back: Michael is standing in front of me. I now recognise him – very clearly.

'Michael, somehow I was gone just now, suddenly I couldn't see you any longer, what was the matter with me?' I ask him.

'They probably had you back down there, but it looks as if they can't really keep you.

'Apparently your brain is rather damaged.

'Therefore, the rest of your body is not working properly. But I can't tell you exactly what's going on, nor can I tell you what will happen next.

'But for now you are here again and I am delighted to be able to tell you more and to answer your questions,' Michael encourages me, beaming happily.

74

'Three hundred joules, and stand back from the patient,' Dr Dirk Bender shouts again, his forehead is already drenched in perspiration.

Again an acoustic signal sounds and again Christian's body rears up, however . . .

'Sister Monika, please inform the family. They should hurry to come here,' the physician on duty, Dr Kirsten Kolbe, calls out, 'immediately!'

75

'A short while ago you said you had talked with Jenny about heaven and hell, so I would like to explain it to you again and maybe even in more detail,' Michael ties in again with my last questions of our joint thread of revelation.

'By the way,' he adds, 'Lara once asked me . . . '

'What??? Lara asked *you* about heaven and hell, how that? Lara is still alive – down there, or has something happened to her???'

I am horror-stricken.

'No, no, everything is all right, of course she is still alive down there. Nothing has happened to her.' Michael puts my mind at rest. 'But she was here once,' he adds 'and I was here to welcome her.'

'She was here?" I am aghast again. 'But I don't know anything about it. I should know that as her father, shouldn't I?'

'Don't you remember? Many years ago Lara was seriously ill. She had just started school when she was taken ill with scarlet fever and she had a very high temperature. One night she was on the verge,' Michael gets straight to the point.

'Yes, that's right. That night we were really worried about her. But I didn't realise that it was that bad,' I slowly recall the incident. 'And you met her here?'

'Yes, Lara was kind of in abeyance, between here and down there. This happens far more often than you might think, by the way, especially with children,' he lectures me. 'I received her just as I do now with you. Lara was terrified at first, and she was very loving and in need of closeness. I told her that she should not be afraid and that she would be taken care of for ever and ever.

'She was most afraid that she might have to go to hell. In her lessons of religious instruction at school they must have talked a lot about it. But I could very quickly put her mind at ease and I told her that there is no such place as "hell", as the legend you down there keep spreading around.'

'So, there is no hell?' I interrupt Michel.

'Slow down, there is no *place* called "hell" as quite a few would like to make you believe down there.

'Many used the threat for the sole purpose of making a lot of money by selling letters of indulgence, while others tried to intimidate their followers, but today...'

I interrupt Michael again: '... but does this mean that with us down there everyone is allowed to do as they please without retribution? Where does that leave justice, if not even here evil deeds committed down there are avenged? Then the term justice is nothing but an empty word.' I am rather enraged.

'Just let me finish my sentence.' Michael remains completely unperturbed, as usual. 'You have to listen more closely. And, besides: you of all people, you, who, before coming here, didn't even believe that anything existed after death, you now complain about the alleged absence of justice *here* calling it utterly unacceptable.

'You down there spurn justice far too often and you try to come out on top by using both your elbows whenever possible.'

Of course Michael is right. And I make an effort to let him go on without further interruptions.

'In principle, we do have something called "hell" here. And most certainly justice does exist here, for lesser sins just as well as for severe ones. However, everything is completely different from what you down there imagine and what you are taught – all of it in the "name of God", of course.

In fact, though, "hell" is not a place, but a damned unpleasant *condition*, believe you me...'

'A condition?' I interrupt him almost in a reflex. 'What do you mean by that exactly?'

'Well, Jenny already told you something about this,' Michael knows more than I am prepared to admit. 'Even if you are not so well versed in the Bible, you surely know this quotation: *"If anyone slaps you on the right cheek, turn and offer him the other also"?'*

'Of course I know it and it's pure rubbish!' I am a little indignant. 'After all, the message is that you should suffer injustice with humility which is completely incomprehensible for most people. This alone is another reason for some down there to leave the Church because they cannot accept this at all.'

'Yes, but this is because you don't really understand the quotation, as is the case with the meaning of so many great religious cultural treasures available to you down there.' Michael returns.

'And why is that?' I am really curious to hear his answer.

'Look: the Jews in the Old Testament, just like 95% of all people – do you notice something? – were right handed. And if you wanted to humiliate someone especially badly you would slap his right cheek with the back of your right hand. But if you wanted to ask your adversary for forgiveness, you had to give him an ever so light brush on his left cheek with the palm of your left hand, more like a caress.

'This was only possible if your adversary agreed, because he then had to present his left cheek to the aggressor. This is what is meant in the Bible. But you just don't recognise it.'

Now I am gobsmacked. How often had I already pondered about this quotation and dismissed it as sheer nonsense. But now it suddenly made sense.

'Michael, you keep quoting from the Bible, why not from other religions? Are they less worthy?' I interject, since this question just crossed my mind.

'Oh no, absolutely not,' Michael deals with it immediately. 'Many religions are indeed great treasures. I just called them "cultural treasures". Of course not everything they claim is always right and it is not always a real "treasure" this being due to the fact that each religion consists of a mixture of ideas arising from a large number of varying sources and roots. Furthermore, some good and also some bad intentions are hidden in their doctrines having been planted there by people.

'Since you grew up with a Christian cultural background, naturally I tend to refer to that. After all, much of it is known to you, although some of it needs to be straightened out.'

Tenaciously I stick to my question: 'You say that other religions are equally important cultural treasures. They often teach completely other values than Christianity and much of it is even contradictory. That doesn't fit, does it?'

'Yes and no, the problem lies elsewhere,' Michael replies with stoical calmness. 'The representatives of nearly all religions claim that their faith is the one and only or even that it was derived directly from God – dictated by God, so to speak. But I tell you: *no religion is "derived directly from God"*.

'Every religion in its entirety is the work of humans. Nevertheless: many of them incorporate divine features in varying degrees. In most of them you can find, at least *indirectly*, notions and perceptions which, over many generations and due to experiences on a higher level, some people down there have indeed learned and then managed to integrate them into their religion.

'Chris, at this very moment you are having such an *"indirect divine"* experience on a *"higher level"*.

'Your daughter Lara has also gone through such an experience.

'And what I tell you and explain to you is also on a "higher level" albeit only "indirectly" from God.

'Many people down there keep having such contacts, so that many people believe they experience something similar. But, in the end it is like playing "Chinese Whispers": even if something was correctly explained here, it could be retold down there later in a completely different way.

'In the course of time all religions *also* developed under the influence of such experiences.

'You can usually recognise very easily which of the various narrative contents and traditions reflect and illuminate realistic experiences and which are just interpretations or objectionable – or even completely absurd – fabrications.

'Wherever the *"basic divine principle proclaiming to love all humans and the world in its entirety"* is not fully implemented or wherever this principle has been lost completely, the "true divine light" is missing. The same applies when devotees claim their religion to be unique and raise this principle to the status of a dogma and when they then advocate violence to impose its alleged uniqueness on many other people or if only possible on all humans. Such elements are *not even indirectly* derived from God.'

'Michael, I am still very curious to know what "hell" means here.' I want Michael to pick up his former thread again.

'Especially those people who have killed or severely exploited others, cheated them, humiliated them, slandered them or damaged them in such a severe and enduring manner that *their life down there* was massively impaired,' Michael starts anew, 'must, of course, take responsibility for their behaviour here.

'They have a very difficult time here until *every single one* of those they have on their conscience, *has forgiven* them for their misdeeds. In the figurative sense all aggrieved persons must be prepared to turn their left cheeks to their offenders. This reflects two biblical connections: the first is the demand of Jesus to turn your left cheek if someone has slapped your right one, the second is the quotation from the Second Book of Moses, where it says: "... *eye for eye, tooth for tooth* ..." [50]. In fact, these two elements contradict each other only superficially:

'Depending on the severity of the injury and on the number of injured people, a very long period of time – as you would express it – may elapse before they all have forgiven their offenders here. By the way, we would express this here more aptly by saying: it would take "much space to pass"; for space and time are also a polar-symmetrical pair – as Einstein already expressed in his formula.

'Here, it is first and foremost the prerogative of the injured party to accept the offered apology by turning his left cheek and then to forgive. This is what is meant by "eye for eye, tooth for tooth".

'But due to the "unconditional and omnipotent love of God"[51] and the desire to develop themselves towards God in the long term, which is inherent in all humans but which too often goes unrecognised at first, *everyone* will eventually *strive* to forgive their offenders, since everyone seeks to "grow spiritually". And the comprehension that you must be able to forgive is part of this.

'To forgive does not mean to forget, however.

'God surely doesn't forget.

'Learning "how to forgive" is written in your Bible in the "concept of salvation", which is the true message about the "Judgement Day" according to your Christian tradition.'

'Then the "Judgement Day" has nothing to do with the resurrection of the dead?' I want to know.

'Yes and no,' Michael answers very patiently. 'The Judgement Day has *nothing* to do with the resurrection if you consider "death" as being the end of your life down there. For this, your Bible gives you the "central message" of the *immediate resurrection* which was disclosed to you by Jesus.

'It follows that the "Judgement Day" must contain a different message from that of your resurrection after death down there, since, as you can see for yourself, death does not exist.

'The Christian Bible aims merely to make clear that real death is something completely different from the end of your life down there. This means that someone is dead only if he turns away from God, which is tantamount to suffering the loss of love and a life agreeable to God.

'Death only takes place when you are spiritually and emotionally dead, when you are simply without love – but not when you merely die physically down there. In the final analysis the "spiritual" death is an "ethical-moral or mental death". It is followed here by the "status of hell". And the salvation from this is the "resurrection on Judgement Day". Hence every single person expects his own individual "Judgement Day" when he finds his way back to God. One of the preconditions for this is the strong will to repent deeply so that all sins can be forgiven. To achieve this he must ask every single aggrieved person for forgiveness of his sins. Then all of them must be prepared to grant him forgiveness, which means they must be prepared to turn their left cheeks. Only when all goes well for the sinner and he is granted forgiveness for all those of his sins which are important here, will he experience his Judgement Day here and will be redeemed. Hence the Judgement Day is something very personal here and not at all some kind of collective event at the end of all days.

'You down there sometimes call this purgatory and you believe that the true hell follows thereafter. But in fact purgatory and hell are the same here. Depending on the severity of the sins they have committed, the sinners can find themselves in an absolutely wretched state which only ends on their Judgement Day by means of final forgiveness. So, there is no further "hell" after that.

'By the way, the moment of salvation on Judgement Day is very similar to that of the Buddhist nirvana, which does not mean a level of "nothingness" but rather one of "eternal blessedness".

'Up until the moment when those with a heavy burden of guilt manage to obtain forgiveness from every single person they have harmed down there, they go through their own personal hell up here.

'Besides: you will certainly have noticed that in accordance with Buddhist tradition the body is washed during the memorial service. This happened at Jenny's funeral, too. Why do they do it? It is done in order to grant mutual forgiveness for trespasses. You see, the important truths are reflected in many religions, they are often just hidden and are expressed in different symbols.'

'Where does that leave the devil described in the Bible?' I throw in.

'The devil is in the details.' Michael has to laugh out loud. 'Yes, indeed, each single sinner harbours his own greater or lesser devil. However, the devil is not an individual person. Each sinner is himself a more or less nasty devil and goes through his own hell until all his sins are forgiven on his Judgement Day.

'This hellish *condition* can be utterly miserable and even gruesome for the sinners depending on the gravity of the misdeeds they committed. They are forced here to experience time and again and in detail the same injuries that they had inflicted on their fellow humans down there, but now they see this from the viewpoints of the injured persons and their relatives and friends who are directly affected.

'They experience the cries of those they killed and also the lamentations of the relatives of the victims – yes, everything and from all of them again and again. For them it is like experiencing recurring horrible nightmares over and over again.

'There was once an American movie shown down there in which a whole day was repeated in an infinite time warp until the main actor finally became "reasonable". The title was "Groundhog Day". If you have seen it you will know very well what I mean.[52]

'And now imagine you keep having terrible nightmares and possibly always the same ones . . .

'This would be a descriptive comparison. But nightmares are more like comedy movies compared with the hurtful situations relived in such vivid detail.

'Very soon, therefore, every sinner will start to plead for a speedy forgiveness from each and every single victim, which will call on the victim to turn the left cheek towards his tormentor. But not everyone will immediately accede to this request. It is solely up to the victim to decide. Of course, at some time or other everyone will do it, because this is part of the process of maturing. But it could indeed take an excruciatingly long period of time.'

'But tell me, Michael, how will someone who was murdered down there find his murderer here, for example?' I want to know.

'You know, Chris, in general, everyone here us able to contact anyone who ever lived down there. This usually needs the approval of *both sides*, though. You may also refuse any contact. It is comparable to your social networks in the internet. There are "friendship requests" by means of which people address others. You can either reject or accept them. It is the same here: you may approve or dismiss such requests, with one exception, however: a guilty offender *cannot refuse* to be contacted by the injured person. Theoretically he would have to suffer the lamentation for all eternity should his victim decide to rebuke him for that long. But that doesn't happen, not even in the most abominable cases, since every single individual here endeavours to improve his own spiritual emotional development – and this also means learning how to forgive, for this is part of his own spiritual growth and it is God's will.

'Moreover, with the growing distance from your life down there you worry less about former matters of importance. Until then, however, it could be a very long and extremely painful, often even torturous way for anyone who has committed evil deeds down there.'

'We down there evaluate crimes differently, depending on the cultural background. Do you have other or your own laws here?' I am curious to know.

'Oh yes, indeed, the benchmarks here are very different from yours down there,' Michael explains to me.

'It is the severity of the *iniquity committed against fellow humans* and the degree of anguish caused thereby which is of paramount importance.'

76

'I shall be pleased to explain it to you in more detail,' Michael continues.

'Basically, the most severe crime of all is, of course, to kill a human being. If you irrevocably take away the highest asset a fellow human being possesses down there, then it is extremely difficult to forgive in most cases – although there is no rule without exception.

'For a start, murderers and killers, war mongers or political and religious leaders – or in general – any humans who command the killing of innocent people or who approvingly accept their death, will certainly be unable to rejoice in their life here.

'On the contrary: they will all find themselves in a state of hell in which they will experience in detail the circumstances suffered by each single one of their victims. They will relive all the agony of their victims and that of the bereaved ones.

'And in this extremely emotional situation and under severe strain, they are surrounded here by people like them, which greatly exacerbates their stress.

'However, there are, of course, exceptions. Everything depends on the individual elements of a crime which may be very different in nature. *In contrast to many cases down there all the facts are laid open here and made transparent.* No one can whitewash himself by bringing forth arguments for his defence which misrepresent the facts. Nevertheless: no perpetrator will be judged by others, not even by God. Every single one experiences in detail the effect that his own malpractice has had on others and hence each of them condemns himself in the end.

'No one can escape his personal hell of emotions when he deserves it.

'As I already said, however, there may be circumstances which justify a killing.

'One example would be in preventing the killing of innocent people. Then it is legitimate to kill, even from our viewpoint here. Up here the protection of the victim always takes precedence over the protection of the perpetrator. The term "prevention" also includes self-defence, but it can also go well beyond this definition, depending on the circumstances.

'Another example is something known to you as "euthanasia". *Human dignity is always inviolable.* Dignity and personal freedom, hence also the free will of humans, are assets which, from our viewpoint here, are absolute and must be strictly respected.

'When a person has the wish to die, then you might try to talk him out of it.

'Maybe *he'll* change his mind. But it is not up to *you* to adjudge his decision.

'Therefore, in individual cases, it may even be legitimate to assist a person to commit suicide, should he explicitly wish to do so but is unable to do it himself, and when the circumstances evoke *your* compassion.

'This may be the case when people suffer from severe and incurable diseases. Even though every individual has the right of free self-determination, this should not be exercised with the aid of profit-seekers who earn their money by exploiting those having the understandable yearning to die due to their personal situation. 'Of course, you should always try to help people who despair of their lives down there, so that they might give up their wish to die. But the ultimate decision is theirs alone.

'Such a wish is often expressed in order to escape further infirmity due to a serious illness. From the sick person's viewpoint the world might look very different than from that of those not directly affected. Therefore it is not for the latter to pass judgement on the decision.

'Apart from killing and inflicting serious bodily harm on fellow humans there are many more offences which also lead to "infernal emotional states" here.

'The following rule always applies: the seriousness of an offence *depends not only on the deed itself*. Just as important is the kind of *responsibility* someone has for his fellow humans down there and, based on this, the extent to which his behaviour affects those entrusted in his care.

'When, down there, national and religious leaders, politicians, directors of companies or other persons carrying great responsibility for many people, possibly even for entire nations, fail to comply therewith then they bear "false witness" in the *true sense* of the biblical commandment. This being due to their having assumed the great responsibility, sometimes even under oath. An oath might be violated by deprivation of personal liberty, breach of trust, blatant mismanagement at the expense of those in their care, by fraud or any other kind of "highway robbery".

'For all that they will some day have to answer to all their victims here. Should such people indeed be responsible for the deliberate destruction or disruption of an individual's life down there causing it to be no longer worth living, then this may even be tantamount to taking a life.

'Depending on the impact a breach of trust has had on the lives of the victims this might also apply to severe forms of defamation, which maliciously impair the lives or freedom of action of others, irrespective of whether shamelessly imposed by someone in a "higher position of authority" or by the proverbial "man in the street". '

'The defamers will feel the consequences of their actions from the viewpoint of the victims and possibly from those of other directly affected persons. They will then evaluate themselves and their behaviour and in the end they will have to beg forgiveness from every single one.

'Anyone who is on a spiritually higher level than his fellow humans will be especially hard hit by his own reprehensible actions. But anyone of comparatively simple mind down there can also cause much sorrow and will have to answer for it here.

'You yourself experienced the consequences of slander a short while ago, when your wife Helen was mobbed in the hospital. Her colleagues sanctioned that her personality may have been harmed for good and that she might have suffered not only mental but also professional damage. I'll give you another example: some weeks ago a doctor came to us who was suffering immensely from being libeled by patients on the internet. They gave him exceptionally low ratings supported by false statements, simply because this physician expected self-responsibility from his patients. For example, he refused to give his patients a sick-leave note, when *they* felt like having a day off work but were not really sick. Or he demanded drastic slimming diets from those who were excessively obese – which was indeed absolutely essential when they wanted to improve their health permanently. But they just called him a bad doctor.

'When large numbers of people read such malicious accusations, then the instigators will later need to ask forgiveness for their misconduct from all those whom they had misinformed. It will be even more difficult for sinners who carry great responsibility and those wielding a disproportionate influence on the public due to their professional work, such as politicians or media representatives.

'If they have harmed other people with deceit and spite – both usually based on envy – then they will have to pay for it here in the same way and in great humiliation.'

'In that case, an awful lot of people here will be rather busy trying to straighten things out – they won't be able to do anything else,' I tease a bit disbelievingly.

'You are right, but time doesn't play a role here. It is here subject to completely different criteria. And your "first new life here" is indeed determined by attempts at cleansing your own conscience.

'In this respect the idea of karma, so widely-spread down there, is basically correct. Justice is demanded and experienced here though and not down there.

'Power and responsibility down there carry greater risks which must be faced so that they don't backfire later. Everyone must learn to deal with their responsibility properly and they must never loose sight of the well-being of those in their care.

'Knowing this should be a strong incentive for everyone to devote themselves to the well-being of dependants in a non-ideological, freedom-loving, pragmatic and justice-seeking manner. Justice does not mean egality, however. Unfortunately many of you misunderstand the issue and strive for enforced conformity.

'However, very many of the rules and laws decreed by those with responsibility down there in the attempt to legitimise their own misdeeds to the world at large and thereby causing more harm to those in their care, are considered as serious offences here. One day those responsible for these actions must face the music here.

'Maybe you remember the biblical Parable of the Talents?[53]

'A man travelling to a far country called his own servants and delivered his goods to them. And to one he gave five talents, to another two, and to another one, to each according to his own ability; and immediately he went on a journey. Then he who had received the five talents went and traded with them, and made another five talents. And likewise he who had received two gained two more also. But he who had received one went and dug in the ground, and hid his lord's money.

After a long time the lord of those servants came and settled accounts with them. The first servant who had received five bags of gold brought the additional other five. The man with two bags of gold came with two more. The third man who had received one bag of gold could only show the one bag. His master said to him: "You are a wicked, lazy servant!" So he took the bag of gold from him and gave it to the one who had ten bags. Then he said: "For to everyone who has, more will be given, and he will have abundance; but from him who does not have, even what he has will be taken away.

'I must admit,' Michael continues without stopping to draw breath, 'that this parable – like many others also – is not easy to understand at first sight.

'Sometimes this is due to faulty interpretation; sometimes it is due to the incorrect translation of earlier written records.

'You only need to know: every human being is different. The freedom and dignity of every single individual are inviolable and hence must be greatly respected.

'All individuals must recognise, however, that they not only have their own free will but that they also carry great *personal responsibility* which must be complied with and which cannot be offloaded on to someone else.

'But although you all carry your own personal responsibility the load is not equally heavy for everyone.

'It differs, for example, in accordance with capability, status, assignment and position, intelligence and knowledge, life-task, area of life and personal environment. It follows that every single person is, without exception, evaluated individually here for their deeds. This is what everyone must do here on their own one day.'

I listen carefully to Michael's explanations and keep on probing: 'Among the acts of grave misconduct mentioned in your list was "highway robbery". Isn't that something which is hardly known in modern times, at least in the part of the world where I live down there?'

'Not at all! Today it is more or less the same as it was in former times, it is just dressed in different clothes and it is often even much worse than it used to be. Look, in the Bible as well as in the Koran, it is considered right and important to give away part of the income which you earned due to your abilities in everyday life – for the poor and for the country in which you live and which provides public services.

'Unfortunately, a completely new mentality of unlimited cash collection has started to spread with you down there. This is completely unacceptable. Every single one of those responsible for this development will have to answer for it one day here.

'It is unacceptable that half or more of the earnings are taken away from individuals who worked hard for their money.

'Such practices are usually known as taxes and duties down there. But in many cases they resemble more downright dispossession.

'Duties extracted by the authorities should all without exception be added together, the sum total then being the actual tax burden. And this sum total alone should be the relevant measure and should not excessively burden the individuals rendering this contribution from their earnings arising from their personal commitment.

'All people must try to adjust their expenditure to match their income and no one can increase both of them constantly in an unreasonable manner.

'This applies to everyone and anyone and also to every national and state authority, every local authority and every business enterprise.

'When this does not work and citizens subjected to these authorities are time and again burdened with exorbitant new duties, then I call this theft tantamount to highway robbery.

'It is hard to believe that those demanding payment of the duties so irresponsibly often point their fingers at those who in one way or the other try to evade such forced and unbearable drains on their resources.

'So the charge of "moral deficiency" should be levelled against those who, despite the authority bestowed upon them by way of function and position failed to fulfill their responsibilities – and this will quite certainly entail consequences here.

'You have plenty of cases down there, too, where billions of taxpayers' money are simply squandered. This is money earned through arduous toil by hard-working citizens over decades. Some duties are not even declared as taxes due to grotesque ideas invented by resourceful highway robbers...'

'Oh yes, I could name you some from my own social circle,' I am in my element. 'The solidarity surcharge, the tax rate that increases automatically, a "death duty" which is played down as inheritance tax, capital levy, tax for sparkling wine, which was invented in World War I...'

Michael laughs: 'You know all this much better than I do, of course. You are probably right if it corresponds to everything I just told you. And I am sure you could immediately name any number of prestigious objects and projects which end up as white elephants.

'Hardly is anybody ever held responsible down there for such scandals. But in fact, none of these rip-off methods will stay unatoned here, though, for they truly harm responsible citizens; poverty among the elderly, for example, is exacerbated thereby, and future generations will have to carry the heavy debt burden. Up here, like an echo, it will all fall back on those individuals who are responsible for it.

'On the other hand, those who try to evade such violation are castigated like lepers and punished whenever possible.

'In some cases this might be justifiable, in many others less so. In this context I would like to quote your Christian Bible, where Jesus says: *"He who is without sin among you, let him throw a stone at her first."*[54] And how many of your politicians or media moguls would have the right to do so?

'The same applies, by the way, for the so popular ideological redistributions which are in reality nothing but blatant expropriation, often based on pure envy.

'All these examples show grave misdemeanors and are in some cases even the nearest thing to downright crimes against humanity.

'Of course, we are talking specifically about examples within *your* immediate environment. But everything I have to say about this applies to all countries in the world – and believe me, some other corners down there have much more severe problems where much less morality is displayed, which doesn't at all diminish the guilt of those entrusted with responsibility for others in your country.

'All those responsible for such misconducts, crimes and misdeeds must later personally justify their actions here.

'They will experience great shame here and they will need to ask forgiveness from every single one of their victims which they must also *want* to do that. That is not an easy task and it will encumber their own progress for a long time.

'By the way, this is also the deeper meaning of the biblical quotation: *"But many who are first will be last; and the last first"*[55].

'The first in this sense are now those who act down there for their own well-being at the expense of others, while the last ones down there are those who make sacrifices in order to help their fellow humans or *genuinely* serve people's needs.

'As I already mentioned, the worst "hell" awaits those, of course, who trample all over the highest asset of human beings by deliberately taking a human life down there. By doing this, they rob the victim of any chance for further development down there. However, their hell is not a place but rather a condition.

'But believe me, that is the worst hell you can imagine. However, it will not last for eternity, since at some time or other the good will outweigh the bad and the evil. This is guaranteed to every one of us by the all-embracing love of God.'

I am deeply moved by Michael's explanations.

77

'He's still not coming back. Another intravenous injection of adrenalin. I'll try again. And if it works, then immediately amiodarone 300 mg . . .' Dr Dirk Bender is under immense stress.

Again he places the electrodes on the chest of his patient and presses them down: "Everybody stand back, and 400 joules please.'

'Professor Schneider's relatives are already on their way, I just managed to contact them,' Sister Monika is back.

'Ask them to wait outside,' Dr Kolbe turns to her.

'I will go and talk to them,' Professor Paland butts in. He entered the room some time ago. 'I shall also ask them whether Mr Schneider has issued a power of attorney to anyone and whether he is an organ donor . . .'

78

All members of the Schneider family have gathered in the waiting room of the intensive care unit with the exception of Sascha and Jasmin who, for understandable reasons, preferred to take a walk in the park of the University Hospital.

Helen is constantly crying and Tom cannot hold back his tears either. Lara tries to comfort them again and again. She, too, has to fight back tears herself.

Bob is as white as a sheet and appears completely petrified.

They are all huddled together in misery.

While they are all trying to come to grips with this sudden and possibly inevitable course of events, Professor Paland joins them. For him it is also an extremely difficult moment:

'I am so sorry, but all our efforts seem to be in vain,' he says quietly. 'Christian Schneider is fighting with death and we are still fighting for his life. But at the moment it looks as if we are losing the battle.'

The crying and sobbing increases, even Lara can't hold back any longer. Bob is the only one who still fights his tears and he still hasn't uttered a word.

'Although it is very difficult for me right now,' Professor Paland continues, 'I must ask you all in this situation whether the patient has prepared an Advance Directive and also whether he wishes to become an organ donor should anything drastic happen. We haven't found anything in his possessions.'

He has hardly uttered the word "organ donor" when they all seem to turn into pillars of salt.

After a short pause Bob is the first one to speak:

'I know that my father wanted to donate his organs should anything happen to him, which seems inevitable now,' he says and appears amazingly collected.

'I must see the organ donor card, though,' replies Professor Paland, 'we are obliged to check this before...'

'Then I'll go home and fetch it. It is not so far. I think I know where Father keeps it,' Bob puts forward and is already leaving to get his father's organ donor card.

'I'll be back in a jiffy,' he calls out.

79

'And all this is known to Lara?' After another short interruption I find my words again.

'Yes,' answers Michael, 'by the way, I welcomed your daughter as Michaela, it seemed more appropriate at the time.'

'Then she knows that death, or what we down there know as death, is only the transition to a new life?' I philosophise.

'Oh yes, and that has had a significant impact on her further life. Have you never noticed that she...'

'Of course,' I interrupt Michael and guess immediately what he is driving at. 'It remained always a puzzle to me up to now why Lara became so devoutly religious, whereas Helen – and I even much less...'

'... whereas you both are not really religious,' Michael interrupts me now. 'But even though Lara joined your Catholic community down there and undertakes a substantial amount of valuable work for the children of the community, she has developed her very own view which seems sometimes rather distanced from the official doctrine. She simply knows more...'

'Nevertheless, I can't always understand her present behaviour. On the one hand she seems strictly Catholic, sometimes she even seems to live like a nun. I never saw her with a boy, for example, when she went through puberty, and I always thought that was the reason. But on the other hand she got involved with this Dr Bender when she was not even eighteen years old...'

'... who is making every effort at the moment, by the way, trying to save your life,' my Guide interrupts me again.

''Oh dear, is he still at it?' I smile at him and continue relatively unimpressed: 'Yes, and now she is pregnant by him. This is not at all consistent with her faith, in my opinion at least. But then she vehemently resisted any suggestion of an abortion. No, somehow I don't think all this really fits together.'

'But of course it does,' intervenes Michael. 'Lara has certainly recognised, that many issues in her Church down there are not being properly communicated, much is misrepresented and in some cases it is even completely wrong and untenable and at the same time incompatible with the biblical sources. There are more than enough reasons for this discrepancy but it doesn't make sense to dive into that right now.

'But Lara also recognised that there are several important central messages which obviously are indeed true. The Christian Easter message is one of such central messages. It proclaims that anyone going through so-called death down there will experience direct resurrection. And she experienced it herself. In the same way as I do now with you, I was able to convey to her the knowledge that there will always be a salvation from your sins even if for many sinners it will demand a lot of hard labour. This is why it is so important to recognise that which from God's point of view would be classified as "significant sin".'

'You have already told me something about this,' I throw in. 'Could you just recapitulate some of the basic rules again?'

'Of course!' Michael shoots back. 'Generally speaking, there is one Golden Rule:

Don't do unto others what you don't want others to do unto you. Hence, all crimes against humanity are categorically severe sins.

Then Michael continues: 'The same applies to the following rule which is known to every Christian:

"You shall love God and your neighbour as yourself." This expresses very nearly everything there is to say. Your life down there is first and foremost defined by one big purely physiological task: your reproduction is of paramount importance, so that the survival of your species and its chance for further evolution is ensured. We already talked about this.

'Human beings, however, have already gone a significant step further. Their spiritual level is admittedly far superior to that of animals. During their life time down there they have already made considerable progress towards our level here.

'And therefore they must already master spiritual duties:

Above all they must learn to love!

'And believe me, this is incredibly difficult.

'How difficult it is for you down there to follow your heart, especially if you have to abandon your once chosen paths. Possibly these paths were only chosen due to social standards and conventions down there. Such conventions are always purely human inventions. But you have to decide individually and on your own whether you are prepared to follow them and whether you are able to do so.

'At the same time you must learn that you should never *entirely abandon* your chosen path. That would be just as wrong.

'For by doing so you would harm others which would then fall back on you again.

'In East Asia it is important to ensure that your neighbour can "save his face". Everyone should do that. It is also important not to abandon paths altogether because you should always give love and not take it away. You see, there are indeed many predicaments and pitfalls. They can turn your life down there sometimes into some kind of terrestrial hell of feelings, I know.' It is the first time I hear Michael sigh.

But then he carries on as usual: 'From all this the next rule follows automatically, it is the one with the most serious consequences.

'You already know it and for all those, who break this rule, the longest and hardest work of all is waiting and they will experience a genuine hell. Whoever deliberately takes someone else's life down there and hence destroys this persons chance of further development, must relive the agony of the victim and his nearest and dearest until they all are prepared to grant him forgiveness of their own free will.

'However, since to forgive is not the same as to forget, all the evil deeds will remain unforgotten in eternity. This could be an opportunity for the perpetrators, however, because it might motivate them to organise their future lives much better and with more care and love.'

'And what happens if someone has millions on his conscience?' I interpose.

'Then he must suffer here the agony of millions and also that of the bereaved ones and ask them all for forgiveness until they have all pardoned him at some time or other. And he will not be able to escape this ordeal, since the spiritual core of everyone, meaning that which life is all about and which lends life its *continuity*, is forever indestructible.'

'And there is no exception?' I ask him.

'But of course, there is no rule without exception,' Michael answers me. 'I already said this and I already mentioned some exceptions. It is, for example, permitted to take a life down there if by doing so an innocent life is saved which would otherwise face the direct threat of annihilation. You might find yourselves in a grey area in some instances with your assessments down there, but this will never be the case here.

'Here is another example: if a criminal spirit down there takes hostages and threatens to kill them if his demands are not fulfilled, then it is permitted to end his life prematurely without detrimental effect. This is considered here to be a case of self-defence. Look: about eighteen months ago a religious fanatic came to me, who had been involved in terroristic actions down there because he felt he was a guardian of an allegedly divine truth. He was killed by a hostage he had to guard and who had been in the custody of this vile group for a long period of time. The hostage was able to free himself by killing this guard who came here and actually demanded that the hostage be punished.

'And even here he overlooked the many murders he had committed because it was all done "in the name of God". Only when I showed him around here to see all the consequences his reprehensible actions entailed and I explained to him that it would now be his Herculean task "ordained by God" to experience all the misery he had caused from the viewpoint of his victims until every single one of them had forgiven him and he had gained salvation for his own soul, only then did he collapse in front of me. The hostage, however, who had caused him to turn up here, has nothing to fear. On the contrary, he is also one on the list of the many victims the terrorist guard has to work through and to beg for forgiveness.

'You know, Chris, I have already told you several times that no one is judged here by anyone else – not even the most abominable mass murderer.

'However, I can't reiterate this often enough, everyone must relive, feel and suffer later everything he has done to others down there until every single one of his victims has forgiven him. And he will never ever be able to forget, neither the images nor the screams of his victims.

'Also all those who are seriously ill and might see no other way out for themselves but to end their own life down there, must come to terms with their decision here. If they ask someone else to help them to die, regardless of the method, and they are determined to go through with it, they will be unable to remonstrate with their helpers for doing so. But they will surely stand their ground here, because they presumably had good reasons.

'If, however, someone decides to commit suicide for trivial reasons, then it would be viewed differently here.

'Here they all must consider themselves liable for their actions and the problems they thought were seriously crippling down there could here prove to be negligible and render the decision a big mistake.

'They will certainly have a hard time here.

'Also the question as to whether an abortion is sinful or not must be evaluated in every individual case. It will always be a very difficult decision and it remains a decision to be made down there.

'There is no right or wrong for this here.

'But here all reasons and motivations are transparent, so that no one can withdraw from this openness and be deluded. No one is judged by anyone else here for this decision. In such a case again, every person must justify his own action solely to himself.

'As long as no independently viable new life is created, no one need ask forgiveness for the decision from anyone.

'In short: your sins down there are subject to different criteria here. Everyone must evaluate their actions here *themselves*. All concomitants are transparent. The seriousness of sins is solely defined by the degree of suffering caused by them to the fellow humans affected. This alone determines the sinners' personal hell in which they will relive and suffer the misery caused by them from the viewpoint of the victims.

'It will end with the remission of the sins by the victims. And this will be *the individual sinner's Judgement Day*.

'Without that no one will reach the next rung on the ladder of their own spiritual evolution.'

80

The third and fourth attempts to jumpstart Christian's heart also fail.

However, Dr Bender's team keeps up their desperate fight – cardiac massage, medication, and, of course, a steady stream of oxygen.

Suddenly Sister Maria steps into the cubicle.

'Dr Bender,' she addresses the Senior Physician, 'one of the patient's relatives started bleeding suddenly, she is said to be five months pregnant.'

'Seven months,' escapes Dirk Bender's lips, and they all look at him in amazement.

'Take Lara to the Gynaecological Ward immediately and call Professor Grüter, I know him well. He and his team are to take care of Lara.'

Dirk briefly stares at his team members as they stare back at him. But then he immediately lowers his gaze again.

'We must continue here, maybe there is still a chance – hand me another shot of adrenaline. I am going to inject this directly into his heart. And then get ready for another defibrillation.'

81

When Bob returns he can just see Lara being taken away on a stretcher.

'What's happened?' he rushes up to her.
'I am bleeding and I could possibly loose my baby,' she cries. 'They're taking me to the Gynaecology Ward.'
'Please, hang on, I am sure you'll make it.' Bob kisses his sister on her cheek.
'I'll see you later,' he calls after her and is already on his way to the intensive care unit where his father is fighting death.

When he arrives he shows Professor Paland his father's organ donor card.
Professor Paland is rather surprised to see that the donor card has a hand-written amendment:
"I am prepared to donate my organs if two neurologists independently of each other declare that I am dead and that this is supported by a ten-minute zero line in the EEG."
Professor Paland carefully reads Christian Schneider's organ donor card.
'My goodness, here is someone who has been given good advice,' he murmurs, quite audible for Bob.
'Yes, a good friend of his works as an orthopaedic specialist not far from here. He probably dictated that to my father,' Bob informs the Head of the Accident Surgery.
'We have been trying to get preconditions like this rubberstamped by the Medical Chamber for a long time now. But they think it is unnecessary.
'However, if there were more guaranteed safety for donors, surely more people would be

prepared to carry an organ donor card,' Professor Paland returns.

'I will see to it that there is one more chance for your father. If all our efforts to keep him alive should be in vain, then I will contact "Eurotransplant" in Leiden, as was his wish.'

There in The Netherlands is the central registry for donor organs which are urgently needed by sick people.

'I'll keep you informed,' Professor Paland throws in while he is already hurrying back to Christian Schneider's cubicle.

82

'What about the death penalty then?' I ask Michael in connection with the subject we had just been discussing.

'These must be absolutely and strictly abolished!' he replies. 'For which there are two good reasons: firstly, it cannot be a true punishment since, as you can see, life goes on immediately for everyone. And secondly, someone's life down there would come to an end without the ability to save someone else's innocent life at the same time. The life of someone who has been killed down there cannot be restored simply by killing the perpetrator and assuming this to be the punishment.

'Of course, it is important to punish humans for their sins when they commit crimes against their fellow humans. The punishment must be hard according to the degree of severity. As I already mentioned every single individual down there carries a great personal responsibility.

'And no-one is allowed to shirk it.

'There are scientists who reject the idea of personal liability. They are of the erroneous opinion that you cannot be held responsible since the brain alone is responsible for your actions. They say that it is only after the human brain decides independently what to do, that its owner is led to believe that he took a "personal decision" himself. These scientists don't believe in the own free human will and they consider the "ego" to be pure illusion. They think that there is no such thing as a "personal decision" and that everything is produced and induced by a completely impersonal, self-sufficient brain.

'Now you can see for yourself, how much rubbish is spread around down there which is then quickly promoted to a scientific dogma.

'Of course, *as a matter of principle*, all individuals have a free will of their own. However, it is limited by certain basic general conditions.

'Among others are the laws of nature, for example. If you wanted to fly like a bird down there you would fall flat on your face right away.

'In the same way social conventions and standards or various rules and regulations imposed by public authorities may restrict your own free will to a greater or lesser degree – which happens regrettably far too often to an unacceptable degree.

'The generally free will of all individuals is inseparably interconnected to the most precious asset of personal responsibility for their own actions.

'I already told you the parable of the bags of gold which is written in your Christian Bible. All those attempting to live up to their personal responsibility and strive to increase and improve the value of their "bags of gold" are pleasing God and are so doing the right thing.'

83

'Thanks for the cue,' I jump in, as I had long since wanted to lead our conversation to the subject of "God". 'Let's talk about God then. You already mentioned him several times. Does that mean he really exists?' Now I really want to know.

'Of course there is a God,' Michael answers. 'But I know as little about him as you do!'

'I don't understand this, how do you know that there is a God and why do we always talk about "him" and not sometimes simply about "her".

'We keep talking about "him" because the term "God" has a male pronoun in your language. But that has nothing to do with the nature of God,' Michael is almost a little peeved; he obviously thinks my question to be unreasonably dumb. But he recovers quickly and continues: 'The existence of God must not be proven, God is recognisable and perceivable in everything that exists. Yet, there is indeed clear analogous evidence that God exists.

'For this purpose I would like to help you along with the aid of mathematics again.'

'With mathematics??? Do you really think there is a mathematical proof for the existence of God?' I ask incredulously.

'No, no proof, God wouldn't need that,' he returns, 'but I a little logical can help: I call it an analogous proof,' he continues. 'You are lucky to have experienced yourself that two independent realities exist which are polar symmetrical to each other, a spiritual one and a material one.

'In fact there are in addition various gradations and hence various levels on both sides, which means that there are not only the spiritual but also the material ones.

'I hope to be able to come back to this later.'

It seems that Michael still doesn't know what will happen with me.

'That is why . . .' so Michael, '. . . we perceive ourselves here to be just as "material" as you down there, although we are not as dense as you are. The reason for this is that the spiritual component here is higher than it is with you down there. I already explained to you that the entire universe is going through a gigantic evolution aimed ultimately at improving the spiritual development. As long as there was no life on earth the spiritual component was relatively small and consisted mainly of "lifeless basic information". This included numbers, simple geometrical forms and the relationships they have to one another.

'The development of appropriate instruments and devices for an interactive evolution was only possible with their help. The maturing "equipment capabilities" then facilitated the gradual development of new and ever more complex informational entities out of the original "basic information" – I already talked about "information clusters" to you. So the spiritual component still grows incessantly, while at the same time the material component decreases *relatively*, in qualitative terms.

'Therefore, I like to use your terms "dense material" and "ethereal material". Of course this is only an oversimplification and certainly also an imperfect description but it helps tremendously to gain an understanding.

'Meanwhile you will certainly have understood the "intrinsic essence of this world". There are two basically different, really existing levels or worlds which are completely different from each other in their *quality* – to express it in a simple term. At any one time they each carry a more or less substantial part of the other within themselves. The development proceeds upwards in steps, however, while the spiritual part is continues to grow, the material part diminishes.

'Both worlds are interdependent just as the famous symbol of Yin and Yang so beautifully depicts.

'You did understand – didn't you? – that the spiritual part is the more comprehensive and stronger reality whereas the material part generated by it is the weaker one.

'The material part is generated by the spiritual reality, finely graduated pursuant to the already accomplished level of development. By means of elementary mathematical logic I was able to explain that to you in a plausible way, right?'

'I understood that and, furthermore, I notice just now that you must be right, otherwise I wouldn't be here, would I?' I agree with him on all points.

'That's exactly how it is,' Michael continues.

'But the spiritual world has, in the true sense, a "root" from which it originates now – again viewed in an elementary mathematical analogy.

'You can easily calculate the square root of all positive numbers; this refers to what I introduced to you as being the +1-reality. The +1-reality I explained to you as being analogous to the material world.'

'Of course, that's obvious,' I am rather bored.

'So it is,' Michael continues undeterred. 'Then you should also be able to calculate the square roots of all negative numbers of the -1-reality which is the polar-symmetrical world on a par with the other one, shouldn't you?'

'That's logical!' I agree and this is nothing new to me with my mathematical background knowledge.

'Every mathematician does it . . .' Michael continues, ' . . . since your computer technology, for example, would be unthinkable without such a procedure. But actually this is only possible by using a trick. For this, we introduce the "imaginary number i". This renders the square root of negative numbers *calculable*. This leads to a logical conclusion, and this is very important now:

'This "imaginary i" and the i-reality connected with it, *must* really exist just as "-1" and "+1" and the worlds connected to it do. Nevertheless, we cannot at all imagine this "i-reality". We know without doubt that "i" actually *is*, so that it must certainly exist.

'But we cannot for anything in the world identify or even know what "i" is and how "i" comes about.'

It dawns on me: 'And you mean that this "i", this imaginary number, which must certainly exist, with which we constantly work, but which we cannot determine, let alone determine in detail, that this is a metaphor for the real existence of God?'

Michael laughs and is obviously delighted since I seem to have understood his lecture.

'That's exactly how it is! God is the origin of everything and anything, just as in this analogy he is also metaphorically the origin of both "comprehensible" number-realities.

'And this has nothing to do with speculation or belief – it is in fact pure knowledge which should become or rather will become accessible to anyone by reasonable reflection.

'However, any further guesswork about God ends here, since this would lead to speculation which would be counterproductive from the start.'

'Is that the reason why Islam forbids depictions of Allah and why in the Christian faith the commandment demands that you shall not make for yourself an image of God?' I want to know.

'Exactly,' Michael continues, 'but such prohibitions and commandments do not mean that you are not *allowed* to make for yourself an image of God, but that you are *unable* to make one, since however you figure it, it will always be completely wrong.

'*God is completely beyond our definition.*

'Nevertheless there are some points which can be narrowed down:

'For example, the term "God" characterizes a superior, higher *"entity"* – compared with the realities we are able to perceive in our world.

'Solely *from, through* and *with* "God" is anything and everything generated. Therefore, as I already mentioned, the term "God" in the singular is reasonable since it leads to the concept of an "entity".

'Furthermore, it is an integral characteristic of the entire cosmic evolution, yes, of the eternal growth of the spiritual. Hence, "God" must also be understood as *the highest spiritual entity* – from our point of view.

'And after all, men and women only exist because on the first step of life sexual reproduction guaranties evolution towards a maximum in variety. But just as *I* can appear here as both male and female at will, *so God must imperatively be both*.

'And something else: your world down there, which you know as a material world, is a comparatively dense material world. The power down there which joins everything together you call energy. A characteristic of this dense material world is *discontinuity* or quantisation.

'The world I am showing you right now, is in contrast a bit more "spiritual world" – or generally speaking "a world of information". But it is by no means "merely" a spiritual world. In fact, it is only a little bit "less material and a bit more spiritual" than yours down there. *Continuity* is the hallmark of everything spiritual or informational – just as life possesses continuity because it does not continually end only to begin anew immediately.

'Much of this may still confuse you, but it complies with what I just told you. The evolution of the universe is associated with the growing chaos of everything material which you know as *entropy*. At the same time and to the same degree everything informational – or spiritual – grows towards ever more complexity. Up here the spirit is already on a higher and more complex level than down there with you. In contrast the material is less pronounced here – but it has not yet disappeared altogether here either. If you were to look closely our world here is only slightly less material, considered from the viewpoint of your physics, than yours really is down there.

'But, it is enough for you to be unable to perceive it with your senses.

'As a general rule every form of matter is exactly encoded by information – even down to its smallest structure and layout. Matter is in principle not at all solid.

'For everyone in *their* world it is, of course, but from an objective viewpoint it is not.

'Just imagine *water*. You know it, of course, in its various forms, which you call aggregate states. You down there are comparable to water in its solid form, which is ice. Snow is a bit fluffier which then melts into water and in the end you have steam.

'All this is still the same water with its common core of information. The differences lie solely in the external appearance, which is due to various forms of condensation resulting from movements.

'In a similar way, new, self-contained worlds are being constantly generated which exist in parallel to one another and possess a very different materiality. They are rather like the Russian Matryoshka dolls which nestle within one another and are hierarchically arranged, so that the next higher one embraces the lower one. Each world differs from all the others solely due to its individual encoding. That is why you can only perceive yourself in your own world with senses which are encoded accordingly.

The most important component of all worlds is information which also acts as an interface between them. In the course of the cosmic evolution information grows from an initially very simple to an increasingly more complex nature. It becomes life and spirit! Information is the central theme which interconnects all worlds in their different materiality. Everything and anyone always belong to *both* fundamental worlds. We gradually crawl up the "eternal ladder of *life's* evolution", but in principle our spirit remains quintessentially the same, even if we change. The same is true for you in the course of your life down there: you are still the same person even if you don't resemble the child you used to be when you are growing old. You call your current step on this eternal ladder "material" because you don't know how many different grades there are.

'Human beings are conceived, they mature until they are born and then they enter a completely new world. Their bodies grow and after about 25 years they reach the peak of their *physical* power.

Thereafter it only goes downhill, slowly at first, picking up speed in the course of time.

'As the inevitable and necessary end of this *cycle*, determined by the "law of entropy" or by "the degree of disorder", death awaits their bodies at the end of "their time".

'But to the same extent their personalities, their internal "spiritual cores", mature incessantly and in a *linear* manner, pointing upwards at all times. And if their "material brains", their physical equipment pools, which are qualified for performing spiritual interactions, are not destroyed by dementia, then they will have reached the peak of their spiritual productivity at the very moment of their "physical death".

'This discrepancy between the cyclical pattern and linearity should really make you think down there:

'Logic should tell you that it is incomprehensible and almost absurd to believe that death is your definite end.

'"Entropy" tells us that death is only the end of your body: your "spirit" will live on for ever.

'Of course, you can find these connections in the Bible again – underlining again its high cultural value and it is rightly called "Holy Scripture". In the Gospel of John it says:

In the beginning was the Word, and the Word was with God, and the Word was God. It was in the beginning with God. All things were made through it and without it nothing was made that was made. In it was life, and the life was the light of men. And the light shines in the darkness, and the darkness did not comprehend it. [56]

If you translate this freely into the language of your time, then you could arrive at the following conclusion:

'In the beginning there was "pure information" and it derived from a "superior intelligence" we call "God". And this was pure information "it-him-herself". And God was the determining factor for everything, for the Creation and for all general conditions. Everything in existence today was created by information. This is where life developed – it is a form of very "complex information in motion". And it is also the determining core, the "light" of every human being. This core can be found everywhere, also in death, for it remains intact and will exist eternally – it cannot be destroyed, not even by death, by darkness.

'Should death, as you call it, cause a life, once created, to cross over from one world to the next, then the core of information it has hitherto differentiated will, of course, remain completely intact – in the case of human beings you would simply say they will keep "the personalities they possess at the time of their deaths" or in a more religious term they will keep *"their souls"*.

'Therefore, we must reconsider the term "reincarnation" in a completely different light than most of you do down there: it is always some kind of *"rebirth" into a different world which is invariably the next higher one* of the truly innumerable, real worlds all of which exist in parallel. Each change entails, however, the loss of some of your "material substance".

'Instead the real core of yourself, your "spiritual part", will grow significantly compared with your previous life: above all it will become more complex and thus "qualitatively more valuable".

'In the next world of your existence your spirit will, of course, automatically assume the somewhat differently encoded "material" structure of this new world which will then determine its new appearance.

'However, on the spiritual level you will not start at zero as would have been the case if the notion of a "reincarnation" were a "rebirth in the flesh on earth".'

'But I have heard . . . ,' I point out, ' . . . that many humans believe in reincarnation in the classical sense simply because they find some external signs – birthmarks or scars, for example – which are believed to be the results of injuries incurred during an alleged former life.

'Others believe in reincarnation because they seem to remember exact situations or places from a former life they suppose to have had and, sometimes, this even seems to be verifiable. And then there are those who think that they have gone back to "earlier lives" by means of hypnosis . . .'

'Although you don't believe in all this you seem to be quite well informed,' Michael returns. 'But there is no truth in it at all. It is all without exception based on *deception* and I'll gladly explain to you why that is:

'Since the core of all things – and thus also that of life – is ultimately pure information which is indestructible and exists eternally, and which becomes ever more complex in the course of time, you can in principle communicate or, as I termed it earlier on, *interact* with it at all times. Since most of the time you don't even notice these interactions and hence you project them back onto yourself. Nowadays you have a similarly growing internet which you can access at any time. Some academics even write their theses on it, thereby forgetting where their information came from.

'Similarly, by means of hypnosis or meditation, some people access much more complex information such as the circumstances in which long deceased people used to live or even their languages. In the process they don't notice that they are not identical with those persons. Sometimes people are put into such a deep trance during hypnosis sessions that these "accesses" become so much easier. And by the way, the efficiency of the brain's filter-function develops within the first few years of childhood. Therefore, children sometimes have the ability to access more complex information than they have later.

'As I already indicated to you, there are different forms of "matter", each with a very different "materiality".

'Their true essence – their core – is always pure information, however. Whatever you perceive with your senses as "matter" is merely a certain structure, encoded by information.

"If you think back to the basics of quantum physics in your own special field of work, it should easily become apparent to you: take any atom, to keep it simple take the hydrogen atom since it has only *one* nuclear particle and *one* electron orbiting it.

'Now consider the huge distance between these two particles. Let's assume the nucleus, the proton, is as big as a cherry. The electron would then be much smaller than a pinhead and would hurtle round the cherry at a distance of approximately two kilometres. Between these two particles there is nothing, no "real" substance except "effect" or "relation" which exactly encodes this immense distance. But that's not enough: due to your knowledge of quantum physics you should know that in reality even these two particles of the atom do not physically exist when at rest.

'Basically they are only forms of "dynamic information" which have come together and whose location and impulse are not simultaneously definable. This means that their existence is "blurred" and is subject to mere probability.

'In other words: what you down there know as matter and which you perceive as being so "solid" is actually just a breath of nothing. It is a kind of "condensation" of some exactly encoded information.

'All of you down there function in the same way.

'And your senses are constructed in the same manner just like all your measuring devices.

'This means that you can only perceive things which exist *within* this "closed code room", regardless of your methods and devices. Once again you find yourselves in a "Platonic cave".

'Whatever "real worlds" exist beyond these boundaries almost completely escapes your perception. Such worlds exist in large numbers, however, and it is only the encoding of their kind of "matter" that is slightly "phase-shifted" compared with yours.

'You should, therefore, not trust your "sensory perception" alone, but rather should you recognise that it doesn't have sufficient capacity for you to reach the "ultimate knowledge". What you need is your "spirit". However, this eludes any sensory perception but is still real.

'However, otherwise you have no chance of real progress. By the way, Immanuel Kant[57] already recognised and described this in the 1780s of your current calendar system. He used the term "reason" instead of "spirit".'

Michael notices that I am looking a little disbelievingly but amazed.

'Do you still have problems to imagine this? Then, dear Chris, let me present another analogy. Maybe this will do better:

'About 150 years ago according to your calendar people only knew visible light but no other kinds of radiation such as radio waves, x-rays or others. Of course, these already existed – just as they do now. But the people then didn't know them, they were not yet discovered at that time.

'As you know today visible light is only a very small section of an immense radiation spectrum. And you still don't know by far the entire spectrum. But since already you have today discovered significantly more about it you have become more open to the possibility that this might not be the end of the story.

The same applies to life and the many "material worlds", which really exist in parallel to one another, differentiated by various encodings.

'Since it is merely their encodings that render them different in nature I call them "phase-shifted".

'In spite of such possibilities of comparison their real existence is not taken into consideration thanks to the pigheadedness of your people down there – at least not before their having been able to take a look into the next level of existence, just like you are doing now. When you then have the chance to return, you are said to have had a near death experience, a kind of extraordinary experience of consciousness.

'But many such people are ridiculed down there, mocked and not taken seriously. Some don't dare to tell anyone about, not even their immediate family.

'Did you never hear about this phenomenon at some time or other and then simply dismiss it?'

Michael's question is probably just rhetorical and he doesn't expect an answer, presumably he knows it anyway. So, without hesitation he continues:

'Actually there are countless worlds existing in parallel to one another which all show only slight differences in their "material structures" – and this also includes yours. They are all self-contained so that sensory contacts between them are almost impossible.

'When they do happen from time to time, then it is due to the fact that not all of them are equal and the spectrum of sensory perceptions can overlap at the fringes. This is why these phenomena remain almost impossible to reproduce.

'Any "safe" contact can only be achieved by means of the underlying "informational core" inherent in all forms of life.

'Just as in this world "parallel lifeworlds" are accurately encoded by information, you encode diverse geometrical forms similarly by means of coordinate systems, for example.

'Any living creature is in its intrinsic core an "information cluster" which eternally strives to develop an ever higher complexity and to become ever more differentiated – or, in other words, it is an "eternally growing spirit".

Without your really noticing it you change now and again from one level of existence to the next higher one. With these changes of levels your visual appearance always changes also. When you undergo the first change from the lowest level, on which you are now, to the next higher one, you suddenly don't live anymore for the people you leave behind: you are "dead".'

Many of you don't even notice the change immediately, because they still see themselves as intact, even though the encoded matter shows a different kind of structure on the new level. You could also say that matter becomes more and more subtle from one level to the next.

'"*Simplex sigillum veri est*" – "Simplicity is the sign of truth". Here again you can recognise the universal basic principle: information keeps growing towards an ever higher organisation, whereas for matter the degree of disorganisation – entropy – increases.

'The ultimate ground of the universe is first and foremost a huge world of information which is differentiating further and further in the course of its own evolution.

'So, Teilhard de Chardin once asked down there very appropriately: *"Are we not all together a God in creation?"* He was absolutely right, since the term "God" describes the all-encompassing, higher and superior *entity*.

'By the way, Muslims are right here when they commit themselves to Allah as the one and only God. Nevertheless the Christian dogma of the Holy Trinity is not entirely wrong. We just have to regard it as being a *symbol*: when simple mathematical logic suggests the real existence of God as the highest entity and the existence of a spiritual and also a material world, then the term "Holy Trinity" *actually* underlines this with *God*father, Holy *Spirit* and finally God's *Son*, who represents the material part of humanity. Consequently, the Son had to die to show people that matter must perish but that its inner core, the information cluster accumulated during their lifetimes, will always survive.

'Should one day some reasonable intellectuals sit down together with a view to starting scientific research whilst keeping in mind that there *can* only be one truth, then your world would become a better place quite soon. This could also finally induce the desire in people to look beyond as many boundaries of their specific areas of expertise as possible and to draw boundary-transcending comparisons. It would then no longer be unnecessary to have to "sell" the never ending flow of unilateral and often daring interpretations as new revelations. And for the many religious dogmatists down there I would even go one step further by saying: even if the indescribable, superior and highest entity, namely "God", already embodies infinity and eternity, the mathematician Georg Cantor[58] succeeded during the 19th century of your calendar system in proving that there is an infinite number of infinities. So, it is irrelevant how much progress you may make one day in looking beyond your own narrow boundaries: you will never be able to know everything.

'Since everything is "information" in its core and higher beings distinguish themselves from the lower ones by their informational or "spiritual" degree of differentiation, you yourselves are, of course, already "spiritual beings" during your lifetime down there.

'You are on the lowest step of your spiritual development and, just like all the many others, you are regrettably unable as yet to realise, where you are actually heading.

And so you have an extremely serious problem down there now: meanwhile you are capable of eradicating mankind completely and to destroy everything by means of relatively simple instruments which are unfortunately almost freely accessible.

'Mankind as a whole is in great danger of jeopardising irreversibly its further development due to people's own stupidity. Sure, evolution would then start all over again down there, this time based on an already acquired higher level of information. It is also certain that it will, therefore, reach your current level significantly faster than before. But it would just as certainly create completely different forms of life.

'Mankind in its current form would be irretrievably lost for ever.

'Therefore, I ask you: does it really have to be like that?

'Have you still not reached a spiritual level which is high enough to enable you not only to recognise the dangers but also to counteract them effectively with combined strength?

'Isn't it about time to leave behind at long last all the radical, political ideologies which stand in the way of the universal uniqueness of the individual along with all shades of dogmatic fanaticism and religious fundamentalism?

'Can't you accept that *your* only true possession, *your* Planet Earth, is essential for *your* survival as mankind and that for this reason *you* must especially respect *your* resources?

'Many of you down there don't understand that after your own deaths the battle for survival will inevitably go on.

'This I why they do not believe that they will have to justify themselves one day in full remorse for their wrongful, destructive actions down there and that they will have to ask their victims for forgiveness.

'This shortsightedness is unfortunately inherent in more and more people down there while they even believe that they themselves are especially "enlightened". Actually this is the root of all evil and also one of the reasons why religious and political fundamentalism is spreading. Human beings are searching for support and they find it there. They see that the "Enlightenment" fails to provide such support. And they feel that the proponents of the Enlightenment are *wrong* when they try to convince them that their very own religion, which has existed since time immemorial, is stupid, obsolete, unrealistic nonsense. But they are unable to put up resistance against the current mass of scientific dogmas the theses of which often are not even proven. In the end they feel deserted and grow frustrated and apathetic.

'On the one hand a ruthless "me first" mentality rules among you down there, because you only believe in the "here and now" and all thoughts of "more than this" are ignored or ridiculed – even if many people do think differently, perhaps those who have made similar profound experiences as you are making right now.

'On the other hand something is emerging at the moment in the form of a sinister polar-symmetrical manifestation, which you justifiably abhor as political and religious radicalism and which you must vehemently and effectively combat, in order to prevent a horrendous disaster to befall mankind.

84

'Chris, now I'll come back to what I already mentioned earlier on:

'I just said that your material world down there is characterised by *discontinuity* and that the force which moves matter in all its various forms and holds it together – in other words that which renders the material world dynamic – is known to you as "energy".

'The force on the other side, which is keeping the polar-symmetrical "spiritual world" in motion and making it dynamic and holding it together – this force is "life" itself. Life is characterised by eternal *continuity*.

'Now I'll come to the "Supreme Being" – and by that I mean God's world which is basically indescribable:

'God's power, which, in the final analysis, facilitated the creation of everything that *is*, which holds it together expertly as a divine power and which will consistently keep developing further and further towards an ever higher spirit in maximum variety, this indestructible and all-encompassing "power of God" is "love".

'*Love* is the highest and strongest power existing in the entire world and on all its levels.

'And that is why at the end of all time at the very latest – whatever that means exactly I cannot tell you, and there might never be an end – in any case each single individual will be granted salvation, regardless of how evil and malicious the individual has been on the way there.'

85

I am still immensely fascinated and would like to learn much more. Of course, I am also curious as to what Michael can tell me about some other notions with which we scientists currently view the world down there and especially those concerning physics.

'Michael, can you perhaps answer some of my questions regarding our modern scientific view of the world?' I urge him hurriedly.

'Of course, go ahead. I hope we'll have sufficient time left,' he replies and he obviously seems to be in a hurry, too.

At the same time I sense somehow that the decision about my near future is imminent. And my feeling also tells me that Michael seems to have a similar intuition.

'You probably know that in September I am expected to deliver a lecture at the World Congress of Physicists which will be followed worldwide.'

'Of course I know that, Chris! That is also a reason why I want to give you as much information as only possible. After all, I really do hope that you'll go back. However, at the moment it doesn't look too good. Should things work out, though, I would hope that you will use the knowledge you have accumulated up here when you return. Only when such understanding has been disseminated soon enough will all of you, mankind as a whole, have a chance to survive down there.'

'Michael, our cosmic view of the world is influenced by materialistic ideas to no small extent simply because we think we have recognised some of the key parameters of cosmic development which obviates the need to search for other concepts, especially metaphysical ones.

'So, we are quite certain that the whole universe started from a Big Bang 14 billion years ago according to our calendar system. There are mainly two key pieces of evidence to support this concept: firstly, the background radiation which we can measure and, secondly, the redshift of light emitted by celestial bodies moving away from us.

'With his relativity theory Albert Einstein asserted that the universe consists of a four-dimensional space-time, namely three dimensions of space and the fourth dimension being time. This space is bent, which was proven many years ago by measuring light passing the sun. So it would seem that the world resembles an expanding lump of sourdough with raisins which are drifting further and further apart.'

Michael laughs.

'Do you know what your Nobel Laureate for physics, Peter Laughlin, said, some years ago in an interview, when the subject of the Big Bang and the many colourful theories about the universe were broached – especially the "string theory" and those of "dark matter" and "dark energy" and many others?'

'No, I can't remember.'

'Can you really not recollect what your son Tom once even read out to you? Fine, then I'll repeat it for you. Laughlin said:

'"... *the Big Bang scenario is nothing but marketing."*

'And in reference to others of his colleagues' notions he said in the same interview: *"Not one of their claims is backed by any experiments. Not one of them has said anything that is true."'*

'Have these chastised colleagues really earned such a slap in the face?' I ask a little perplexed.

86

'Let me give you a few logical hints to help you along. Then you might recognise that Laughlin was not altogether wrong,' Michael continues and he seems to become ever more urgent. I have the impression that, while he is speaking to me here, he simultaneously realises what is happening down there

– so as if he has a button earphone and is listening to minute-to-minute stage directions.

'Imagine a one-dimensional line. It needs a sheet of paper on which it can be drawn. The sheet is a two-dimensional plane which is surrounded by a three-dimensional space.

'Apart from the universe – which some consider to be a three-dimensional *open* space without really knowing what that might be – you only know *closed* three-dimensional bodies, such as you yourself are one. Now, it is a characteristic of three-dimensional space that it is *always closed*. From a purely logical point of view, therefore, you need an additional "real" four-dimensional space. Now we might, of course, conclude that this would theoretically continue forever. That would be the case, however, only if *closed* real four-dimensional spatial objects actually existed. But they don't. Therefore, four-dimensionality is the end of the story, since it is *not closed but open*, thereby strictly following the specifications defined by the law of polar-symmetry. *Where there is finiteness there must also be infiniteness,* which by the way also applies to eternity. Three-dimensional space is a closed, finite space, the four-dimensional space on the other hand is infinite and open.

Many years ago a scientist who sadly received little acknowledgement already postulated that a "true" four-dimensional space must exist.[59] And another scientist, who even lives not far from you, picked up the hypothesis and, supported by his own research, he advanced the concept further and improved it significantly.[60]

'Just imagine two infinite planes which intersect perpendicularly. Hence you have a real open four-dimensionality of the mathematical formula x^2y^2.

This corresponds with the actual realities of the universe, an infinite 4-D-space which accommodates all three-dimensional closed bodies, as is every sun, every human being and every animal. Since the actual "core" – or let me express this in other words – the central content of our cosmos is "information", you can easily imagine that in this *open four-dimensional space* everything is perfectly structured by numbers. This will ensure that everything is situated in the right place – similar to a coordinate system – and that it moves just as you perceive it.

Universal space is a space which is exactly structured by "information". And here the numbers from 1 to infinity play an equally important role as some simple geometrical forms do in their relationships to one another.

'Did you know that the relationship between the area and the circumference of a square and its internal circle is a number sequence which starts with 2-7-3?'

'No, I would have to calculate that. But why do you ask? I don't recognise the significance.'

'Maybe you will notice that the background radiation you mentioned has exactly this value. It shows 2,73... Kelvin, this is a bit above the point of absolute zero. And to the chagrin of all cosmologists it is isotropic, meaning it is constant and evenly distributed in all directions throughout the universe.

'You were so proud when you detected ever so slight fluctuations and immediately wild speculations ensued. But this 2,73... Kelvin sequence is not a smooth number, it is an irrational, infinite number. This means that minimal fluctuations are allowed "in nature".'

'Something else: This minimal operating temperature of the universe is simply essential as it makes movement possible at all. But even if this radiation seems weak to you, it is in fact exceptionally *strong*. You physicists probably disregard this deliberately, in order to salvage ideologies stuck in a dead end: should galaxy clusters indeed be racing away from one another at an almost unrealistic speed, as you ask the world to believe, then the background radiation actually ought to be much weaker and it should even decrease in the course of time.

'But that is not the case, and you keep quiet about it. The background radiation is just as strong as could be expected of a stationary *two-dimensional surface*.

'That is the case here. Do you notice something?

'Of course, the relationship between a square and its inner circle would have a different value in a different arithmetic system than the decimal system. But since it is the result of the relationship between two simple geometrical forms, the arithmetical system is irrelevant.

'When I now tell you that this number sequence can be found all over the world in certain key positions, then it is about time to ask yourself whether there isn't a much greater truth behind it all.

'And that's how it is: *the driving force behind all this is "information"*.

'It is important to realise that the number sequence 2-7-3 constitutes a "limit of feasibility", which was demonstrated by your scientist countryman[61] whom I already mentioned. Many years ago he developed a unique conceptual model based on the biblical command "grow and multiply": he imagined himself in the role of the creator "on the drawing board" and started with drawing the smallest but finite point, the circle, onto an empty sheet of paper. Following strictly logical principles he then made it multiply and grow. After only three steps something amazing materialised: he now had four circles and when he connected their central points, a square was created in the two-dimensionality of his sheet of paper.

'This square has the same relationship to the original circle, drawn into it as an inner circle, as has 1,273 to 1. So this results in the already known, universally decisive number sequence 2-7-3.

'The three steps he had to take to arrive here, not only produced all important triangles but also the "golden section" with the also infinite number sequence 6-1-8 as the result of a continuing division.

'As you know, this value is tremendously important for all "optimal dimensions" in the world. By means of only the four first ordinal numbers 1 to 4 and the two number sequences 2-7-3 and 6-1-8, all based solely on geometrical relationships which he found in his intellectual model, he was able to show that all laws of nature known to you can be explained with an error rate of less than 1%.

'All this he developed on a two-dimensional sheet of paper which represents a, while strictly following logical principles including the universal regularity of the polar-symmetry.

'If we were now to develop "space" by means of this two-dimensionality, again in a strictly logical manner, it would be wrong to simply choose another "point" outside this surface, since thereby you would create a three-dimensional closed body such as a pyramid.

'From a logical perspective it would be much better to raise the sheet of paper into a vertical position.

'And by doing so, we create the precondition for a "real" four-dimensionality. As I already told you, it consists of two planes which infinitely intersect each other at right angles.

'In about 2002 according to your calendar system you physicists down there changed your previous opinion that the universe is finite. You are right. In fact it is infinite.

'Now I must also contradict you in your perception of a "four-dimensional space-time, since the universe is already spatially truly four-dimensional.

'It was Albert Einstein, by the way, who long since pointed out that his famous formula $E = m c^2$, as you know it, only applies to a stationary system.

'In fact, however, the whole world, and this includes the "material part" you experience through your sensory perceptions, is an extremely dynamic system.

'The cosmic operating temperature is responsible for this.

'Therefore we must multiply all factors in Albert Einstein's formula by itself, meaning we must square it. Then it would read: $E^2 = m^2 c^4$.

'When "c", the speed of light, appears in the fourth power in the dynamic system, then the same must also apply to the other "physical units" contained therein.

'Basic physics in any school teaches that speed is distance divided by time. This shows that in reality *four real space dimensions and another four real time dimensions which are polar-symmetrical to them* must exist, to the detriment of your misconstrued concept of a four-dimensional space-time.

'With such a perception you are barking up the wrong tree. You know, Chris, Isidore of Seville[62] once said correctly: *"At the beginning was the number..."* and a bit further: *"Take from all things their number and all shall perish."*

87

'Now a few words concerning your other questions,' Michael appears increasingly strained.

'Big Bang? No, that is entirely your own invention. There never was a Big Bang. The universe is still developing and there is constantly something new emerging.

'Your satellites diligently photograph the births of stars, but no one asks why it is that not all stars, including these new ones, were created in the Big Bang if there ever was one.

'*In the beginning was* "information" or, as it says in the Bible, *"the Word"*. And *the Word was with God, and the Word was God"*. Exchange "Word" for "information" and you have a good approximation. I already explained that earlier.

'Your problem down there seems to be that, although ever more scientists are recognising increasing contradictions, none of them is prepared to reject one or the other thesis, because they are afraid to be left isolated and not to "belong" any longer. A small number of them *determine* what must be believed, no matter whether it is true or not. As you can see, the background radiation of the universe as one of the two most important arguments for a Big Bang already drops out, since it is of "informational nature". It is encoded by an infinite number sequence which in general stands for the "boundaries of feasibility" in the world. This results from the simple geometrical relationship between the "development of a unit in the smallest circle and the square of the multiplicity".

'A second important evidence for the Big Bang for you down there is the redshift of light emitted by faraway celestial bodies which reaches the earth.

'Just as you hear the tone of a fire engine horn growing lower once it has passed you, you imagine that the wave length of light increases as the source of light moves away.[63] And red light has longer wave lengths. Hence it is assumed that all galaxy clusters are moving apart. Although this is in general correct, it is still *no evidence* for the Big Bang. Celestial bodies still emanate red light, for example, when they just grow old. And the light of very distant bodies also appears to us redshifted *in itself*. They need not even be moving away from you at great speed.

'Finally, the wave length of light can also change due to various forces taking effect while it is heading towards you. All these things are already known to you, but the theory of the Big Bang *must* be maintained, since in this case it applies again: *"It cannot be what may not be".*'

'What about the "string theory" then?' I dare ask. 'There is a whole generation working on it meanwhile and they believe it to be the "be all and end all".'

'Do you seriously believe that?' Michael is winking at me. 'Actually, you can answer this question yourself now. The strings are simply another attempt to explain unexplainable phenomena in a purely material manner.

'But by now you should be able to think differently. For example, there is a large number of smallest particles which exist in two oppositional states – in different polarisations, for example. Now you have discovered that, when you measure one of the states or manifestations of a particle, it is only the *other* state which is measurable in subsequent computations irrespective of the distance between them at the time. Now you rack your brains as to how it is possible that these particles "know" of each other although they are light years apart?[64]

'I already explained to you in answer to one of your questions that here among us *I* can indeed show several new arrivals around simultaneously.

'And yet it is always me who accompanies them.

'I can divide myself, because I can send my personality anywhere, since it is my "informational core". This is not yet possible for you down there due to your consisting of denser material. Here, however, it can be done.

'I would like to add two not entirely perfect by definitely plausible examples here: with a suitable receiver you can watch several TV stations at the same time down there today. Or think of a complex website in your present day internet. You can copy it or you can mail the link and anyone interested can see or download it at the same time. They all watch the same things simultaneously. If you now fantasise a little you can imagine that you aren't just looking at a website on a two-dimensional monitor but rather that you have a complex three-dimensional body of information in front of you, then it will all start to make sense to you.

'Keep in mind now that the smallest particles down there do not really have a material component. They more or less consist of pure information – which is everywhere at the same time. An example of pure information is the photon, the smallest particle of light. A twin photon carries two different kinds of information. Then it soon becomes clear: when I select one of the two, then somewhere else only the other one is available. Incidentally, you also interpret light as being simultaneously a wave. This impression is created because "actual space" as a four-dimensional information space is structured by numbers.

'So light simply follows the coordinates by multiplying them with the information of the photon. In the same way gravitation is clearly regulated as an effect which is polar-symmetrical to light.

'Your string theories merely cloud your minds and obliterate the truth. You can bin them without a second thought.

'Don't be angry with me when I say that so clearly, but you must learn to rethink. Someone I showed around here about two years ago, a well-known physicist from your country, demanded a paradigm change down there.[65] Unfortunately, we are still waiting for it.

'This shows that not every renowned physicist down there is on the wrong track, but there are many.'

So I learn that it would be better to pack up the strings again.

'Chris, may I answer one question which you haven't asked yet and which I was waiting for?' Michael surprises me after a short break.

'Certainly, what is it, Michael?'

'Well, the first question asked by most people I talk to here is whether they are alone in the universe as human beings or whether there is life anywhere else, especially as intelligent or even higher developed life.'

'Of course, that also interests me. But didn't you answer that as an aside in the positive right at the beginning? I seem to remember it.'

'True, I did. You know, Chris, after everything I have told you up to now, we should rephrase this question, for now you know that there must be countless numbers of beings, mostly on all those many parallel levels of existence, many of which are on a spiritually higher level, and they do indeed exist. After all, many of those have led their first life down there, like you are doing. In fact there are indeed countless celestial bodies with life on your dense material level.

'And yet a great number of those are inhabited by beings who are spiritually far more advanced compared with you down there. However, all these celestial bodies are so far apart from one another that it is inconceivable that you will ever be able to meet on your level, that is on a physical level. You would probably just annihilate one another anyway.'

'Yes, Michael, I am afraid that is true.'

88

'And now, dear Chris, it's your turn: you must decide...'

Utterly surprised I look at Michael.

'Me? What should I decide?' I ask back

'Come here, I'll show you something.'

Michael leads me through a long glass passage to another sphere in this huge building.

Something completely unexpected assails me – and I am instantly deeply moved.

Through a large glass wall as you would find in a police station I look from here into another room. There I can see Helen, Bob and Tom sitting together. They are all inconsolable with tears rolling down their cheeks.

They are weeping because of... *me*!

I look to the other side. There is also a glass wall showing a different room. It is in a hospital. And there is Lara. What? Lara is in hospital? What's the matter with her?

'What happened?' I ask Michael aghast.

'She was bleeding. You know, all the stress about you really got at her. She might lose the baby, because she can't come to terms with you dying.'

'Because I am dying?' I inquire hastily.

'Yes, she can't get over the fact that it might not be possible to save your life. That really weakened her and her body reacted in this way,' Michael explains to me, as always in a stoic calm.

I walk a bit further and can see into a third room.

But there . . . I can see . . . myself.

'That old basket case down there – is that me?' I ask Michael, I am absolutely shocked. 'With all those tubes, white as a sheet and with no sign of movement?'

Gathered around this "being" are numerous people and I quickly recognise Dirk Bender, although he is turning his back to me.

He is frantically drumming on my chest.

Others watch the monitors, loading syringes and . . .

Then I see these waves flickering wildly across one of the monitors.

'That is not my heart twitching, is it?' I want to know.

'Yes, Chris, that is your heart. And can you see Doctor Bender? He is desperately trying to bring you back, but . . .'

'Yes, I noticed. But he probably won't succeed.' I complete the sentence and feel a bit more relaxed.

'It rather looks like that, but he can't manage it because the key for the success of his efforts lies exclusively in your hands:

'You are carrying the key to your own eternity.

'Only you can help him to succeed, thereby ensuring that you will be a grandfather soon and that your daughter won't loose her baby.

'At this moment it is entirely up to you whether your sons and Helen, who all love you so much and who are weeping for you down there, whether they will be happy again.

'It is entirely up to you whether your wife will suffer a total collapse because she lost you and also whether your son Bob will be able to get over his sorrow over the death of his beloved Jenny more easily when you are able to pass on to him the warm regards she sends him.

'And it is entirely up to you now whether Dirk and Lara will still have the chance to become a happy couple.'

'But you said you don't have any influence on any of that . . .' I point out to Michael. I am rather deeply moved by all this and very uncertain what to do.

'That's right, *we* can't influence anything but *you* could. You have your own free will,' he returns. 'But you have to decide quickly. There is not much time left. For most of these decisions the time frame is quite limited. And yours is running out fast.

89

It seems to be hopeless. Beeeeeeep . . .

The ventricular fibrillation of Chris Schneider's heart has ended in a cardiac arrest in spite of all the desperate efforts to rescue him. Zero line in the ECG, asystole.

'Let us prepare the organ removal, I have his organ donor card. We just have to follow a few guidelines, get the EEG and two colleagues from the Neurology Department,' Professor Paland calls to the emergency team assisting Dr Bender.

'I can't give up yet. One more last attempt, I'll try it with heart massage again,' Dirk Bender shouts back.

He doesn't even wait for Professor Paland's answer.

'Another syringe with adrenalin, please' he yells to the nurse standing beside him. 'Once more directly into the heart.'

'Mr Bender, there is no point in continuing all this. His brain is probably . . .'

'I'll try just one more time,' Dirk Bender is overriding his boss firmly now. 'Please get everything ready.'

Applying forceful pressure to the breastbone he works in a strong and fast rhythm downwards on Christian Schneider's ribcage.

No one noticed that Helen meanwhile entered the intensive care cubicle. She pushes past the assistants and takes Christian's left hand. Tears are running down her face. She throws herself on her husband and cries out with fervour, sobbing noisily:

'Christian, please come back, stay with us, we all need you so much.'

90

'Did you see that? Did you hear your wife Helen?' Michael asks and looks around. But Chris seems to have disappeared suddenly.

'Chris... Chris? Are you gone already?'

Obviously Chris decided to go. Michael would have talked him into it anyway. But now he releases a sigh of relieve.

'I hope he hasn't forgotten everything when he arrives down there,' Michael thinks. 'It would be helpful if he could pass on some of the knowledge he gathered here. Down there so many people are manoeuvring themselves into so many dead ends,' he mumbles and then he vanishes.

There are further missions awaiting him.

91

'Helen, please step to one side, otherwise I can't continue,' Dirk Bender calls out.

Dirk doesn't give up.

Professor Paland is still standing in the cubicle door and he obviously seems angry.

He is not used to his staff not following his instructions. And there seems to be no chance of success. The ECG monitor shows a zero line. The artificial respiration is still working and simulates something like a small remainder of life.

Let him rest in peace, he thinks and hopes that Dr Bender recognises this as well.

At the same moment there is a sound: beep – interval – beep – interval – beep, beep – interval – beep, beep, beep – interval - beep, beep, beep, beep – interval - beep, beep, beep, beep, beep, beep, beep, beep, beep, beep, beep, beep...

Suddenly a completely unexpected wave appears on the ECG monitor equalling heart beats which slowly gain speed and become more regular.

'We got him, we got him back, quickly now, another dose of intravenous adrenalin,' Dr Bender shouts enthusiastically and Helen firmly presses Chris's left hand.

'I just hope we can keep him here,' Dirk Bender still fears that his patient might slip away again. He looks at Professor Paland who stares back at him in unbelieving amazement and is speechless.

'Mrs Schneider, stay with him, I think it was good that you came,' Professor Paland says to Helen and relief is spreading over his face.

'Try to stabilise him,' he addresses his assistants and leaves the room.

Shortly after, he returns with Bob and Tom: 'It might be a good idea when both sons are here as well. Who knows, maybe our colleague here notices what is going on, who knows...'

He leaves the intensive care cubicle again.

Over the next two hours Christian Schneider's pulse and blood pressure normalise.

Of course, he is still receiving artificially respiration and he is still unconscious.

A computer tomography of the skull is scheduled for the following day to establish whether his brain suffered any visible damage by the whole procedure.

Helen and his sons stay with Christian; they hold his hands and talk to him. Meanwhile Tom has informed Sascha and Jasmin about the state of affairs. But they both wanted to wait for Tom and went to a restaurant in the neighbourhood.

The door to the intensive care cubicle opens and Professor Paland comes in again

'I just dropped in at the Gynaecological Department and told your daughter the good news. I also had a talk with Professor Grüter,' Professor Paland says and makes the impression of being quite happy.

'I am really glad to be able to tell you that the bleeding doesn't seem to have been as serious as expected. It even stopped suddenly. Nevertheless, your daughter or sister respectively must stay with us for another few days so that we can monitor her. However, there is no immediate danger for her and her baby.

On his way out he turns round again and smiles: 'I also informed my colleague Mr Bender, I hope that is all right for you. Anyway he was delighted and he looked very happy.'

Then he leaves the room and one of the intensive care nurses enters to check all the instruments.

92

'Hallo, Michael, here I am. Nice to see you again.' I offer Michael my hand while he is simultaneously explaining to a newcomer something about his new surroundings.

'That's nice of you to drop by again – to say goodbye, I assume?' Michael is pleased and is not the least little bit amazed to see me again. 'Are you all right?' he asks.

'That remains to be seen. Tomorrow they'll be giving me another check-up, but I hope that my "old machinery" will soon be back in working order, at least for the next few years,' I express myself carefully.

'I am pretty sure about that,' Michael laughs. 'And I seem to have heard that we will meet again in about thirty years, unless you have another accident. But then someone else might come to pick you up.'

'Don't you dare!' I smile at Michael. 'But explain to me now why I am here again. I thought I had already made up my mind to go back to life and you said it was entirely up to me?'

Michael is amused: 'You don't have to be clinically dead, sometimes it also works when stress hormones in your brain keep the access "open". I know of some people amongst you down there who show up here more often than *we* would like.

'When your body experiences exceptional situations, and that can easily happen due to severe physical or mental stress, then your brain "opens". Sometimes this also happens while someone is meditating, or when people are lost in prayer or during deep hypnosis.

'You know, during your lives down there the primary role of the brain is *also* to keep you *away* from "spiritual influences" which might otherwise confuse you and complicate your lives. After all, you must all master your lives down there and for doing this your brain needs a certain concentration which is – how shall I put this – "as little impaired as possible".

'In normal circumstances your brain filters off a tremendous amount of all kinds of external information, including that from the spiritual side.

'Keep in mind that many of your ancestors are here, your parents, for example, who would have loved to welcome you here right away but they couldn't. Then there are your grandparents and many, many others. You already met Jenny. But many of those who knew you and who loved you, would gladly support you down there and help you through difficult situations from here. Of course, they would like you to notice that as well. However, that would strongly interfere with you and your further development.

'In other cases it could be the other way round: some spirits here may even want to do harm or just fool around.

'But that shouldn't happen – at least not as a general rule. Sometimes we don't notice and now and again we look the other way. And sometimes the brain of a human being, still alive down there, is simply too porous. If that happens people perceive more than we would like – or even more than they would have liked.

'In general, however, evolution has taken excellent precautions and with the brain it has created an amazing *"reduction filter"*.

'Nevertheless, in certain situations the brain becomes more porous like a permeable membrane. In most cases this only lasts for a short period of time and disappears again. When children grow up, it takes time until these filtering skills become effective. And another example: when close relatives die, this phenomenon may occur more frequently. In those cases you down there sometimes talk about "*after* death experiences". I know, of course, that you always considered this as utter nonsense up to now. But I sincerely hope that you have learned your lesson now.

'I certainly have learned a lot and I thank you for it, Michael,' I am eager to answer him.

'Due to all these attempts to bring you back to life,' Michael continues, 'you have produced and have had injected such large quantities of stress hormones like adrenalin and cortisol that your brain is still porous enough at the moment for you to be able to turn up here again. But don't worry they will dissipate soon enough and then everything will be back to normal.'

'What a pity, I really enjoyed talking with you here – and it was tremendously interesting. I have learned an awful lot from you and I am looking forward to seeing you again one day.'

I am still holding his hand.

'You will have to come back one day,' Michael laughs. 'But now I would like to remind you of my request. Do you remember what I mean?'

'You asked me for something?' I have to think hard about his. 'I am sure you could manage on your own anyway, couldn't you? But I would be delighted if I could fulfill one of your wishes. What was it again?' I ask him a bit surprised.

'Well, when you are really fit again, then I would like you to . . .'

93

The next day, Helen, Bob and Tom are sitting together at Lara's hospital bed. The previous day Professor Paland had informed Lara immediately about the good news concerning her beloved father.

Of course, she is overjoyed to hear that her father's condition seems to have greatly improved and that the worst which seemed so inevitable has been averted.

She wants to see her father as soon as possible.

The door to her room opens and Dirk Bender enters.

'Hallo everyone,' he calls from a distance before shaking hands with each of them. He sits down on Lara's bed and gives her a kiss on her cheek.

'I have already heard everything about your heroic actions yesterday,' Lara smiles at him. 'I'm also well again and our baby is fine, here is the ultrasonic image.'

Lara speaks almost without taking a breath, she is in such high spirits.

'I know, I just talked with my colleague Mrs Kramer, your physician in charge. I am very glad that we succeeded after all. Your father has been stable since last night and we are rather surprised, since for a long time it didn't look too promising at all.

'Something must have helped us . . . ' Dr Bender is pondering and he smiles fondly at Lara.

Lara looks back at him just as fondly.

'You know, I am convinced that there is more between heaven and earth than we all want to believe,' she says rather smugly. 'Maybe someone gave Dad a kick,' and then she adds in a low voice, inaudible for all the others, 'maybe Michaela had something to do with it . . .'

'But I wanted to tell you all something else,' Dirk Bender picks up the conversation again, looking at Helen, Tom and Bob and holding Lara's hand in a tight grip.

They all gaze at him. The air in the room seems to crackle and an intense suspense draws close.

'Everything will be fine,' he pours out. 'We just received the result of the cranial computer tomography, the picture of Christian Schneider's skull. There is no new additional damage and the bleedings have all been drained off thoroughly and are diminishing rapidly.

An expression of great joy crosses their faces.
They all keep up their animated discussion; they are almost unhinged with happiness.

94

Christian Schneider remains in a coma for quite some time.
The awakening process takes another two weeks, but he soon manages to breath on his own.
When he opens his eyes for the first time, Lara is sitting at his bedside holding his hand and she smiles at him.

'What . . . about . . . your baby?' are the first words he gets out laboriously stammering.
'Everything is fine!' Lara answers and Christian Schneider drops back to sleep, his mind settled.

Lara is surprised. She asks herself why it is that the very first thing her father wants to know is how her baby is doing, although he was so vehemently against her carrying it to term.

And how on earth could he possibly have known that she very nearly lost it while he was clinically dead?
These questions keep bothering her.

95

Off we go, heading to New York.

Every five years the world's most renowned physicists meet for a congress organised by their new world association.

For the 100th anniversary of the organisation it was decided to meet in New York.

I see this symposium as a priceless honour this year and at the same time it poses a great challenge for me. After all, I am to present the ceremonial address for this 100th anniversary.

When I was invited to do this the previous year, I was much moved and it was clear to me right from the start that I would talk about the state of our current cosmological view of the world, one of my favourite subjects since early childhood.

With this invitation a life dream was fulfilled. And now the event was drawing close. But at the same time everything had changed.

I needed many more weeks to recover from the helicopter crash I had survived thanks to lucky circumstances. Later the doctors told me that they had to resuscitate me twice and that it was touch-and-go whether I would survive or not. I remained in a coma for quite a while thereafter.

Meanwhile all my injuries have healed quite well, thank heaven. I am left with slight pains in my left shoulder now and again. Sometimes my short-term memory still plays tricks on me, but I am optimistic enough to hope that it will also improve soon.

Due to the long time I had to spend in the University Hospital and subsequently in the Rehabilitation Centre in Aachen, the preparations for my presentation in New York didn't progress too well.

It was also questionable whether I would recover in time to be able to undertake such a long journey after I had returned to life. However, I politely but vigorously declined all suggestions to give my presentation at the next congress in five years time and I decided to struggle through at all costs.

The pilot of the helicopter, my former class mate Max Kauder, was able to leave the hospital before me. He, too, is well again.

His injuries were far less severe and they didn't need to resuscitate him.

It was established that in fact some youngsters pointed a very strong laser beam at the helicopter thereby completely blinding us and causing the accident. Based on the statements of some witnesses they were caught later. Now they have to stand trial and severe penalties are awaiting them.

To my utter delight Lara made Helen and me happy grandparents three weeks ago. Her healthy daughter was born without further complications. Lara named her Jenny, to our son Bob's delight, whose girlfriend Jenny had died under such tragic circumstances in May. Bob will even be her godfather and he is already smitten by his nice.

Mother and child are well. They both still live in our house. Helen thinks this is truly wonderful and she spends every free minute with the little one.

Lara and Dirk have found each other again. Dirk played a significant role in my rescue, as I was told later, and this certainly helped his and Lara's reconciliation. There is also the rumour that they are planning to get married. At least they are meanwhile looking for a suitable joint flat in Aachen.

We are all happy about this turn of events. At least then one of our children will stay in the neighbourhood and Helen would have the chance to take care of our grandchild now and then.

Of course, Lara and Dirk also like this aspect which would give them sometimes the opportunity to spend time just with each other.

96

Since the organisers of the World Association of Physicists were so very pleased to hear that after my hard battle back to health I have recovered sufficiently to be able to deliver the ceremonial speech at the anniversary congress next Sunday, they generously offered to pay not only for my trip to New York but also for my whole family to accompany me.

As an expression of my sincere gratitude to Dirk, Jasmin and Sascha, who had done so much for my family and me over the last few months, I invited them all to come with us. And so the short trip Helen and I had planned, developed into a one-week tour with the entire family and partners.

At lunchtime today we will all depart from Düsseldorf on a direct flight to New York John F. Kennedy Airport.

Even our little granddaughter Jenny, only a few weeks old, will accompany us and Helen's family in Boston is looking forward to getting to know their German great-granddaughter. Helen is especially excited about meeting her elderly parents again at long last and to be able to embrace her brother and his family.

They haven't seen one another for far too long a time.

Eight adults and one baby are on their way to cross the ocean to the country of unlimited possibilities.

Apart from our little Jenny who will be taken care of on Saturday by a babysitter – also provided by the congress organisers – they will all attend my representation.

I am very proud and overjoyed.

97

After a pleasant eight-hour flight we arrive in New York in the afternoon. None of us feels at all tired, even Lara is friendly and peaceful thanks to the long sleep she had during the flight.

To my utter surprise immigration is a smooth and swift procedure today, although the US immigration office has the not altogether undeserved reputation of being rather awkward at times. After we all managed to retrieve our luggage we are taken to our hotel in the mini-bus waiting for us which has just enough seats for us all. Our hotel is "The Standard" located on the south-west side of Manhattan Island.

This very comfortable eighteen-storey hotel offers excellent views on all sides over this impressive city. It bridges a relatively new recreation area known as "High Line".

This "High Line" is a former nearly three-kilometre long elevated railway viaduct. In 2006 it was decided to convert it into a park which has become very popular in the meantime. In 2009 the first construction phase was finished and opened to the public. Further parts were successively redesigned and the last part was finished in September 2014.

Today it is possible to leisurely stroll along it from 34th Street to 11th Street; most of the stretch runs parallel to the Hudson River.

At the northern entrance lies the rather new and gigantic "Javits Convention Center" which is home to many exhibitions and big congresses such as the one we will go to.

Via the "High Line" we can walk from our hotel to the Congress Centre and back at our leisure without being encumbered by the sometimes chaotic New York traffic.

After having checked in at our hotel we lie down for a little snooze, but only for a little while. You shouldn't take too long a rest after such a flight since then your body, being pretty much confused by the six-hour time-shift, won't adjust fast enough to the new day-and-night rhythm.

Since the weather is still beautiful at this time of year we agree to meet in the evening for a stroll along the "High Line" and have dinner together afterwards in a nice restaurant.

98

Probably due to my imminent presentation I am too agitated to sleep, so I get up again and climb off my American king-size bed after only fifteen minutes.

I wander through the hotel to stretch my legs and to have a look around.

In the lobby I meet Lara, who is also unable to sleep while Dirk is taking care of their little daughter in their room.

'Lara, I must apologise to you. You have given birth to a wonderful daughter and we are delighted to have a grandchild. I want to thank you for this. I am terribly sorry that I exerted so much pressure on you not to carry the child to term.' Tears are welling up in my eyes.

'That's all right, Dad. You had your opinion and it was well-founded. But I had my opinion and it was just as well-founded. After all it is my child, so I had to decide what to do.' Lara answers calmly and, I think, in a very reflected and prudent manner.

Then she continues: 'You know, many years ago I experienced something which I won't forget for the rest of my life. And up to now I haven't told anyone about it. I was still a child and I was very sick at the time...'

'Lara, you had scarlet fever,' I interrupt her. 'And there came the night when we were really very frightened; you almost died.'

Lara looks at me with wide eyes.

'And you recall that just now?' she asks rather perplexed.

'My dear child, I think you were closer to death than to life at that time. Michaela told me so...'

With this Lara freezes to a pillar of salt.

Her mouth is wide open and her eyes stare at me in unbelieving amazement.

She knows, she never ever told me or anyone else anything about this experience.

Unperturbed I continue: 'Yes, Lara, I was on the other side as well. And I also met Michaela who is also Michael simultaneously, by the way. It is easy for her to switch from one gender to the other. Therefore, for me as a male it was Michael, to you as a girl it was Michaela who appeared.

'She told me about you and she also showed me how bad it was with you and how you very nearly lost your little Jenny.

'All this happened when I was clinically dead and Dirk was repeatedly trying desperately to bring me back to life.'

Lara can hardly shut her mouth. She lets a beat of silence pass, looking at me lovingly, before she stammers:

'Now . . . well . . . now I realise why you asked after my – still unborn – baby immediately after briefly regaining consciousness during your long coma.'

'Did I indeed do that? I can't even remember. I don't recall either that I woke up from time to time.'

'Yes, you did. I was holding your hand and you suddenly opened your eyes and asked immediately how my baby was. Then you went back to sleep.'

We hug each other firmly and give free rein to our emotions. Lara understands that I have changed drastically. And she also knows why.

99

After a beautiful joint evening with a delicious dinner at a popular Hudson River pier we fall into our beds dead tired.

I admire little Jenny who accompanies us to almost all our activities and who is so sweet and peaceful. I hardly ever hear her cry.

The next day, it is Friday the 16th September, after a generous breakfast in the hotel, I take the "High Line" and walk to the Javits Convention Center where the congress is starting today with a reception. The congress will last for four days till next Monday.

The very next day, Saturday, the festive gala evening will take place, and at 7 o'clock in the evening I am to deliver my speech to the delegates and a large number of invited guests, among them many relatives – just like my own – who are already waiting with great expectancy. Very nearly 1,000 scientists from all over the world have registered for this evening. They want to discuss the latest ideas concerning matters of physics and to exchange and debate their views.

Modern cosmology, subject of my presentation, is only a small part of it but it is by no means a marginal issue. For most of the members of my audience it is a science in itself which still leaves very many questions open.

During the champagne reception the heads and organisers of the event introduce themselves.

Thereafter I am asked, as the speaker, to say a few words and I address the visitors with a warm welcome. Then I invite them to attend my speech on the following festive evening which will take place in the largest hall of the building.

A multi-course dinner will be served and a small ensemble of musicians will accompany the event with classical music between the short speeches to be held during the congratulatory reception at this centenary celebration.

All this will be followed by dancing to light music after dinner.

When the visitors give me applause, I reach for the microphone again and thank everybody for the ovation and I promise them an exciting presentation for the next day.

The anniversary conference proceeds thereafter with numerous scientific contributions.

I listen to some of them with great interest, but before the first day of the congress is over I start to look for my family again.

100

On the way along the "High Line" I meet Bob. He is all on his own, looks rather sad and pensive walking in the early gathering darkness.

If I hadn't walked up to him and addressed him he wouldn't have noticed me.

I can see that he must have been crying since his eyes are still red.

'What's wrong with you, Son?' I ask. 'Shall we sit down somewhere and enjoy the setting sun?'

Without giving me an answer he is making a beeline for a bench nearby which offers a breathtaking view across the Hudson which gleams silver in the evening sun.

'You know, Dad, somehow everyone is happy and well again. You have recovered, thank heaven, and you will present your speech tomorrow. Mum managed to fend off the mobbing attacks and Tom's role within the family is more accepted than ever. Then Lara has given birth to a healthy little daughter and everything seems to be all right again with Dirk. I am really very happy about all this.

'But what about me?'

'I know you lost your beloved Jenny,' I interrupt him, 'and that is really awful. We are all very sad about that.

Lara wanted to give you a sign of love when she named her little daughter after your girlfriend Jenny.'

'Yes, I know, and I am very grateful to her. Nevertheless, this doesn't bring Jenny back to me. And I miss her so much.'

'Unfortunately, no one can replace her,' I agree, 'but can't you imagine that Jenny might somehow still be alive somewhere else and that she might still feel a close connection with you?'

Bob looks at me incredulously with wide eyes.

'This from you, from your mouth?' he asks, with an almost uncomprehending gaze. 'From you of all people, Dad, you, who never really wanted anything to do with religion and spirituality?

'It was always you who made fun of Lara and her beliefs when she contradicted you and challenged your perception of the world yet again.'

'That's right,' I answer him, meekly, 'but I think I have grown out of it over the last few months.

I have matured and my severe accident has played a major role in it.'

Bob now looks completely stunned.

101

Quietly I tell Bob of my experience during the time of my resuscitations while I was clinically dead and while I subsequently lay in a deep coma.

I tell him about Michael and Michaela, about some misunderstandings and misinterpretations concerning God and the world which we should finally bury and, of course, I tell him that there is indeed something more waiting for us than just our life down here.

I also tell him about the great responsibility we have down here which we mostly don't recognise – a great responsibility for us, for our neighbour and for mankind as a whole.

I also tell him that one day we will have to account for everything we have done and to justify our actions, and, while no one else is judging us, we will judge ourselves until every single one of those we have wronged down here has forgiven us.

Finally I allow a silence to develop.

Bob has become very quiet and doesn't utter a single word.

Motionless he looks at me as if he is waiting for me to tell him more.

'Bob . . . ,' I continue in a low voice '. . . before I met Michael+Michaela I saw Jenny, your Jenny...'

Suddenly Bob starts to cry bitterly.

'That's totally absurd. Why do you try to console me like this? Haven't you already told me enough strong stuff?

'A lot of what has been the purpose in our lives up to now, our entire scientific notion of the world, you just turn everything upside down.

'And now this on top of everything else. It is quite interesting to hear what people dream when they are under stress like you, but that has nothing to do with reality,' Bob snorts derisively.

'All right, maybe you did see Jenny in your dream – I sometimes dream about her, too.

'But . . . Jenny is dead, for crying out loud, she is dead. When will you get your head around that? Don't make it any worse for me now than it already is.'

'Bob, please calm down. Let me at least tell you what Jenny said to me – in my dream then if you like.'

Bob is still sobbing his heart out, but he lets me go on.

'Jenny asked me to tell you word for word that she loves you very much, that "they are alive" and that "they are well". I am to tell her family the same. And she also asked me to give you her kind regards.

'Nice going, Dad, dream on . . .'

'I didn't expect you to believe me,' I go on, 'therefore I asked Jenny to tell me something that only you would know about.'

'Yes, and, did she?' Bob insists, in a rather harsh voice, but obviously interested.

'Jenny just said: "Tell him the first of May in Paris, Sacré Coeur." Does that mean anything to you, Bob?'

Now all barriers are washed away.

A hoarse sob forces its way out of Bob's mouth. He buries his head in my lap. I can hardly calm him down.

Very slowly he sits up again, falls into my arms and gives me a firm hug.

Gradually he disentangles himself from me and looks deep into my eyes. He then murmurs quietly:

'As you know, Jenny and I went to Paris together on the first weekend in May, shortly before she died, just like Mum and you had intended to do before Jenny's accident destroyed your plans.

'The first of May was a Sunday. And Jenny was so eager to visit her favourite church in Paris this morning together with me, Sacré Coeur on Montmartre. So we went.

'From our hotel we took the Metro to Anvers and then we dived into the hustle and bustle around Montmartre and made our way up to Sacré Coeur.

At the entrance we had to join a queue so that I had already lost my enthusiasm. But Jenny held me by the hand. She didn't let go and kept smiling all the way.

'It didn't take as long as I had feared. We sat down in one of the pews at the back and Jenny snuggled up to me.

'And then she started: "Bob, I must tell you something." And she looked lovingly at me. "Bob, I went to see my gynaecologist the other day. I want to show you something." She rummaged around in her handbag and took out a small, crumpled piece of paper.

'I've been carrying this around with me ever since. Here it is, Dad,' and with this Bob retrieves this small sheet from his pocket, more like a foil than a piece of paper.

I take it from him and I know immediately that it is an ultrasonic picture.

'Jenny showed this picture to me and told me that she was pregnant – already third month. I haven't told anyone. And I kept it to myself even when Jenny died...'

And tears are welling up in his eyes again.

This time *I* remain motionless and give him a bear hug.

My thoughts are circulating wildly and I recall clearly the situation when Jenny spoke to me and sent her words to Bob, shortly before we arrived at the gigantic complex building where I met Michael+Michaela.

I also remember exactly that she used the plural. She didn't say "I am alive" and "I am well", no, she said very clearly "we are alive" and "we are well".

I recollect that at the time I was wondering a little what she meant by that but I hadn't really thought about it.

But now it becomes quite clear:

Would Jenny be able to carry her child, yet unborn at the time of her death, to term up there, where she is now?

I remember now Michael's+Michaela's words when he+she mentioned that everything, really everything and anything, every atom, every cell and every being – as well as any deed – leaves informational traces up there.

They are traces of "existence". Everything remains preserved, just not in its dense matter form as we perceive it down here with our senses.

It is similar to the internet:
Nothing is ever forgotten.

We need quite a while before we can pull ourselves together and go back to the hotel where the others are probably already waiting for us. Bob seems far more relaxed now and we are smiling at each other.

102

The time for my presentation in front of nearly two thousand people in the Great Hall of the New York Javits Convention Center is drawing close.

Clad in festive garments all eight of us stroll along the High Line from our hotel The Standard to the Congress Center.

The weather is beautiful again and the sun is slowly setting over the Hudson River. I am hanging on tight to the bag with my laptop.

Already in the entrance hall of the Center we are welcomed with a glass of champagne which is flowing in abundance. While Helen, Lara, Bob and I are standing together, Tom and both his friends Jasmin and Sascha are wandering around exploring the surroundings.

Many renowned scientists, among them a number of Nobel Prize winners, are strolling past and shake our hands.

After some friendly smalltalk with other guests we amble together to the Great Hall. It is a feast for the eyes. The guests are welcomed with beautiful flower arrangements on festively decorated large round tables, all perfectly laid for the dinner later. Liveried waiters show us to a table for twelve near the stage where the eight of us take our seats together with the President and the Vice President of the World Association with their partners.

Gradually the hall fills up and at 7 o'clock on the dot the festive evening is formally opened by the first piece of music. Probably in my honour the orchestra plays Ludwig van Beethoven's[66] "Ode to Joy" which has advanced to become the National Anthem of Europe.

After a short address by the Chairman of the Association welcoming the numerous guests, the orchestra plays "Over the Rainbow"[67] and then I am asked to give my ceremonial lecture.

Accompanied by friendly applause I get up and approach the lectern in a relaxed mood. I ask the lady in charge of the technical equipment to insert the first slide of the presentation I have prepared into the projector.

The title of my presentation, as already announced in the congress volume, appears against the background of a New York skyline which I took myself from the "Top of the Rock", the observation platform on the 70th floor of the world-famous Rockefeller Center.

"Our World in the 21st Century"

First of all I welcome the Chairman of the World Association and the active management, I praise the excellent organisation of the conference and address the Mayor of the City of New York and also all the guests who have found their way to attend this event.

I thank the Management for inviting me to give the ceremonial lecture – a great honour for me – and for firmly maintaining this invitation during the last few months which were so difficult for me and my family due to my accident.

My special thanks finally go to my family and also to our friends who accompany us and who helped us tremendously during that awful time and I am delighted to have them here with us today.

Yes, and then I really start:

'Ladies and gentlemen, I am grateful and pleased to have this opportunity of giving you all a few, deep insights into our universe over the next sixty minutes, insights which might be new and unexpected for most of you.

'I would even go a step further and I do hope for you to gain insights which might even help to change the world and our lives forever.

'The last few months of my life were dominated by serious injuries, by a deep coma and two resuscitations. My life was suddenly at stake and I came perilously close to not being able to be here today at all.

'But I assure you all that this was the most important time of my life up to now.

'It was a time during which I was allowed to gain entirely new impressions of our world. Some of those have completely altered my perception of many of the issues about which we believe that we know all there is to know.

'Others will force us to adopt completely different viewpoints which might seem utterly unexpected to many of you here.'

While speaking these words I look into numerous attentive faces turned to me and I fancy that I can notice the growing amazement spreading over them.

'These new insights, which I would now like to introduce to you with great passion and from the depth of my heart, are simultaneously an explicit mandate to all of you.
'Our world is moving closer and closer to a possible collapse if we don't finally learn to change our views as a matter of urgency and to accept *our own* responsibility for everything we do – and not just lay the blame on the broad community of all the others, as, unfortunately, many people keep doing.
'No, actually, and this is what I want to pass on to you all, every single one of us, we must all accept responsibility *for ourselves* since *every single one* of us, we are all carrying *personal responsibility* for ourselves, for our neighbours and for everything that renders our still beautiful world so liveable in.
'And every *single one* of us, we all carry this responsibility *beyond our deaths* and we will all be confronted one day with our actions and also - especially – with our possible failures and we will have to explain ourselves. It will be *our* mission to comprehend this and to relay this message to the world. In order to do this we need today more than anything else a paradigm shift and a change in awareness.'
On many faces I detect now the first signs of a certain perplexity.

But at the same time I sense that "from above" someone is giving me a friendly smile...

Without further ado I continue:

'And therefore, ladies and gentlemen, I gave my presentation today a second title.

'And that is, in my opinion, for all of us, for every single one of us, most important and a mandate to master the future of this world with determination and bravery – and at the same time also our own future.

And this subtitle is:

Our Key to Eternity!

Footnotes

[1] RWTH = Rheinisch Westfälische Technische Hochschule, the name of the Aachen University.
[2] Stephen Hawking (*1942), British physicist and astrophysicist. Quoted from the German newspaper "Welt am Sonntag", 22 May 2011.
[3] The scientists Saul Perlmutter, Brian Schmidt and Adam Riess were awarded the Nobel Prize in Physics 2011 for "discovering dark energy".
[4] The original quote reads: "Sire je n'avais pas besoin de cette hypothèse". This is the reply the French astronomer Pierre Laplace (1749-1827) gave to Napoleon's question as to where in his Mécanique Céleste (celestial mechanics) God has his place.
[5] Robert B. Laughlin (*1950), Nobel Prize in Physics 1998 for the discovery of the quantum Hall effect, quotes from "DER SPIEGEL" 1 (2008).
[6] Giordano Bruno (1548-1600), Italian priest, philosopher and astronomer.
[7] Rainald von Dassel (ca. 1114-1167); between 1159 and 1167 Archbishop of Cologne and Archchancellor of Italy appointed by Emperor Frederick I Barbarossa. After the conquest of Milan he brought the relics of the Three Kings to Cologne as spoils of war.
[8] Johann Wolfgang von Goethe (1749-1832), German poet, ennobled 1782.
[9] Friedrich Wilhelm IV (1795-1861), member of the Hohenzollern dynasty, Prussian King 1840-1861.
[10] Max Planck (1858-1947); German physicist; father of Quantum Physics, awarded the Nobel Prize in Physics 1919.
[11] Johann Philipp Gustav von Jolly (1809-1884), German mathematician and physicist, successor to Ohm at Munich University.
[12] Immanuel Kant (1727-1804), German mathematician and philosopher. Spent most of his life in Königsberg (East Prussia), today Kaliningrad (Russia).
[13] From: DER SPIEGEL 33, 2014, "Immer jauchzend, nie betrübt" ("Always jubilating, never saddened"), an article on the subject "Biology".
[14] Source: FOCUS 33 (2014).
[15] Alexander von Humboldt (1769-1859), German natural scientist, who gained experience and knowledge by his worldwide travels, one of the fathers of geography.
[16] Charlemagne (747-814). King of the Franks 768-814, First Emperor since ancient times (800). Commissioned the building of the Aachen Cathedral.
[17] Stevenson, Ian, „Children who remember previous lives", USA (1989)
[18] TV-programme „PSI", ARD, Autumn 2003
[19] Allan Kardec (1804-1869), French teacher and spiritualist, author of numerous books, creator of the term "reincarnation", mentioned for the first time in his book "Livre des ésprits" (1857)
[20] Bible, New Testament, Gospel of Luke 23:43, New King James Version.
[21] From: DER SPIEGEL 49, 1998. A similar wording can be found in the Vatican Congregation for the Doctrine of the Faith 17 may 1979, published by the German Bishops Conference, Bonn.
[22] The believe in complete death goes back to the protestant theologian Karl Barth (1886-1968).
[23] Bible, New Testament, Gospel of John 3:4-7, Jubilee Bible 2000.
[24] C. Richard Dawkins (*1941), British biologist, author, atheist and agnostic. Dismisses everything religious as being pure fantasy. Examples are "The God Delusion", 2006, "Why we believe in God(s)" 2011.
[25] LHC = Large Hadron Collider. This is a particle accelerator at CERN ("Conseil Européenn pour la Recherche Nucléaire" (European Organization for

Nuclear Research). The LHC is located underground near Meyrin, a municipality of the Canton of Geneva in Switzerland.

[26] Higgs boson is an elementary particle named after the British physicist Peter Higgs. It is electrically neutral, has zero spin and decays ultra fast. It is assumed that a Higgs field exists throughout the universe which causes existing particles to acquire mass when passing through.

[27] Hans Grässel (1860-1939), famous German architect of schools and graveyards.

[28] Bible, New Testament, Gospel of John, 11:25, New King James Version.

[29] Blaise Pascal (1623-1662), French mathematician, physicist and philosopher and theologian after his "experience of enlightenment" (1654).

[30] Bible, New Testament, Gospel of John, 3:4-7, Jubilee Bible 2000.

[31] Bible, New Testament, 1 Corinthians, 15:40, 42, 44, 46, 47, 49, 51-52, New King James Version.

[32] Bible, New Testament, Gospel of Luke 23:43, New King James Version.

[33] Socrates (469-399 B.C.), Greek philosopher.

[34] Plato (428-348 B.C.), Greek philosopher, student of Socrates and teacher of Aristotle.

[35] Aurelius Augustine (354 and 430), Bishop of Hippo in today's Algeria, philosopher, Latin Church Father, Saint.

[36] Francis of Assisi (1181-1226), Italian founder of the Franciscan Order and Saint.

[37] Dietrich Bonhoeffer (1906-1945), Protestant theologian, involved in the German resistance against Nazism. Executed in a concentration camp.

[38] Henri Nouwen (1932-1996), Dutch priest, philosopher and psychologist, university professor at Harvard.

[39] Konrad Adenauer (1876-1967); first Chancellor of the Federal Republic of Germany 1949-1963; simultaneously Foreign Minister 1951-1955; Lord Mayor of the City of Cologne 1917-1933 and 1945.

[40] Holland is actually only the northern part of The Netherlands bordering the North Sea. Even in The Netherlands, but primarily in Germany and in many other countries, the name Holland often stands as a synonym for the whole of The Netherlands, since after the Thirty Years War, which ended in Munster with the Peace of Westphalia, Holland was the richest and most influential province of the "Republic of the Seven United Provinces".

[41] ADAC is an abbreviation for "Allgemeiner Deutscher Automobil Club" (*General German Automobile Club*), the largest automobile club in Germany.

[42] Pierre Teilhard de Chardin (1881-1955); French Jesuit, theologian, philosopher and natural scientist.

[43] Albert Einstein (1879-1955), German physicist and Nobel Prize Winner. Extract from his letter to the author Eric Gutkind in 1954.

[44] Albert Einstein "Letters to and from Children" in: Shaun Usher "Letters of Note", Canongate Books, Edinburgh (2013).

[45] Plato (428-348 B.C.), Greek philosopher, student of Socrates and teacher of Aristotle.

[46] Martin Luther (1483-1546); German Reformer. He inadvertently contributed to the schism within the church, for which he is considered to be the co-founder of the Christian Protestantism and thus also of the Protestant Church in Germany.

[47] Bible, Old Testament, Wisdom of Solomon, 11:20, King James Version.

[48] Panpsychism is a metaphysical theory according to which all objects possess a kind of soul or basic conscience.

[49] Albert Einstein (1879-1955), German physicist and Nobel Prize Winner; originator of the theory of relativity. His most famous formula is $E = m c^2$, which basically states the interchangeability (equivalence) of matter and energy.
[50] Bible, Old Testament, Second Book of Moses (Exodus), 21:24, New King James Version.
[51] Although the term "almighty" is normally used in the sense of "being all powerful", a quite different, plausible interpretation should apply here, which would give better sense in the context of this book: similar to a meal which might be very rich and lies uncomfortably heavy in the stomach, so this interpretation of "almighty" means that "God's love" is the "elementary power" inevitably present in every single one of us, even though often hidden, and will thus have the compulsive desire to unfold and develop at some time or other.
[52] "Groundhog Day", American Movie (1993).
[53] Bible, New Testament Gospel of Matthew, 25:14-30, New King James Version: The Parable of the Talents, similar also in the Gospel of Luke, 19:12-27.
[54] Bible, New Testament, Gospel of John, 8:7, New King James Version.
[55] Bible, New Testament, Gospel of Matthew 19:30, New King James Version.
[56] Bible, New Testament, Gospel of John, 1:1-5, New King James Version, slightly altered in accordance with the German version of the Bible as translated by Luther. Because it is said "the word WAS God", in original versions "it" is used here in contrast to English ones, where "him" is used.
[57] Immanuel Kant (1724-1804); German philosopher of the Enlightenment.
[58] Georg Cantor (1845-1918), German mathematician.
[59] Peter Plichta (*1939), German chemist and mathematician, author.
[60] Various books by the author, see literature references at the end of the book.
[61] Various books by the author, see literature references at the end of the book.
[62] Isidor of Seville (560-636), Bishop of Seville. He collected the knowledge of antiquity still available in the western Mediterranean and compiled it in an encyclopaedia of the early Middle Ages, *Etymologarum sive originum libri XX*
[63] 'Doppler-Effect', named after Christian Doppler (1803-1853), Austrian mathematician and physicist
[64] Bell's Theorem (named after John Bell); EPR paradox, named after Albert Einstein, Boris Podolsky and Nathan Rosen, who did not believe in the mere randomness for the appearance of central events on an atomic and subatomic level. With the Aspect Experiment in 1972, Allan Aspect investigated pairs of twin photons with different polarisations. When one photon of the pair was caught by a filter, then at any arbitrary distance it was only possible to measure the other one with the matching polarisation.
[65] Hans-Peter Dürr (1929-2014); German physicist. He was the Director of the Max-Planck-Institute in Munich until 1997 (Werner Heisenberg Institute).
[66] Ludwig van Beethoven (1770-1827), German composer. He completed his 9th Symphony in 1824. The last movement with the choral finale, a setting of the poem "An die Freude" (Ode to Joy) by the German poet Friedrich Schiller (1759-1805), is today the so-called European National Anthem, or better that of the European Union (EU).
[67] "Over the Rainbow", music H. Arlen, lyrics E.Y. Harburg, was sung for the first time in 1939 by the American actress Judy Garland (1922-1969) in the movie "The Wizard of Oz" based on the novel "The Wizard of Oz" written by L. Frank Baum.

Prof. Dr. med. Walter van Laack

1. Books in English language:

Our Key To Eternity (Novel)
ISBN 978-3-936624-18-2 (SC), 308 p. (2016)
ISBN 978-3-936624-31-1, E-Book (2016)

To Perceive The World With Logic
ISBN 978-3-936624-08-3, Softcover (SC), 340 p. (2007)
ISBN 978-3-936624-09-0, E-Book (2008)

Nobody Ever Dies!
ISBN 978-3-936624-03-8, (SC), 272 p. (2005)
ISBN 978-3-936624-22-9, E-Book (2013)

A Better History of Our World
Vol. 1, "The Universe"
ISBN 978-3-8311-1490-0, (SC), 188 p. (2001)
Vol. 2, "Life"
ISBN 978-3-8311-2597-5, (SC), 236 p. (2002)
Vol. 3, "Death"
ISBN 978-3-936624-01-4, (SC), 276 p. (2003)

Key To Eternity
ISBN 978-3-8311-0344-7, (SC), 256 p. (2000)

2. Books in German language:

Unser Schlüssel zur Ewigkeit (Roman)
ISBN 978-3-936624-16-8, Taschenbuch (SC), 316 S. (2015)
ISBN 978-3-936624-27-4, E-Book (2015)

Mit Logik die Welt begreifen
ISBN 978-3-936624-04-5, Taschenbuch (SC), 380 S. (2005)
ISBN 978-3-936624-07-6, Festeinband (HC), 380 S. (2005)
ISBN 978-3-936624-23-6, E-Book (2013)

Wer stirbt, ist nicht tot!
ISBN 978-3-936624-12-0, (SC), 272 S. (Neuauflage 2011)
ISBN 978-3-936624-13-7, (HC), 272 S. (Neuauflage 2011)
ISBN 978-3-936624-21-2, E-Book (2013)

Eine bessere Geschichte unserer Welt
Band 1, "Das Universum"
ISBN 978-3-8311-0345-4, (SC), 196 S. (2000)
Band 2, "Das Leben"
ISBN 978-3-8311-2114-4, (SC), 248 S. (2001)

Band 3, "Der Tod"
ISBN 978-3-8311-3581-3, (SC), 276 S. (2002)

Der Schlüssel zur Ewigkeit
ISBN 978-3-9805239-4-3, (HC), 288 S.,1. Aufl. (1999)
ISBN 978-3-89811-819-4, (SC) , 288 S., 2. Aufl. (2000)

**Plädoyer für ein Leben nach dem Tod
und eine etwas andere Sicht der Welt**
ISBN 978-3-89811-818-7; (SC), 448 S., 2. Aufl. (1999/2000)

**Schnittstelle Tod –
Wo stehen wir nach 40 Jahren NTE-Forschung?**
ISBN 978-3-936624-30-4, Taschenbuch (SC), 92 S. (2016)
ISBN 978-3-936624-32-8, E-Book (2016)

Schnittstelle Tod – Was spricht für unser Weiterleben?
ISBN 978-3-936624-19-9, Taschenbuch (SC), 100 S. (2014)

Schnittstelle Tod – Warum auf ein Danach vertrauen?
ISBN 978-3-936624-14-4, Taschenbuch (SC), 120 S. (2012)

Schnittstelle Tod – Aufbruch zu neuem Leben?
ISBN 978-3-936624-10-6, Taschenbuch (SC), 148 S. (2010)

Supplied by: Book-on-Demand (BoD)
In de Tarpen 42, D- 22848 Norderstedt, Fax +49-40-534335-84
Web: www.bod.de   Email: info(at)bod.de

for:

van Laack GmbH, Aachen, Book-Publishers (HRB-Aachen 5584)
Managing Director: Prof. Dr. Walter van Laack
Partner: Dr.-Ing. Dipl.-Wirt.-Ing. Alexander van Laack,
Martin van Laack, M.Sc., Prof. Dr. Walter van Laack

Roermonder Str. 312, D- 52072 Aachen – Fax: +49-3212-9319310
Web: www.vanLaack-Book.eu – www.van-Laack.de – www.vanLaack-Buch.de
Email: webmaster(at)van-Laack.de

www.ingramcontent.com/pod-product-compliance
Lightning Source LLC
Chambersburg PA
CBHW021136230426
43667CB00005B/142